Supreme Court Economic Review

VOLUME 25

Supreme Court

THE UNIVERSITY OF CHICAGO PRESS
Chicago and London

Economic Review

EDITORS

Murat C. Mungan with
Keith N. Hylton

Sponsored by the Law and Economics Center at
the George Mason University School of Law

INTERNATIONAL STANDARD SERIAL NUMBER: 0736-9921
INTERNATIONAL STANDARD BOOK NUMBER: 978-0-226-64653-4
The University of Chicago Press, Chicago 60637
The University of Chicago Press, Ltd., London
© 2019 by The University of Chicago. All rights reserved.
Printed in the United States of America

Supreme Court Economic Review

The *Supreme Court Economic Review* (SCER) is an international peer-reviewed academic journal specializing in law and economics. The journal has frequently published work focusing on economic and social science analyses of judicial decision-making, institutional analyses of law and legal structures, political economy and public choice issues regarding courts and other decision-makers, and the relationship between legal and political institutions and the institutions of a free society governed by constitutions and the rule of law. The series also publishes special symposium issues that build on SCER's traditional focus on the intersection between law and economics. Contributors include renowned legal scholars, economists, and policy-makers.

Please direct any correspondence to:

Editor, Supreme Court Economic Review
George Mason University Antonin Scalia Law School
3301 North Fairfax Drive
Arlington, Virginia 22201-4498

Supreme Court Economic Review

Table of Contents

Error Costs, Legal Standards of Proof, and Statistical Significance

Michelle M. Burtis[*]
Jonah B. Gelbach[†]
Bruce H. Kobayashi[‡]

The relationship between legal standards of proof and thresholds of statistical significance is a well-known and studied phenomenon in the academic literature. Moreover, the distinction between the two has been recognized in law. For example, in Matrix v. Siracusano, *the court unanimously rejected the petitioner's argument that the issue of materiality in a securities class action can be defined by the presence or absence of a statistically significant effect. However, in other contexts, thresholds based on fixed significance levels imported from academic settings continue to be used as a legal standard of proof. Our positive analysis uses simple null and alternative hypotheses to demonstrate how statistical significance thresholds and legal standards of proof represent alternative approaches to balancing error costs. Within this framework of simple hypotheses, we show that thresholds based on fixed significance levels generally are not consistent*

[*] Michelle M. Burtis is vice president of CRA International.

[†] Jonah B. Gelbach is professor of law at the University of Pennsylvania Law School.

[‡] Bruce H. Kobayashi is the associate dean for research and faculty development and professor of law at the Antonin Scalia Law School at George Mason University. The authors would like to thank Ron Allen, Luke Froeb, Jon Klick, Murat Mungan, Michael Pardo, Jeff Parker, Steve Salop, Steve Yelderman, and participants at the University of Michigan Law School's Law and Economics Colloquium, and the Law and Economic Center's *Supreme Court Economic Review* Research Roundtable on the Economics of Legal Error for helpful comments. The opinions expressed are the authors' and do not reflect the views of CRA or any of its respective affiliates.

Electronically published: December 7, 2018

with existing or optimal legal standards of proof. We also show how the statistical testing and legal standards of proof can be reconciled by replacing fixed significance-level hypothesis testing with likelihood ratio tests.

1. INTRODUCTION

A primary issue for courts faced with evaluating statistical evidence offered by experts in litigation is how to draw legal inferences from statistical results. One approach taken by some courts is to use the standard tools of *statistical inference* to make *legal inferences*. For example, in a discrimination dispute, the existence of a significant statistical disparity among workers in hiring and salaries, after accounting for other factors, has been used to determine whether plaintiffs have met their burden of production for a prima facie case of disparate impact discrimination.[1] Similarly, courts use evidence of statistically significant abnormal returns at the time of a corrective disclosure to determine the existence or absence of price impact in class action securities litigation.[2]

One principal question addressed in this article is, when and under what circumstances is the use of standard tools of statistical inference consistent with the applicable legal standard of proof that applies to the case?[3] Economists, statisticians, and judges import from research settings fixed significance levels—usually 5%, but sometimes 1% or 10%—and use them to make legal inferences.[4] When a research standard such as the 5% significance level is used to make legal inferences, is the resulting decision consistent with satisfaction of a legal standard of proof such as "more likely than not"? A second question is, if levels of statistical significance used in the research context do not generate results that are consistent with the applicable legal

---

[1] See, e.g., *Ricci v. DeStefano* (557 U.S. 557, 587 [2009]), where the Supreme Court described a showing of statistically significant difference as prima facie evidence of "disparate impact" under U.S.C. § 2000e-2(k)(1)(A)(i).

[2] See *Halliburton Co. v. Erica P. John Fund, Inc.* (*Halliburton II*), 134 S.Ct. 2398 (2014); defendant may present evidence of nonsignificant abnormal returns at class certification stage to show the lack of price impact. See also Fisch, Gelbach, and Klick (2018); Brav and Heaton (2015).

[3] The process of fixed significance level null hypothesis testing is described in detail in sec. 3. See also Ziliak and McCloskey (2008), documenting the arbitrary nature of the standard fixed significance level test and criticizing its use generally, including uses in academics, science, and law.

[4] See, e.g., Stock and Watson (2011): "In many cases, statisticians and econometricians use a 5% significance level" (77–78); and Wooldridge (2002): "Suppose we have decided on a 5% significance level, as this is the most popular choice" (124). See also Ziliak and McCloskey (2008), discussing the history of significance tests.

standard of proof, does another fixed significance level generate such consistent results?[5]

In answering these questions, we will assume that both parties' positions can be represented by simple, rather than composite, hypotheses. In that context, the answer to both questions in the previous paragraph is no. Although both legal standards of proof and statistical significance levels can be characterized as normative choices made to minimize the sum of error costs and direct costs, with simple hypotheses there is no a priori fixed level of statistical significance that will generally coincide with the applicable legal standard of proof. That is, even though one can express the applicable legal standard of proof in such a way that it can be understood in terms of fixed significance level in a given case, the level of statistical significance necessary to achieve this result varies across cases and circumstances. Thus, with simple hypotheses, there is no one level of statistical significance that generally corresponds to the legal standard of proof in a context-free way.[6]

Others have pointed out the divergence between statistical and legal standards of proof. Indeed, there is a large literature examining the distinction between legal standards of proof and statistical significance thresholds.[7] Moreover, the distinction between statistical sig-

---

[5] Some courts have considered experts' use of alternative fixed significance levels. For example, in *In re: High-Tech Employee Antitrust Litigation* (No. 11-CV-02509-LHK, 2014 U.S. Dist. LEXIS 47181, at *22, *48 n.24 [N.D. Cal. Apr. 4, 2014]), the plaintiffs' expert argued that a 50% significance level "suggests that it is more likely than not that the compensation of employees were decreased during the period of the agreements." See also Johnson, Leamer, and Leitzinger (2017). The court in *In re Photochromic Lens Antitrust Litigation* (MDL Docket No. 2173, 2014 U.S. Dist. LEXIS 46107 [M.D. Fla. Apr. 3, 2014]) also considered statistical evidence offered by plaintiffs that did not meet the "conventional 5% significance level." Plaintiffs argued that a significance level of 50% would "avoid false negatives, or what statisticians refer to as 'type 2 errors'" (*In re Photochromic Lens Antitrust Litig.*, 2014 U.S. Dist. LEXIS 46107 at *102). The court in *Photochromic* (2014 U.S. Dist. LEXIS 46107 at *104) did not accept the defendants' arguments regarding the impropriety of using a higher fixed significance level, noting, "Although his studies test the boundaries of reliable evidence permitted under *Daubert*, as well as the Supreme Court's directive in *Comcast* that statistical models prove with precision impact and damages on a classwide basis, I cannot agree that Dr. Singer's use of a 50% measure of statistical significance, by itself, is sufficient justification for denying class certification."

[6] In sec. 5.4, we note circumstances in which this result changes importantly when composite hypotheses are allowed.

[7] See Peresie (2009) analyzing differences between EEOC 80% rule and statistical significance); Garaud (1990) discussing the distinction between legal and statistical significance; and Cohen (1985) using error cost analysis to determine appropriate level of confidence in civil litigation. See also Finkelstein and Levin (2014, 193–97), King (2007), and Lempert (2009).

nificance thresholds and legal standards of proof has been explicitly recognized by the courts. For example, in *Matrixx Initiatives, Inc. v. Siracusano* (563 U.S. 27 [2011]), the court unanimously rejected the petitioner/defendant's argument that equated the materiality standard in a securities fraud case with evidence of "statistically significant" adverse effect of its product on the rate of anosmia (the loss of smell).[8] Courts also have criticized the use of fixed significance thresholds in antitrust cases.[9] However, in other contexts, courts continue to use standard fixed significance level hypothesis testing as a legal standard of proof. For example, in disparate impact discrimination cases, courts continue to use fixed significance level thresholds based on the 5% two-tailed test used by academics in research contexts as the legal standard of proof to prove a prima facie case of discrimination "by a preponderance of the evidence" (Garaud 1990, 467).[10] Securities litigation constitutes another example; on remand following

[8] The court held that available information could indicate a reliable causal relationship between two variables even if that relationship was not statistically significant. In that case, Matrixx, who sold an over-the-counter cold remedy, had information that the remedy was associated with anosmia. The issue before the court was whether Matrixx was required to disclose information regarding a relationship between the use of its product and anosmia. Matrixx contended it did not have such an obligation because the information available to it did not indicate a statistically significant relationship. However, the Court found that the lack of a statistically significant relationship did not necessarily mean that there was not a reliable causal relationship between its product and anosmia and that Matrixx's failure to disclose the information was an omission of a material fact. See also Gastwirth (2012).

[9] The court in *Photochromic* (2014 U.S. Dist. LEXIS 46107) found that "there is not, however, any 'precise level in the law' at which statistical significance is sufficient to permit the inference derived from a correlative study. And most courts have rejected the arbitrary application of a 5% threshold."

[10] For a recent example, see, e.g., *Jones v. City of Boston*, 752 F.3d 38 (1st Cir. 2014). See also *Alison Palmer v. George P. Shultz*, 815 F 2d 84 (D.C. Cir. 1987) (prima facie evidence of disparate impact under Title VII required differences in selection rates that were statistically significant at a 5% level). Numerous other Title VII cases have used statistically significant difference in outcomes as evidence of disparate impact and discrimination. See King (2007, 277; describing that many lower courts have adopted the criterion of 2 or 3 standard deviations, which can correspond to a .05 statistical significance level as a bright-line rule). See also *Vuyanich v. Rep. Nat'l Bank of Dallas*, 505 F. Supp. 224, 348 (N.D. Tex. 1980]), *vacated on other grounds* 723 F.2d 1195 [5th Cir. 1984]), "it has become a convention in social science to accept as statistically significant values which have a probability of occurring by change 5% of the time or less." Also, the Court in *Castaneda v. Partida*, 430 U.S. 482, 496 n.17 [1977] noted that "as a general rule . . . if the difference between the expected value and the observed number is greater than two or three standard deviations, then the hypothesis that the jury drawing was random would be suspect to a social scientist." For other cases, see *Bennett v. Total Minatome Corp.*, 136 F.3d 1053 [5th Cir. 1998]; *Segar v. Smith*, 738 F.2d 1249, 1282 [D.C. Cir. 1984]; *Cooper v. Univ. of Tex. at Dallas* (482 F. Supp. 187, 194 [N.D. Tex. 1979]).

Halliburton II (134 S.Ct. 2398), the trial court used statistical significance as the basis for determining dates on which it was appropriate
to certify a Rule 23(b)(3) class action.[11]

This article provides an analysis of the statistical significance tests
and their relationship to the applicable legal standard of proof and attempts to clarify the consequences of a choice of statistical significance levels in such settings. Economic analyses characterize legal
standards of proof as relative comparisons between competing hypotheses put forward by the litigating parties. The positive analysis
demonstrates how a legal standard of proof and statistical hypothesis
testing using a fixed statistical significance level represent alternative
and generally inconsistent ways to allocate error costs. We also show
how reconciling legal standards of proof and statistical thresholds can
be achieved by replacing fixed significance levels with likelihood ratio tests that compare the relative properties of the sampling distributions of the competing hypotheses put forward by the parties.[12]

The organization of this article is as follows. Section 2 presents an
example that illustrates the potential differences between legal standards of proof and statistical significance. Section 3 sets out the error
cost analysis framework as well as the derivation of optimal legal standards of proof. The analysis then examines the conditions under which
existing legal standards, such as the preponderance rule, are optimal
standards. In section 4, we describe the standard use of null hypothesis
testing under fixed significance levels. Section 5 examines the relationship between statistical significance levels and legal standards of
proof. Section 6 concludes.

---

[11] See Fisch et al. (2018) for a discussion of the role of statistical significance in that
case.

[12] The evaluation of the merits of any statistical analysis requires a normative
analysis of the relative frequency and costs of these errors and should inform the
choice of the optimal test and significance level. A full treatment of this last issue
is beyond the scope of this article. In addition, this article does not address many other
issues related to the use and interpretation of statistical models in legal settings, even
though there can be interplay between those issues and the way in which statistical
inference is performed. For example, at the summary judgment (or trial) phase of a litigation, the issue of liability may be assumed by an expert who is calculating damages
with a statistical model. Such an assumption can affect the way in which statistical
inference is performed. Another example is that at the certification phase of a class
action, where both plaintiffs and defendants generally assume the allegations in the
complaint when evaluating the issue of whether impact can be determined with common evidence, a defendant might not put forward its own, competing, statistical model,
and therefore inferences based on the plaintiffs' model gain more importance than in
circumstances where a competing model is available.

2. THE DIFFERENCE BETWEEN LEGAL AND STATISTICAL SIGNIFICANCE ILLUSTRATED

To illustrate the ways in which legal and statistical thresholds can diverge, consider a challenge to a qualification test administered to applicants for a job. A class of unsuccessful female applicants alleges that the qualification test generates an adverse impact. A court or federal agency must determine, as a preliminary matter, whether there is evidence that the administration of the test has a disparate impact on female applicants. One approach is the four-fifths rule contained in the Uniform Guidelines on Employee Selection Procedures, jointly adopted in 1978 by the US Civil Service Commission, the US Department Labor, US Department of Justice, and the US Equal Opportunity Commission (29 C.F.R. §1607.4(D)):[13]

A selection rate for any race, sex, or ethnic group which is less than four-fifths (4/5) (or eighty percent) of the rate for the group with the highest rate will generally be regarded by the Federal enforcement agencies as evidence of adverse impact, while a greater than four-fifths rate will generally not be regarded by Federal enforcement agencies as evidence of adverse impact. Smaller differences in selection rate may nevertheless constitute adverse impact, where they are significant in both statistical and practical terms or where a user's actions have discouraged applicants disproportionately on grounds of race, sex, or ethnic group. Greater differences in selection rate may not constitute adverse impact where the differences are based on small numbers and are not statistically significant, or where special recruiting or other programs cause the pool of minority or female candidates to be atypical of the normal pool of applicants from that group.

Consider a setting with 82 total test takers, of whom 50 are male and 32 are female. To meet the four-fifths threshold, it must be the case that the female passing rate, q_F, is less than 0.8 times the male passing rate, q_M. Defining the ratio of female-to-male passing rates as $\rho = q_F/q_M$, this means that plaintiffs meet the four-fifths threshold if they show that $\rho < .8$. Suppose 45 of 50 male respondents and 21 of 32 female respondents achieve a passing score on a qualifying test. The male passing rate is $q_M = 45/50 = .90$, and the female passing rate

---

[13] The Uniform Guidelines do not have the force of law but are cited and sometimes followed by courts. See Peresie (2009) discussing courts' treatment of the four-fifths rule and comparing and reconciling the four-fifths rule and tests of statistical significance. See also Finkelstein and Levin (2014, 193–97) for an example of divergence between the four-fifths rule and statistical significance threshold.

$q_F = 21/32 = .66$. In this example, the ratio of female-to-male passing rates is $\rho = q_F/q_M = .729$, which falls below the four-fifths threshold of $\rho^* = .80$.

Statistical significance at the 5% level can also be measured in terms of the value of ρ. With the numbers just given, the threshold value for significance at the 5% level is .80—precisely the same as the four-fifths threshold.[14] Because $\rho = .729$ is less than the 5% significance threshold, which is .80 in this example, the estimate of ρ is statistically significant at the 5% level. Furthermore, the natural logarithm of $\rho = .729$ has a p value of .010, so it would be found statistically significant at any level above .01.[15] Because the critical threshold from the four-fifths rule ($\rho^* = .80$) is the same as the threshold from a 5% one-tailed test of significance ($\rho^{**} = .80$), the two tests yield the same qualitative result in this example: each yields evidence of adverse impact.

However, the two thresholds are not generally the same. Consider an alternative setting with 170 applicants, of whom 100 are male and 70 are female. Suppose the pass rates by sex are 90% (90 of 100) for male applicants and 74.3% (52 of 70) for female applicants. In this setting, $\rho = .825 > .8$. Thus, the ratio of the selection rates lies above the four-fifths threshold, and use of the four-fifths rule would not yield evidence of adverse impact under the Uniform Guidelines. However, the difference between .825 and 1 is statistically significant under commonly used statistical significance levels. The natural logarithm of $\rho = .825$ has a p value of .007 and is statistically significant at standard significance levels. The threshold from the four-fifths rule ($\rho^* = .80$) is smaller and harder to satisfy than the threshold from a 5% one-tailed test of significance ($\rho^{**} = .90$). Under the uniform guidelines, ratios between .80 and .90 that do not fall below the four-fifths rule may constitute adverse impact. The Uniform Guidelines' treatment of statistically significant ratios above 80% recognizes the arbitrary

[14] Because the ratio ρ is not normally distributed, the natural logarithm of ρ ($\ln(\rho)$), which is approximately normally distributed, is used to calculate the test statistics (see Finkelstein and Levin 2014, 177–78). Because $\ln(\rho)$ evaluated at 1 equals 0, testing whether $\ln(\rho)$ is different from 0 is equivalent to testing whether the observed ratio ρ differs from 1. Thus, under the null hypothesis of no difference in the test pass rate, the distribution of $\ln(\rho)$ will have mean equal to 0. A commonly used estimator for the variance of $\ln(\rho)$, as applied to this example, is consistently estimated by $\sqrt{[(1-q_F)/n_F q_F] + [(1-q_M)/n_M q_M]}$, which equals .136. Multiplying that by -1.645 yields a critical value for $\ln(\rho)$ of $-.224$ for a one-sided 5% significance test. Exponentiating that critical value yields a critical value for ρ, which is .80.

[15] The p value is the probability of observing an outcome equal to or more extreme than the observed value when the null hypothesis is true (see Federal Judicial Center 2011, 250). In this case, the null hypothesis is that males and females pass the test at the same rate, so that $\rho = 1$ and $\ln(\rho) = 0$.

nature of the four-fifths rule and the desirability to address selection rate ratios above 80% in cases where the differences in selection rates are both economically significant and based on a large-enough sample so that the rates can be measured with requisite precision (Peresie 2009).

The opposite inconsistency can also occur. To see this, consider a setting with 16 applicants—10 male and 6 female. Suppose the pass rates are 90% (9 of 10) for male applicants and 50% (3 of 6) for female applicants so that the ratio of the selection rates falls below the critical threshold from the four-fifths rule ($\rho = .556 < \rho^* = .80$). However, the natural logarithm of $\rho = .556$ has a p value of .08, which means it is not statistically significant at the 5% significance level. In this example, the threshold from the four-fifths rule ($\rho^* = .80$) is greater than the threshold from a 5% one-tailed test of significance ($\rho^{**} = .50$). Use of this test of statistical significance to determine adverse impact requires the female selection rate to be less than half of the male selection rate; under the Uniform Guidelines, ratios that are below .80 but above .50 may not constitute adverse impact. The Uniform Guidelines' treatment of selection rates that are below the four-fifths threshold but lack statistical significance recognizes and considers the imprecision generated when estimating the impact of the test based on a small number of observations.

The four-fifths rule was designed to be an easy-to-administer and practical rule of thumb rather than a standard carefully crafted to balance the interests of employers and employees (Peresie 2009). Although simple rules of thumb can be useful in some settings (see generally, Ehrlich and Posner 1974; Kaplow 1992), the Uniform Guidelines' consideration of statistical significance recognizes that strict adherence to the four-fifths rule of thumb can produce erroneous decisions. However, the guidelines do not provide detailed or precise guidance on when deviation from the four-fifths rule is warranted. Moreover, when courts reject use of the arbitrary four-fifths rule of thumb, they invariably replace it with another arbitrary test: a test of statistical significance that incorporates an arbitrary (often 5%) significance level.[16]

The example in this section illustrates the several issues addressed next. The first is how to design legal decision rules that are not simple or arbitrary rules of thumb. The second is how to determine the appropriate significance level and decision threshold when designing statistical decision rules. The third is how to reconcile the applicable legal

---

[16] See Peresie (2009) discussing the courts adoption of the four-fifths rule vs. tests of statistical significance. The arbitrary nature of the 5% significance level is discussed in detail in sec. 4.

standard of proof and thresholds from statistical decision rules so that they produce consistent results.[17]

The analysis in this article moves beyond a comparison of arbitrary rules and incorporates the economic literature on optimal legal standards of proof set to balance error costs and their relationship to existing legal standards (see sec. 3). The analysis then examines the design of statistical decision rules (see sec. 4). The analysis then examines how such statistical decision rules can be made consistent with the applicable legal standard of proof (see sec. 5).

3. ERROR COST ANALYSIS AND THE DESIGN OF LEGAL RULES

In this section, we present an error cost analysis of optimal legal standards of proof. Section 3.1 sets out the standard of proof. Section 3.2 sets out the loss function used to evaluate standards of proof. Section 3.3 derives the optimal statistical standard of proof under specific but, we think, reasonable assumptions about legal standards. Section 3.4 examines mathematical representations of legal standards of proof and the conditions under which these legal standards of proof are optimal standards.

3.1. The Standard of Proof

We consider the case where the litigants put forward competing hypotheses (H_0 for the defendant and H_1 for the plaintiff) to explain the evidence, which consists of the realization x of a random variable X with a density function $f(X|H_0)$ if hypothesis H_0 is true and $f(X|H_1)$ if hypothesis H_1 is true. Figure 1 illustrates the two conditional sampling distributions under the litigants' competing hypothesis (see generally, Kaplow 2011, 2012, 2014; Cheng 2013; Demougina and Fluet 2006).

Suppose that the plaintiff has the burden of proof or production. Suppose also that the standard of proof is a threshold value x^T that determines whether the plaintiff has met her burden. Because the sampling distribution of X under the plaintiff's hypothesis H_1 is centered

[17] Peresie (2009) recognizes the arbitrary nature of both the four-fifths rule and the 5% level of significance and suggests a rule in which plaintiffs would be required to show that the ratio of the female-to-male selection rates ρ is less than some threshold value ρ^* and that the difference between the observed ρ is statistically significant. To adjust for the additional burden such a rule would place on the plaintiff, Peresie suggests ad hoc upward adjustments to both the threshold value ρ^* (increasing is above .80) and the level of significance (raising it from .05 to .10).

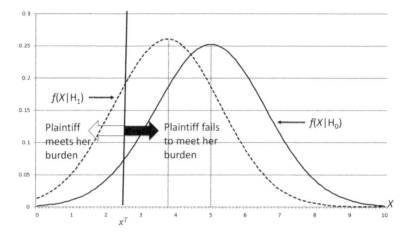

Figure 1. Litigants' competing hypotheses and the standard of proof x^T

to the left of the sampling distribution of X under the defendant's hypothesis H_0, realized values of $x \leq (>) x^T$ favor the plaintiff (defendant). Table 1 sets out the decision rule associated with the standard of proof.

3.2. Error Cost Analysis and the Loss Function

A preliminary matter is the choice of a "loss function" to evaluate alternative statistical tests and legal standards of proof. The performance of these alternatives will be determined by the specific loss function chosen to evaluate the tests. A common objective used to evaluate evidentiary and other procedural systems is to choose the system that minimizes the sum of two types of costs—expected error costs and the costs of the test (see generally, Posner 2003, 563; Allen 2003, 4). For concreteness, we adopt this approach while recognizing that reasonable alternatives might exist.[18]

The error cost matrix in table 2 summarizes the outcomes when the standard of proof is x^T, as suggested earlier. There are two correct outcomes (the boxes on the diagonal) for which the true hypothesis is accepted. There are two types of error—type I error and type II error. Type I errors (when the plaintiff's hypothesis H_1 is accepted when H_0 is true) occur at a rate $\alpha(x^T)$ and generate a cost K_I when they occur. The specificity of the test is the rate of correct negatives and is equal to $1 - \alpha(x^T)$. Type II errors (when the defendant's hypothesis H_0 is ac-

---

[18] For alternative approaches to optimal burden of proof rules based on the provision of incentives for underlying behavior, see Kaplow (2011, 2012, 2014), Hay and Spier (1997), and Sanchirico (1997).

Table 1.   Standard of Proof

Relationship between Realized Value and Threshold	Legal Inference
$x \leq x^T$	Plaintiff has met her burden of production or proof: Reject H_0 and accept H_1.
$x > x^T$	Plaintiff has not met her burden of production or proof. Reject H_1 and accept H_0.

cepted when H_1 is true) occur at a rate $\beta(x^T)$ and generate a cost K_{II} when they occur.[19] The sensitivity of the test is the rate of correct positives and is equal to $1 - \beta(x^T)$.

An ideal test would always avoid both types of errors. However, the extent to which an actual test approaches this ideal is limited by available information and the prohibitive costs of acquiring additional relevant and determinative information.

If $P(H_0)$ and $P(H_1)$ are the prior probabilities that the defendant's and the plaintiff's hypothesis is true, respectively, minimization of expected error costs plus the cost of the test is achieved by choosing a standard of proof x^T that minimizes the following loss function (LF):

$$LF(x^T) = P(H_0)[\alpha(x^T)K_I] + P(H_1)[\beta(x^T)K_{II}] + C, \qquad (1)$$

where C is the resource cost of applying the standard of proof to the parties and to society. C is assumed not to vary between alternative decision standards, but it could be avoided if the legal system used a standard of proof that does not require evaluation of evidence.

3.3. The Optimal Standard of Proof

In this section, the standard of proof x^* that minimizes total expected error costs and direct cost is derived. Minimizing the loss function set out in equation (1) requires taking the derivative of equation (1) with respect to x^T and setting it equal to 0. This yields the following first-order condition:

$$\frac{\partial LF(x^*)}{\partial x^*} = P(H_0)\frac{\partial \alpha(x^*)}{\partial x^*}K_I + P(H_1)\frac{\partial \beta(x^*)}{\partial x^*}K_{II} = 0. \qquad (2)$$

---

[19] The loss function does not explicitly include the benefits of correct positive and negative decisions. Following the standard convention in the decision-theoretic literature, we assume that the loss parameters are normalized so that gains may be assumed to equal 0.

Table 2. Error Cost Matrix

	H_1 Is True $(P(H_1))$	H_0 Is True $(P(H_0))$
Test positive $(x \leq x^T)$	Correct positive	False positive
	(Sensitivity = $1 - \beta(x^T)$)	(Type I error rate = $\alpha(x^T)$)
		(Cost of type I error = K_I)
Test negative $(x > x^T)$	False negative	Correct negative
	(Type II error rate = $\beta(x^T)$)	(Specificity = $1 - \alpha(x^T)$)
	(Cost of type II error = K_{II})	

Solving the first-order condition (2) yields the following condition:

$$-\frac{\frac{\partial \beta(x^*)}{\partial x^*}}{\frac{\partial \alpha(x^*)}{\partial x^*}} = \omega/\pi, \tag{3}$$

where $\omega = (K_I / K_{II})$, the ratio of the cost of type I and type II errors, and $\pi = [P(H_1)] / [P(H_0)]$, the prior odds in favor of H_1.

Figure 2 adds the error rates $\alpha(x^T) = F(x^T|H_0)$ and $\beta(x^T) = 1 - F(x^T|H_1)$ to Figure 1, where $F(X|H_0)$ and $F(X|H_1)$ are the respective distribution functions associated with the density functions $f(X|H_0)$ and $f(X|H_0)$.

To evaluate the left side of condition (3), note from figure 2 that the incremental change in the type I and type II error rates as the threshold x^T is increased are $[\delta\alpha(x^T)] / \delta x^T = f(x^T|H_0)$ and $[\delta\beta(x^T)] / \delta x^T = -f(x^T|H_1)$. Thus, for any choice of the standard of proof threshold x^T (i.e., any choice whether optimal or not), the ratio of first derivatives that enters the optimality condition (3) equals the likelihood ratio (LR) evaluated at x^T:

$$-\frac{\frac{\partial \beta(x^T)}{\partial x^T}}{\frac{\partial \alpha(x^T)}{\partial x^T}} = \frac{f(x^T|H_1)}{f(x^T|H_0)} \equiv \text{LR}(x^T). \tag{4}$$

Substituting equation (4) into equation (3) and evaluating at the optimal standard of proof threshold x^*, we see that at the optimal standard of proof, the likelihood ratio must satisfy the following condition:

$$\text{LR}(x^*) = \omega/\pi. \tag{5}$$

Because of the assumption that neither ω nor π varies with the standard of proof, the optimal standard of proof involves setting the likelihood ratio equal to a constant, the value of which depends on

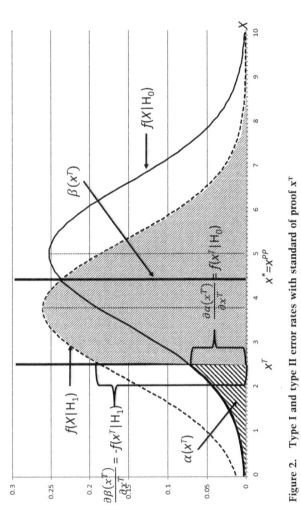

Figure 2. Type I and type II error rates with standard of proof x^τ

the relative costs of type I and type II errors (ω) and the prior odds in favor of the alternative hypothesis (π).[20]

3.4. Legal Standards and Optimal Standards

In this section, we describe the conditions under which the optimal standard of proof x^* derived in equation (5) coincides with mathematical representations of actual legal standards. We consider the conditions in which the preponderance standard, expressed as posterior odds equal to 1, is an optimal standard that minimizes expected error and direct costs. Next we consider heightened standards of proof.

Preponderance. The preponderance standard is a widely used standard of proof in civil cases. A common mathematical representation of the preponderance standard is that the plaintiff has met his or her burden under the standard when the probability of the alternative hypothesis is greater than .5. For example, Judge Frank Easterbrook, writing for the 7th Circuit in *Brown v. Bowen* (847 F.2d 342, 345 [7th Cir. 1988]), suggested the following interpretation of the preponderance standard: "The trier of fact rules for the plaintiff if it thinks the chance greater than 0.5 that the plaintiff is in the right." This suggests the following absolute probability representation of the preponderance standard:

$$p(H_1 | x) > .5. \tag{6}$$

The use of this absolute probability standard as a mathematical representation of the preponderance standard has been criticized by those skeptical of the use of probabilistic models of evidence and by those who are not.[21] The latter critics suggest the absolute probability representation be replaced by a ratio that compares the probabilities of the narratives offered by the plaintiff and the defendant. In these models, the preponderance standard is met for the plaintiff when the ratio of the conditional posterior probabilities evaluated at x is greater than 1 (see Kaye 1983):

$$\frac{p(H_1 | x)}{p(H_0 | x)} > 1. \tag{7}$$

Note that when there are only two competing alternatives, so that $p(H_1 | x) + p(H_0 | x) = 1$, condition (7) and the absolute probability condi-

---

[20] See Mungan (2011) for an economic model that endogenously generates asymmetric error costs.

[21] See Allen and Pardo (2007) discussing the reference-class problem; Cheng (2009) describes mathematical criteria to address choice of reference class.

tion (6), that $p(H_1|x) > .5$, are equivalent statements. In addition, the ratio of the posterior probabilities in condition (7) equals the conditional odds of H_1 given x.

Using Bayes's rule, condition (7) is equivalent to

$$\frac{p(H_1|x)}{p(H_0|x)} = \frac{p(x|H_1)}{p(x|H_0)}\frac{P(H_1)}{P(H_0)} = LR(x) \times \pi > 1. \tag{8}$$

Solving for LR(x) yields the preponderance rule as a likelihood ratio test (see Kaplow 2014, 14):

$$\text{Find for the plaintiff when } LR(x) > LR(x^{\text{PP}}) = 1/\pi. \tag{9}$$

Comparing the preponderance standard (9) to the optimal standard derived in equation (5), it is easy to see that the two will coincide when the cost of type I and type II errors are equal, so that $\omega = 1$ (see Cheng and Pardo 2015). Indeed, the Supreme Court, in describing the preponderance standard in *In re Winship* (397 U.S. 358 [1970]), suggested (albeit in dicta) that such a weighting is appropriate in certain civil cases: "In a civil suit between two private parties for money damages, for example, we view it as no more serious in general for there to be an erroneous verdict in the defendant's favor than for there to be an erroneous verdict in the plaintiff's favor. A preponderance of the evidence standard therefore seems peculiarly appropriate for, as explained most sensibly, it simply requires the trier of fact to believe that the existence of a fact is more probable than its nonexistence."[22]

Table 3 depicts the error cost matrix in a civil case that incorporates the assumption that $K_I = K_{II} = K$, so that $\omega = 1$. Thus, when $\omega = 1$, the preponderance standard (9) is an optimal standard (see Cheng 2009):

$$\text{Find for the plaintiff when } LR(x) > LR(x^*) = LR(x^{PP}) = 1/\pi. \tag{10}$$

Finally, consider the special case of a diffuse or noninformative prior, that is, where $P(H_0) = P(H_1) = .5$, so $\pi = 1$. Coupled with the assumption that $\omega = 1$, condition (10) becomes

$$LR(x) > LR(x^*) = LR(x^{PP}) = 1. \tag{11}$$

As figure 2 is drawn, x^{PP} is the level of proof when the parties' competing densities are equal, reflecting the assumption that $\omega = \pi = 1$. Under these conditions, minimizing the loss function (1) is equivalent to minimizing the total error rate $(\alpha(x^T) + \beta(x^T))$.

[22] See also Pardo (2013), citing *Grogan v. Garner* (498 U.S. 279, 286 [1991]), explaining that the preponderance standard "results in a roughly equal allocation of the risk of error" (561).

Table 3. Error Cost Matrix in a Civil Case

	H_1 Is True $(P(H_1))$	H_0 Is True $(P(H_0))$
Test positive $(x \leq x^T)$ (liable)	Correct positive (Sensitivity $= 1 - \beta(x^T)$)	False positive (Type I error rate $= \alpha(x^T)$) (Cost of type I error $= K_I = K$)
Test negative $(x > x^T)$ (not liable)	False negative (Type II error rate $= \beta(x^T)$) Cost of type II error $= K_{II} = K$	Correct negative (Specificity $= 1 - \alpha(x^T)$)

For a given choice of proof threshold, using the statistical evidence entails a total loss of $[(K/2)(\alpha(x^T) + \beta(x^T)) + C]$. The best feasible alternative would be to not use statistical evidence at all, instead settling for an approach that leads to total error probability of 1. Three examples of such a decision rule are as follows: always determining the issue either for the plaintiff $(\alpha = 1, \beta = 0, \alpha + \beta = 1)$, always determining it for the defendant $(\alpha = 0, \beta = 1, \alpha + \beta = 1)$, and flipping a fair coin $(\alpha = .5, \beta = \frac{1}{2}, \alpha + \beta = 1)$. Each example yields a total cost of $K/2$. Thus, total error costs are lower when the test is used if

$$[(K/2)(\alpha(x^T) + \beta(x^T)) + C] < K/2 \tag{12}$$

or, equivalently, whenever

$$\alpha(x^T) + \beta(x^T) < 1 - 2C/K.^{23} \tag{13}$$

To illustrate how moving the standard of proof threshold affects the loss function, consider again the evidence and threshold x^T depicted in figure 2. At x^T, $-[(\delta\beta(x^T) / \delta x^T) / (\delta\alpha(x^T) / \delta x^T)] = LR(x^T) > 1$ or, equivalently, $(\delta\alpha(x^T) / \delta x^T) < -(\delta\beta(x^T) / \delta x^T)$. Thus, moving the threshold incrementally to the right will increase the type I error rate by less than the decrease in the type II error rate so that the total error cost rate $(\alpha(x^T) + \beta(x^T))$ and thus total error costs $(K/2)(\alpha(x^T) + \beta(x^T))$ will fall. This will be true for any threshold $x^T < x^{PP}$. Similarly, for any $x^T > x^{PP}$, moving the threshold incrementally to the left will increase the type II error by less than the decrease in the type I error rate. As a result, $x^{PP} = x^*$ when $\pi = \omega = 1$.

[23] As just noted, this calculation assumes—via the assumption that $\pi = \omega = 1$—that the legal system is operating with diffuse priors and is indifferent to whether errors operate in favor of plaintiffs or defendants. A system with nondiffuse priors and that was not indifferent would have a boundary condition weighted toward one party type's interests.

We use this following example to illustrate the differences between legal standards and statistical standards of proof next. The use of the likelihood ratio criterion in equation (11) is merely an example of when there are symmetric error costs and diffuse prior probabilities and is not a normative argument that the legal system *should* adopt such priors as a proper presumption or that such a prior should be adopted in applying relative probability tests.[24]

Beyond a Reasonable Doubt. The analysis can also be applied to heightened legal standards of proof. Table 4 depicts the error cost matrix in a criminal trial. The criminal error cost matrix differs from the civil matrix in two primary ways. First, commentators have suggested that in the context of a criminal trial, the cost of a type I error is many times the cost of a type II error.[25] Second, criminal trials incorporate a presumption of innocence. Both the normative weighting of type I and type II errors and the presumption of innocence are consistent with the high "beyond a reasonable doubt" (BRD) standard of proof placed on the prosecutor in criminal trials, as well as the robust procedural protections given to criminal defendants.[26]

Rewriting equation (5), the optimality condition may be expressed as $LR(x^*)\pi = \omega$. Recalling that Bayes's theorem implies that the posterior odds in favor of the alternative hypothesis, $p(H_1|x) / p(H_0|x)$, equals $LR(x) \times \pi$, the optimal standard of proof induces an equality between the posterior odds and ω. When the costs of type I errors are presumed to be greater than the cost of a type II error, $\omega = \frac{K_I}{K_{II}} > 1$. In addition, suppose that the presumption of innocence is reflected in the prior odds π.[27] If we use the Blackstone (1765, 352) ratio ($\omega = 10$), the posterior odds for the BRD standard of proof to be an optimal standard are $p(H_1|x)/p(H_0|x) = LR(x^{BRD}) \times \pi = LR(x^*) \times \pi = 10$. Thus, to convict,

---

[24] See Cheng (2009) arguing for use of a diffuse prior. But see Hay and Spier (1997), suggesting optimal burden considers the proportion of negligent defendants and the parties' relative costs of producing evidence; and Johnson et al. (2017), arguing for a Bayesian approach to legal and statistical standards of proof that incorporates nonstatistical evidence into the prior.

[25] Blackstone (1765) wrote that "it is better that ten guilty persons escape than that one innocent suffer" (352). See also Clermont (2009) examining different approaches to standards of proof in civil vs. common law countries.

[26] These protections include the right to counsel as set out in *Gideon v. Wainwright* (372 U.S. 335 [1963]), the notice requirement from *Miranda v. Arizona* (384 U.S. 436 [1966]), and the requirement from *Brady v. Maryland* (373 U.S. 83 [1963]) that prosecutors disclose material exculpatory evidence in their possession.

[27] For a general discussion and analysis of the presumption of innocence, see Scurich and John (2017), noting prior scholarship suggesting the presumption of innocence requires $P(H_1) = 1/N_r$, where N_r is the count of some appropriate reference class. This would imply a prior odds ratio $\pi = N_r - 1$.

Table 4.   Error Cost Matrix in a Criminal Trial

	H_1 Is True $(P(H_1))$	H_0 Is True $(P(H_0))$
Test positive $(x \leq x^T)$ (guilty)	Correct positive	False positive
	Convicting the guilty	Convicting the innocent
	(Sensitivity $= 1 - \beta(x^T)$)	(Type I error rate $= \alpha(x^T)$)
		(Cost of type I error $= K_I = K$)
Test negative $(x > x^T)$ (not guilty)	False negative	Correct negative
	Letting the guilty go free	Acquitting the innocent
	(Type II error rate $= \beta(x^T)$)	(Specificity $= 1 - \alpha(x^T)$)
	(Cost of type II error $= K_{II} = \omega K, \ \omega > 1$)	

the posterior odds would have to be greater than 10, which equates to requiring that $p(H_1|x) = .909$ to convict when H_1 is the only possible alternative to H_0. Similarly, if $\omega = 19$, the posterior odds for the BRD standard of proof to be an optimal standard are $p(H_1|x)/p(H_0|x) = LR (x^{BRD}) \times \pi = LR(x^*) \times \pi = 19$. This equates to requiring that $p(H_1|x) = .95$ (a numerical threshold often linked to the BRD standard) to convict when H_1 is the only possible alternative to H_0.[28]

A similar analysis could be applied to model an intermediate civil standard of proof (e.g., the clear and convincing evidence standard used in some civil cases). Note that under this formulation, the optimal critical likelihood ratio $LR(x^*) = \omega/\pi$ can differ from the preponderance threshold of $LR(x^{PP}) = 1$ from equation (11) due to asymmetric error costs ($K_I \neq K_{II}$, so $\omega \neq 1$) or from a nondiffuse prior/presumption ($P(H_0) \neq P(H_1)$, so $\pi \neq 1$). Thus, an optimal heightened civil standard ($LR(x) > LR(x^{CCE}) = LR(x^*) > 1$) can incorporate the civil presumption ($\pi = 1$) and asymmetric error costs (where $\omega > 1$), symmetric error costs ($\omega = 1$) and a heightened presumption ($\pi > 1$), or both. If such a standard requires that $p(H_1|x) > .75$, though, it necessarily implies that $\omega = 3$ whenever $\pi = 1$ and the null and alternative hypotheses are the only possibilities, so that the clear and convincing standard coincides with the optimal standard when $LR(x) \times \pi > LR(x^{CCE}) \times \pi = LR(x^*) \times \pi > 3$ (Kaplow 2012, 779). The same analysis can also generate relaxed crit-

---

[28] See, e.g., Newman (2006) commenting on quantification of the BRD standard as equal to a "95% chance that the defendant is guilty" (267). See also Gastwirth (1992, 57) reporting average probabilities associated with legal standards of proof from judicial survey.

ical likelihood ratios $(\mathrm{LR}(x^{\mathrm{ALT}}) = \mathrm{LR}(x^*) < 1)$ when the asymmetry in error costs and/or the presumption/priors are reversed.

4. HYPOTHESIS TESTING AND STATISTICAL INFERENCE

4.1. Null Hypothesis Statistical Testing

Economists, as well as other social scientists, have offered expert opinions in litigation that utilize null hypothesis statistical testing.[29] A null hypothesis statistical test (NHST) is a commonly used method of statistical inference that incorporates elements of two different statistical approaches pioneered by Ronald A. Fisher (1966) and by Neyman and Pearson (1933; N-P). An NHST analysis used in litigation may offer some statistical result and associated fixed level of statistical significance—usually 5%. The inferential focus of such an analysis is whether the difference between an observed outcome and the outcome under the null hypothesis is statistically different from zero at a 5% level of statistical significance.

Fisher's (1966) NHST method was designed as an objective way to evaluate scientific evidence and focuses exclusively on specifying a null hypothesis and examining the data under the assumption that the null hypothesis is true.[30] Fisher promoted the use of fixed significance null hypothesis testing as a tool for identifying interesting results from scientific research, that is, those results with a low probability of occurring by chance under the null hypothesis. Results that failed to achieve statistical significance were to be ignored.

Fisher's exclusive focus on the null hypothesis and statistical significance, at the expense of any alternative hypothesis, was intentional. He explicitly rejected the notion that the costs of false negatives (type II errors) should influence how the threshold of "significance" is set: "The notion of an error of the so-called 'second kind,' due to accepting the null hypothesis 'when it is false' may then be given a meaning in reference to the quantity to be estimated. It has no meaning with respect to simple tests of significance, in which the only available expectations are those which flow from the null hypothesis being true" (Fisher 1966,

---

[29] Although in decline in some areas of scientific inquiry, NHST using fixed significance levels is still the dominant paradigm in economics and many other disciplines. For a discussion of these issues and the use of alternative statistical inference tools, see Fidler et al. (2004).

[30] "In relation to any experiment we may speak of this hypothesis as the 'null hypothesis' and it should be noted that the null hypothesis is never proved or established but it is possibly disproved in the course of the experimentation. Every experiment may be said to exist only in order to give the facts a chance of disproving the null hypothesis" (Fisher 1966, 16).

17; see also Ziliak and McCloskey 2008, 144; Meyerson and Meyerson 2010, 823–24). Fisher was also the most influential proponent of the use the .05 or 5% significance test, or "rule of two": "The value for which P=.05, or 1 in 20, is 1.96 or nearly 2; it is convenient to take this point as a limit in judging whether a deviation is to be considered significant or not. Deviations exceeding twice the standard deviation are thus formally regarded as significant" (R. A. Fisher, quoted in Ziliak and McCloskey 2008, 45).

Fisher's 5% significance threshold originally was used as a convenient standard that set out an arbitrary but objective minimum level of precision for declaring research results "important" (Ziliak and McCloskey 2008, 45–46; see also Meyerson and Meyerson 2010). Indeed, under the Fisher approach, arbitrary significance levels other than 5% could be used, did not need to be specified in advance, and could be applied a posteriori to a given set of data.

N-P's alternative approach to statistical inference attempted to improve on significance testing through a focus on applied decision making and tests of acceptance between competing hypotheses. N-P used the term "significance" to denote the probability of a false positive or type I error. Like Fisher, N-P also used "convenient" significance levels, including .05, to set an acceptable level of type I errors. However, unlike Fisher's approach to significance levels, which could be applied a posteriori, the N-P approach required an a priori choice of a significance level. N-P's approach also required the specification of an alternative hypothesis in addition to specifying the null.

N-P's explicit consideration of alternative hypotheses in turn allowed consideration of "effect size" as well as the explicit consideration of the rate of type I and type II errors and the ability to establish tests that would have the highest power. Given the choice of the rate of type I error and an alternative hypothesis, type II errors were to be controlled by ensuring that the sample size was sufficient given the stated effect size of the alternative hypothesis.

Descriptions and definitions of an NHST vary, but it can be described as a general set of "cookbook" procedures used to carry out statistical testing rather than a precise methodology for conducting statistical inference. Although application of an NHST varies, it does encompass a certain set of procedures that incorporate elements of both Fisher's and N-P's approaches without attempting the difficult task of reconciling inconsistent approaches into a unified methodology.[31]

An NHST generally begins with the specification of a null hypothesis and a choice of an arbitrary significance level, with the 5% signif-

---

[31] For a discussion of the two approaches being complementary rather than contradictory, see Lehmann (1993).

icance level commonly used. An alternative hypothesis is also specified. However, the level of specificity of the alternative hypothesis varies. The most common, or what we refer to as the "standard," approach is to use a nonspecific alternative hypothesis (e.g., when the alternative is the negation of the null hypothesis or a one-directional alternative, known as a "composite alternative"). If the alternative hypothesis is not specific, then an NHST will more closely resemble Fisher's approach to significance testing.

A more specific alternative hypothesis will allow consideration of statistical power and effect size and will more closely resemble the N-P approach to tests of acceptance. As we set out in more detail next, our approach to applying an NHST to make legal inferences more closely follows a modified N-P approach using tests of acceptance. Our approach relies on specifying an alternative hypothesis and allowing for consideration of statistical power and effect size. However, because the sample size is effectively fixed in many legal settings, our approach also emphasizes implementation of the trade-off between type I and type II errors implied by the applicable legal standard for a given sample size.

4.2. Null and Alternative Hypotheses

To illustrate the NHST approach to hypothesis testing and to compare this approach to the general error cost framework set out in section 3, we use the following example throughout the remainder of the article.[32] Suppose that an employer fills N vacancies by hiring 30% women and 70% men.[33] A nonhired female applicant sues the employer under Title VII for discriminating against women.[34] The

---

[32] The basic structure of the example is taken from Rubinfeld (1985, 1058).

[33] The analysis sets aside the four-fifths rule of thumb for disparate impact discussed in sec. 2 to focus on the preponderance standard used in general civil litigation. Our analysis also focuses on hiring outcome statistics rather than the effect of specific selection mechanisms. This focus and the binomial probability models used in the example in the article may be relevant if the selection mechanism responsible for the disparate treatment is not observable. For example, suppose that a firm fills 10 slots by offering the jobs to the first 10 applications pulled out of a large drum. However, the employee who is responsible for placing the applications in the drum systematically and clandestinely places the applications of some women at the bottom of the drum. In this case, the observed selection rate for men and women will both be 1. For an example of such a process in the context of race and jury selection, see *Swain v. Alabama* (380 U.S. 202 [1965]) (black persons in the jury pool had different colored tickets than whites).

[34] Title VII of the Federal Civil Rights Act of 1964, 42 U.S.C. §§ 2000e et seq. See generally, Peresie (2009) and Garaud (1990).

complaint alleges that the employer's hiring practices had a disparate impact on women.[35] With respect to the issue for which statistical evidence is probative, the plaintiff's initial burden of production is to prove, by a preponderance of evidence, that the number of women hired is lower than expected.[36] This can be achieved by showing that the number of women hired is lower than expected and that the difference is significant given the court's choice of significance level (see Garaud 1990, 467).

The inferential problem for both legal and statistical analysis is to decide when the observed outcome (a lower-than-expected number of women hired) favors an alternative hypothesis that the employer is discriminating against women over the null hypothesis that the employer hired employees without regard to the applicants' sex.[37] Under a fixed significance level NHST approach to statistical inference, the null hypothesis of no discrimination is rejected in favor of an alternative hypothesis of discrimination when the observed outcome x is less than a threshold x^C determined by an arbitrarily set fixed level of statistical significance. As set out in section 3, evidentiary standards and burdens of proof and production, such as the preponderance of evi-

---

[35] See *Griggs v. Duke Power Co.*, 401 U.S. 424 (1971).

[36] The Supreme Court's most recent word is that statistical evidence alone is not sufficient to make out a prima facie case—the plaintiff must describe the policy that allegedly gives rise to statistical imbalance. For example, the court in *Texas Dept. of Housing and Community Affairs v. Inclusive Communities Project, Inc.* (135 S.Ct. 2507, 2523 [2015]) stated that "a disparate-impact claim that relies on a statistical disparity must fail if the plaintiff cannot point to a defendant's policy or policies causing that disparity." Of course, statistical evidence cannot itself "point to a defendant's policy or policies causing" the statistical evidence itself. For exposition's sake, we shall assume that the plaintiff can make the requisite showing regarding defendant's policies. As to the required statistical showing itself, the plaintiff need only prove discrimination to the preponderance standard. As the court in *Bazemore v. Friday* (478 U.S. 385, 400 [1986]) explained, "a plaintiff in a Title VII suit need not prove discrimination with scientific certainty; rather, his or her burden is to prove discrimination by a preponderance of the evidence." The Supreme Court has never held that statistical significance at any particular level is required to meet this standard, though some lower courts have (see Garaud 1990, 467, citing *Palmer v. Schultz* (815 F.2d 84, 96 [D.C. Cir. 1987]) where the court stated that"statistical evidence must meet the 5% level . . . for it alone to establish a prima facie case under Title VII").

[37] The inquiry here is a preliminary one—whether the plaintiff has met his initial burden of production for a prima facie case. The general principles analyzed in this article can be applied to other types of preliminary thresholds such as the plausibility standard to decide motions to dismiss in *Bell Atlantic Corp. v. Twombly* (550 U.S. 544 [2007]) and *Tellabs Inc. v. Makor Issues & Rights* (551 U.S. 308 [2007]), the standard for summary judgment under *Matsushita Electric Industrial Co., Ltd. v. Zenith Radio Corp.* (475 U.S. 574 [1986]), or the burden of proof for final adjudication. This issue is discussed in sec. 5.5.

dence, also use threshold levels of the same observed outcome to determine liability. Key issues are to analyze how these alternative threshold values are determined and to provide a framework for evaluating both the consistency and performance of alternative thresholds.

As noted, the NHST approach to statistical inference compares one hypothesis (the null hypothesis, denoted H_0) to an alternative hypothesis (denoted H_1) or to a set of alternative hypotheses. We describe in more detail the concepts of null and alternative hypotheses and present an example that is used to illustrate the concepts and alternative approaches to statistical inference.

The Null Hypothesis. The null hypothesis is the hypothesis to be tested; in the parlance of statistics, the null hypothesis will either be rejected or fail to be rejected. It is commonly defined as the hypothesis that any observed difference (e.g., between two sample means or a sample mean and baseline value) is related to random chance and not systematic causes.

In the gender discrimination example, the null hypothesis is that the employer hires N employees without regard to sex from a large pool of equally qualified applicants. In the pool of qualified applicants, p_0 is the proportion of qualified applicants who are female and $1 - p_0$ is the proportion of qualified applicants who are male. In terms of the defendant's hypothesis discussed in section 3, the null and defendant's hypotheses would be the same.

The firm actually hires x women and $N - x$ men. Let X be the random variable representing the number of women hired so that under the null hypothesis, X has approximately a binomial sampling distribution, with a probability density function given by

$$f(x : N, p_0) = \binom{N}{x} p_0^x (1 - p_0)^{N-x}.{}^{38}$$

(14)

---

[38] For a discrete random variable, such as a count of the number hired, the usual term is the "probability mass function"; the term "probability density function" is used when the random variable of interest has a continuous distribution. Because nothing important will be changed by ignoring this distinction for purposes of our discussion, we use the term "density" throughout. Note also that the sampling distribution for the number of women hired, X, is only approximately binomially distributed because the pool of qualified applicants is sampled without replacement. The precise distribution is a hypergeometric one, but using a binomial distribution here will simplify the discussion without changing anything important (a general rule of thumb is that the binomial sampling distribution for counts can be used when the population is at least 20 times as large as the sample, a condition likely met in most applications).

The binomial density function gives the probability of hiring exactly x women for the N open slots. The expected number of women hired if H_0 is true is $\mu_0 = Np_0$, and the variance equals $\sigma_0^2 = Np_0(1 - p_0)$. For example, if the firm hires $N = 10$ qualified workers without regard to the sex of the applicant from a qualified pool that is half female and half male, the probability that a given hire will be a woman is $p_0 = .5$ under H_0.[39] Thus, under the assumption that the relevant pool of qualified workers is half male and half female, the null hypothesis is equivalent to a null hypothesis that $p_0 = .5$, so the expected number of women hired equals $\mu_0 = Np_0 = 5$ and the variance equals $\sigma_0^2 = Np_0(1 - p_0) = 2.5$. Figure 3 depicts the sampling distribution of the number of women hired under H_0, that is, when $p_0 = .5$ and $N = 10$. In the figure, the horizontal axis measures the number of women that could be hired, x, which can range from 0 to 10. The vertical axis measures the probability X takes on each of these values, when the null hypothesis is true.

The null sampling distribution in figure 3 illustrates that even when the firm hires applicants without considering the sex of the applicant, it is not the case that a given hiring cycle always will produce an observed outcome where half of new hires are men and half are women. In fact, when an employer selects 10 qualified workers without regard to sex and the qualified pool is half men and half women, we would expect the event that 5 women are hired to occur a shade less than a quarter of the time.

In the hypothetical example set out at the beginning of this section, the employer hired 70% men and 30% women. With $N = 10$, this means 3 women and 7 men would be hired for the 10 vacancies. The probability of this outcome ($x = 3$) under the null hypothesis is 11.72%, and the probability that three or fewer women will be hired is 17.18% (the sum of the four relevant probabilities). The significance of these numbers is addressed next.

The Alternative Hypothesis. Under an NHST, the alternative hypothesis is the hypothesis that is favored when the null is rejected. There are several types of alternative hypotheses. These include nonspecific compound hypotheses that are used in the standard approach to an NHST, which include nondirectional alternative hypotheses, one- and two-tailed directional alternative hypotheses, and

[39] Our examples set $p_0 = .5$. When the qualified pools are not 50% female and 50% male, then p_0 will deviate from .5. See *Wards Cove Packing Co. v. Atonio* (490 U.S. 642, 650 [1989], citing *Hazelwood School District v. United States* (433 U.S. 299, 308 [1977]; [alterations and omission in original]), for the proposition that "the proper comparison [is] between the racial composition of [the at-issue jobs] and the racial composition of the qualified . . . population in the relevant labor market."

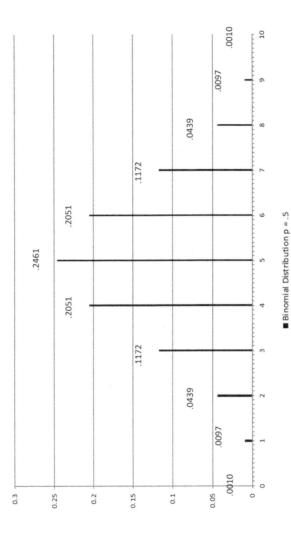

Figure 3. Binomial sampling distribution of the number of women hired (X) under the null hypothesis ($p_0 = .5$ and $n = 10$).

point hypotheses.[40] Nondirectional alternative hypotheses, such as the negation of the null hypothesis, are often used in settings in which the only concern is whether the null hypothesis is true. Directional alternative hypotheses can be one-tailed, for which only one tail of the region of rejection is of concern, or two-tailed, for which both regions of rejections are of concern. In the discrimination example just set out, a nondirectional alternative hypothesis would be $p_0 \neq .5$. But such a two-tailed alternative hypothesis makes no sense in an employment discrimination lawsuit. To see this, suppose the employer-defendant actually hired 9 women out of 10 total hires. Even though this is a very unlikely outcome if the employer hires in a sex-neutral way, it is unlikely in a way that would provide evidence the employer *favors* female plaintiffs rather than discriminating against them. No court would direct or uphold a verdict against the employer under such conditions. The relevant alternative hypothesis would be a directional one, often known as a one-tailed alternative hypothesis (that women are hired less than half the time, or $p_1 < .5$).

Our analysis in this article relies on the third general type of alternative hypothesis, the point or specific alternative hypotheses.[41] In point alternative hypotheses, the sampling distribution under the alternative hypothesis is a fully defined distribution with no unknown parameters. Although their explicit use in empirical analysis is relatively rare, specific alternative hypotheses are fundamental to the N-P approach to statistical inference and the associated determining concepts of statistical power, effect size, and optimal likelihood ratio tests under the N-P lemma.[42] Use of point or specific alternative hypotheses is also helpful to understanding the relationship between statistical inference and legal inference discussed in section 3. Both Kaplow's (2011, 2012, 2014) approach to legal decision rules—based on N-P likelihood ratio tests—and Cheng's (2009) relative probability approach use specific alternative hypotheses. Recent approaches to legal inference and burdens of proof incorporate specific explanations

---

[40] As noted earlier, hypotheses that encompass more than one possibility are called "composite hypotheses." Composite hypotheses may include any number of point hypotheses.

[41] This article does not consider composite hypotheses. For an approach to balancing type I and type II error costs in such situations, see Gelbach and Kobayashi (2018).

[42] In terms of the example that was just set out, the N-P lemma states that when performing a test between two specific hypotheses, H_0 and H_1, the likelihood ratio test that rejects H_0 in favor of H_1 when the likelihood ratio evaluated at x is greater than some threshold likelihood ratio is the most powerful test for a given significance level. Under some conditions, the N-P lemma can be generalized to composite alternative hypotheses (though it generally cannot when the alternative is simply the two-tailed negation of a point-null hypothesis).

of the evidence, the legal analog of point hypotheses. Pardo and Allen's explanation-based reasoning and the process of inference to the best explanation make use of a finite set of specific explanations, generated by the parties in the first stage of the two-stage explanation-based inferential process.[43]

Table 5 provides example data for a null hypothesis and three specific alternative hypotheses based on the discrimination example. The table lists the values of the sampling distribution density function for the null and each of the alternative distributions, as well as the ratio of the density function for each of the specific alternatives relative to the null, that is, the likelihood ratio (Rubinfeld 1985, 1058–9).

Panel a of table 5 provides probabilities under the null hypothesis, just described—the hypothesis that the firm hires qualified employees without regard to gender. Panel d represents the specific alternative hypothesis that the firm does not hire women at all (H_1^d). The number of women hired is generated by a binomial sampling distribution with parameter $p_1^b = 0$. Panel c represents the specific alternative hypothesis that the firm discards applications submitted by married women, and thus, when it hires women, hires only those who are single (H_1^c). Assuming 40% of qualified women are married and 60% are single, the probability that a woman is hired under this alternative hypothesis is 3/8 (or .375).[44] The number of women hired will be generated by a binomial sampling distribution with parameter $p_1^c = .375$. Finally, panel b represents the specific alternative hypothesis that the firm hires only those women without children (H_1^b). Assuming 20% of qualified women have children, the probability that a woman will be hired under this alternative hypothesis is 4/9, or $p_1^b = .444$.[45] Figure 4 shows the binomial sampling distributions for the four hypotheses in table 1.

---

[43] Pardo and Allen (2008) discuss factors that determine the inferential interests and the level of detail of the explanations; Allen and Stein (2013) distinguish "relative plausibility theory" from mathematical approaches to evidence; and Pardo (2013) explains how inference to the best explanation explains evidentiary law.

[44] Under H_1^c, suppose that all applications from qualified married women are discarded. The remaining set of applications is then forwarded to the hiring committee, and 10 are randomly picked. Maintaining the assumption that 50% of the applicants are women and 50% are men, under H_1^c, 40% of the women (2/5) and 20% of the total files (2/10) are discarded, and $p_1^c = .3/.8 = .3750$. The same probability can be derived from a sequential process where applications from qualified married women that are randomly picked are not considered and thrown back into the large pile of applications, whereas applications from qualified men and single women are approved.

[45] Under H_1^b, suppose that all applications from women with children are discarded. Thus, under H_1^b, 20% (1/5) of the women and 10% of the total files (1/10) are screened out, and $p_1^b = .4/.9 = .444$.

Table 5.   Null and Specific Alternative Hypotheses

NUMBER OF WOMEN HIRED (X)	*a.* NULL (H_0) $f(X\mid H_0)$	*b.* ALT. (H_1^b) $f(X\mid H_1^b)$	$LR(X)$	*c.* ALT. (H_1^c) $f(X\mid H_1^c)$	$LR(X)$	*d.* ALT. (H_1^d) $f(X\mid H_1^d)$	$LR(X)$
0	.0010	.003	3.0	.009	9.0	1	1,000
1	.0097	.023	2.3	.055	5.5	0	0
2	.0439	.081	1.8	.147	3.3	0	0
3	.1172	.173	1.5	.236	2.0	0	0
4	.2051	.241	1.2	.248	1.2	0	0
5	.2461	.231	.9	.178	.7	0	0
6	.2051	.154	.7	.089	.4	0	0
7	.1172	.070	.6	.031	.3	0	0
8	.0439	.021	.5	.007	.2	0	0
9	.0097	.004	.4	.001	.1	0	0
10	.0010	.0003	.3	5.5E-05	.1	0	0
Probability a woman is hired	$p_0 = .5$	$p_1^b = .444$		$p_1^c = .375$		$p_1^d = 0$	

4.3. Null Hypothesis Statistical Testing and Fixed Significance Levels

Using an NHST with a fixed significance level α entails rejecting the null hypothesis whenever the observed number of women hired has a p value less than α. Consider the discrimination example just set out. Examining figure 3, the one-tailed p value associated with observing three or fewer women hired equals .1718. If the conventional α = .05 significance level is applied to this outcome, the deviation of 3 of 10 women hired from the expected 5 of 10 under the null hypothesis is not statistically significant, because the p value is .172, which exceeds the value of α (i.e., .05). Even if only 2 of 10 women were hired, the deviation from the expected 5 of 10 would not be statistically significant at the conventional .05 level (p = .055 > α = .05). Only observed outcomes where 0 or 1 of 10 women would be statistically significant based on a test that required p values below α = .05.

Thus, the threshold of statistical significance based on p values < .05 is between 1 and 2 women hired out of 10 and is illustrated in figure 5. Figure 5 shows the distribution of outcomes when the null is true. When the null hypothesis is true, the α = .05 significance test

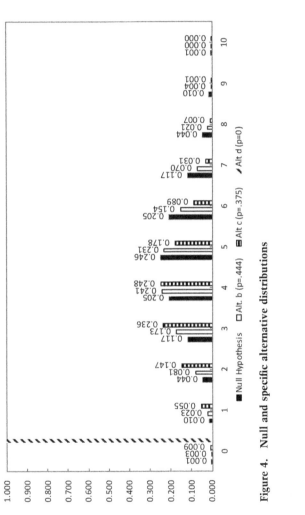

Figure 4. Null and specific alternative distributions

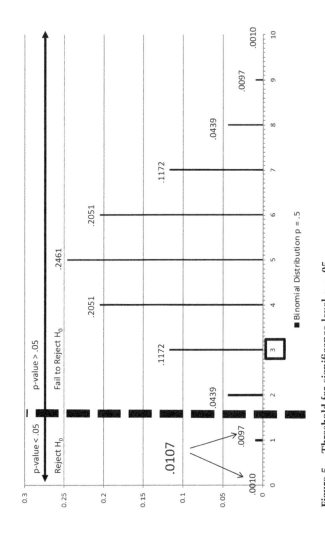

Figure 5. Threshold for significance level α = .05

erroneously rejects the null when 0 or 1 of 10 women is hired. As table 3 indicates, these outcomes are false positives or type I errors. This type of error occurs under the null hypothesis with probability .0107.

Setting the significance level at α ensures that the type I error rate will be no greater than α. In the discrete binomial example illustrated in figure 5, setting the significance level at α = .05 actually results in a type I error rate of less than .05, due to the discrete nature of the binomial distribution. Figure 6 illustrates a situation in which setting α = .05 fixes the type I error rate to be equal to α = .05. Figure 6A superimposes the normal approximation onto the binomial distribution in the case of N = 10.[46] With a normal distribution, an α = .05 significance level corresponds to a one-tailed critical value equal to 2.40 (or 1.645 SD below the mean).[47] Figure 6B shows the lower-tailed normal distribution cutoff for an α = .05 significance level. When the null hypothesis is true, rejecting the null hypothesis when $x < x^C$ = 2.401 will erroneously reject the null hypothesis 5% of the time when x is a normally distributed continuous variable.[48]

4.4. Type II Error and Statistical Power with a Fixed α = .05 NHST

The fixed α = .05 NHST considers only type I error and the sampling distribution under the null hypothesis. Thus, in a fixed N setting, this approach ignores the rate and costs of type II error as well as the distribution of the alternative hypothesis. Determining the rate of type II errors associated with a fixed α = .05 NHST requires explicit consideration of the applicable sampling distribution under the relevant alternative hypothesis. To illustrate the power associated with fixed α = .05 NHST, suppose that the plaintiff alleges that the firm's hiring practices discriminate against married women, whereas the defendant insists it does not discriminate at all. The null hypothesis remains the same, and the alternative hypothesis is now described by

---

[46] The normal approximation with N = 10 is used for convenience to illustrate why α is the rate of type I error. However, in general, the normal approximation is not accurate for small values of N. The normal approximation is usually viewed as appropriate when $Np > 10$ and $Np(1 - p) > 10$, conditions that are not met in this example.

[47] Using the standard deviation from the underlying binomial distribution, with N = 10 and p_0 = .5, which equals $[Np_0(1 - p_0)]^{1/2} = [10(.5)(.5)]^{1/2}$ = .158, 1.645 SD equals 2.599, and 1.96 SD equals 3.097. The left-hand cutoff for an α = .05 one-tailed test equals 5 − 2.599 = 2.401, and the left-hand cutoff for a two-tailed test equals 5 − 3.097 = 1.903.

[48] When the null distribution can be approximated by a normal distribution with known parameters (μ_0 = Np_0, σ_0^2 = $Np_0(1 - p_0)$), a standardized test statistic ($Z = (x - \mu_0) / \sigma_0$) can be calculated and compared with the applicable cutoff for the fixed α null hypothesis test. For an α = .05 one-tailed test, the null hypothesis is rejected if $|Z| > 1.645$.

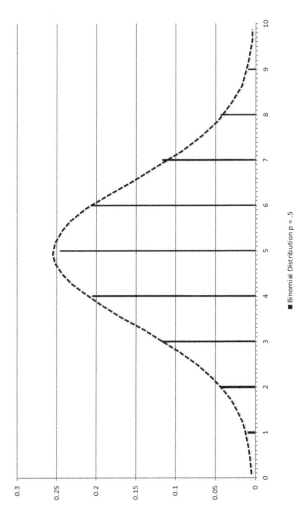

■ Binomial Distribution p = .5

Figure 6. (A) Normal approximation of null distribution and α = .05; (B) normal distribution critical values for a one-tailed test.

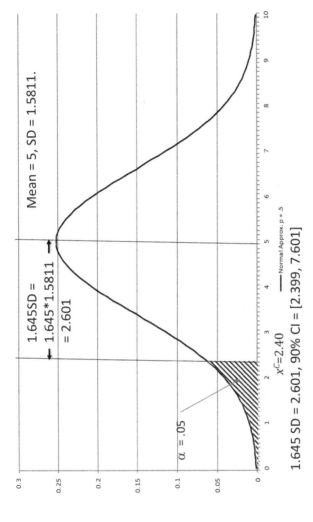

Figure 6. (*Continued*)

33

H_1^c. Under H_1^c, the plaintiff alleges that the firm discriminates against married women, who make up 40% of the qualified pool of female applicants. The relevant sampling distribution is a binomial distribution with parameter $p_1^c = .375$.

Figure 7 shows both the null and the alternative distributions of X given H_1^c when the firm attempts to fill the 10 vacancies ($N = 10$). As shown, a fixed $\alpha = .05$ NHST will result in a critical value that rejects the null hypothesis of no discrimination if one or no woman is hired. This results in a probability of erroneously rejecting the null when the null is true equal to .0107. This type I error rate is calculated by adding the probability of observing fewer than two women hired when the null is true, that is, adding the frequencies from the null distribution to the left of the cutoff. A type II error occurs when the fixed $\alpha = .05$ NHST fails to reject the null when the alternative is true. The type II error rate is calculated by adding the probability of observing two or more women hired when the alternative is true, or adding the frequencies from the alternative distribution to the right of the cutoff. The type II error rate of the fixed $\alpha = .05$ NHST is .9363 in this case, so under H_1^c the sum of type I and type II error rates is .947. Thus, if the goal is to minimize the sum of error rates, with $N = 10$ a fixed significance level of $\alpha = .05$ only barely improves on a noninformative test such as a coin flip.

5. LEGAL AND STATISTICAL SIGNIFICANCE COMPARED

In this section, the error cost analysis discussed in section 3 is compared with the fixed significance level NHST discussed in section 4. The fixed significance level NHST is conceptually different than the error cost analysis. The standard approach to a fixed $\alpha = .05$ NHST begins with the application of the standard or conventional significance level of 5%. The fixed $\alpha = .05$ NHST considers only type I error rates and the null distribution in fixing the type I error rate at 5%. The rate and costs of type II errors, as well as the distribution of the alternative hypothesis, are ignored.

In terms of the error cost matrix illustrated in table 2, fixing the significance level at α is equivalent to setting the type I error rate at α irrespective of the level of type II error β. Table 6 illustrates the error cost matrix for the disparate impact discrimination example when a fixed $\alpha = .05$ NHST is used. Suppose that the legal standard to prove a prima facie case of disparate impact is a statistically significant deviation in the number of women hired relative to the expected number under the null hypothesis. A type I error is the rejection of the null

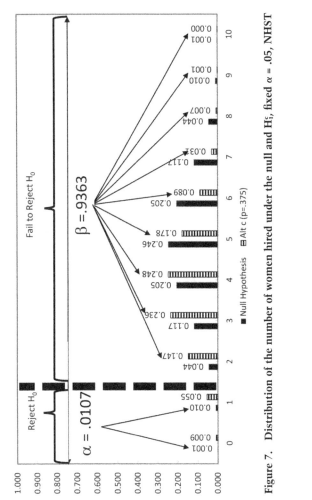

Figure 7. Distribution of the number of women hired under the null and H$_i$, fixed α = .05, NHST

Table 6. Error Cost Matrix in a Fixed α Null-Hypothesis Statistical Test

	Alternative Is True (Firm Discriminates against Women)	Null Is True (Firm Picks Employees without Regard to Sex)
Test positive $(x \leq x^c)$ (statistically significant)	Correct positive	False positive
	Correct inference of statistical discrimination	Incorrect inference of statistical discrimination
	(Power/sensitivity = 1 − $\beta(x^c)$ = ?)	(Type I error rate = $\alpha(x^c)$) = .05)
Test negative $(x > x^c)$ (not statistically significant)	False negative	Correct negative
	Erroneous, no inference of statistical discrimination	Correct, no inference of statistical discrimination
	(Type II error rate = $\beta(x^c)$ = ?)	(Specificity = 1 − $\alpha(x^c)$ = .95)

hypothesis (a positive test, finding there is a significant deviation) when the null hypothesis is true (i.e., the firm hires qualified workers without regard to sex). A type II error is the failure to reject the null hypothesis (a negative test, failing to reject the null) when the null hypothesis is false (the firm discriminated against women when making employment decisions).[49] The thresholds for significance levels are set without consideration of the rate of type II error or any reference to or consideration of the potential alternative distributions (see Ziliak and McCloskey 2008).

In contrast, the error cost analysis presented in section 3 considers both type I and type II error rates, the distributions of both the null and alternative hypotheses, as well as the costs associated with avoiding the two types of errors. As discussed next, given these differences, the two approaches generally will produce different tests and different outcomes. To the extent that legal standards and procedures consider the costs of both type I and type II errors, it would be mere coincidence if a standard that fixes the rate of one type of

[49] There is a preference among many statisticians for using the term "do not reject" or "fail to reject" rather than "accept" the null hypothesis (see, e.g., Hogg, Tanis, and Zimmerman 2015, 360). This preference reflects the ability of scholarly researchers to reserve judgment on the true state of affairs. Courts do not have that luxury, of course; see *Daubert v. Merrell Dow Pharmaceuticals, Inc.* (509 U.S. 579, 597 [1993]), "Scientific conclusions are subject to perpetual revision. Law, on the other hand, must resolve disputes finally and quickly."

error (type I errors), without considering either the relative cost or the rate of type II errors, just happened to minimize the applicable loss function.

For expositional purposes, we focus in this section on the civil standard of preponderance of the evidence with diffuse priors. Under these conditions, the preponderance test is identical to the $LR(x^*) = 1$ optimal test that minimizes sum of the error rates $\alpha + \beta$. This section compares this mathematical formulation of the civil legal standard under these conditions and the fixed α statistical test.

5.1. Fixed α = .05 NHST versus $LR(x^*)$ = 1, Minimum $\alpha + \beta$ Tests

Figure 8 depicts the properties of the $LR(x^*) = 1$ test that minimizes $\alpha + \beta$ when the null hypothesis of no discrimination (p_0 = .5) is tested against the alternative H_1^c hypotheses that the firm does not hire married women (p_1^c = .375) and N = 10. The $LR(x^*) = 1$ test rejects the null hypothesis when fewer than five women are hired. In contrast, as shown in figure 7, the fixed α = .05 NHST rejects the null hypothesis when fewer than two women are hired, thus $x^C < x^{PP} = x^*$.

Note that although the $LR(x^*) = 1$ test has a higher type I error rate ($\alpha(x^*)$ = .3770) than the fixed α = .05 NHST depicted in figure 5 ($\alpha(x^C)$ = .0107), it will have a much lower type II error rate ($\beta(x^*)$ = .3057) than the fixed α = .05 NHST (with a $\beta(x^C)$ = .9363). As a result, the sum of $\alpha(x^*) + \beta(x^*)$ = .6827 for the $LR(x^*) = 1$ test is lower than the sum of $\alpha(x^C) + \beta(x^C)$ = .947 for the fixed α = .05 NHST.[50]

The same trade-offs are illustrated in figure 9. On the horizontal axis is the *specificity* of the test, or the rate at which the test correctly fails to reject the null hypothesis when the null is true. The vertical axis measures the *power* of the test, or the rate at which the test correctly rejects the null when the alternative hypothesis is true. A perfect test would have power and specificity of 1 and is located at the upper right corner of the figure. Under the circumstances posited in the example, such tests are unattainable with a finite number of observations. Given the cost and limitations of information in determining an outcome, there will be a set of feasible tests that differ in terms of the rates of errors and the costs associated with administering and participating in the test. Determining which of the many feasible, but imperfect, tests is preferred will depend on the relative cost of type I and type II errors.

[50] In addition to producing higher error costs, the α = .05 fixed significance level test would not satisfy the boundary condition (13) for a cost-effective test, and its use would result in losses plus direct costs that are higher than if the test were simply not performed. This is due to the very high type II error rate associated with this test.

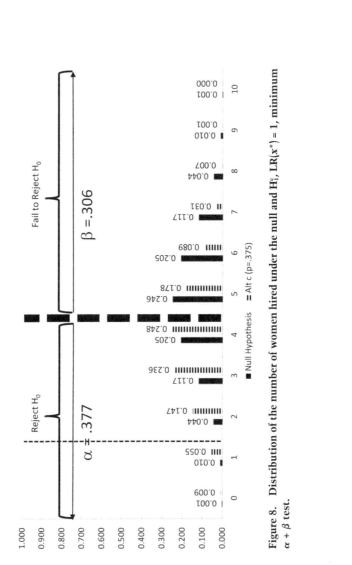

Figure 8. Distribution of the number of women hired under the null and H_i^c, $LR(x^*) = 1$, minimum $\alpha + \beta$ test.

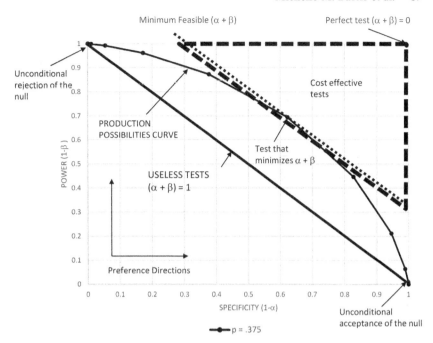

Figure 9. Loss function and feasible significance tests for H_i^c

Combinations of power and specificity that are attainable with a finite ($N = 10$) number of observations are depicted in the figure and lie along the curve labeled the "production possibilities curve." This curve contains the possible combinations of specificity and power as the threshold cutoff of the number of women hired is moved from greater than 10 (unconditionally accept the null) to less than 0 (unconditionally reject the null). The former lies at the bottom right corner of figure 9 and yields a test with perfect specificity and no power. The latter lies at the top left corner of figure 9 and yields a test with no specificity and perfect power. These tests are in the set of non-informative or "useless" tests, that is, those that have a likelihood ratio equal to 1 for all values of X. Such tests return results (positive or negative) that are the same whether the null or alternative is true.[51]

Figure 9 depicts, in the area labeled "cost effective tests," the set of tests that satisfy the boundary condition (13) under the assumption that $2C / K = .3$. Finally, figure 9 depicts the test on the produc-

---

[51] Such tests include per se rules (tests that always come out one way), as well as random tests (e.g., deciding guilt or innocence through the outcome of a coin toss) (see Finkelstein and Levin 2014, 88).

tion possibilities curve that minimizes $\alpha + \beta$. Under the assumption that $\pi = \omega = 1$, tests with equal levels of expected losses given by equation (1) lie along line with slope of -1. Among the feasible tests, the test that minimizes the total error cost rate $\alpha + \beta$ is the test for which the slope of the production possibilities curve is tangent to the minimum $\alpha + \beta$ line (the dashed line in fig. 9). This test is the $LR(x^*) = 1$ test that rejects the null hypothesis when the number of women hired x is less than 5. The $LR(x^*) = 1$ test, based on the binomial probabilities from the null and alternative H_i^c binomial distributions, yields a type I error rate $\alpha(x^*) = .377$, a type II error rate $\beta(x^*) = .306$, and a total error rate $\alpha(x^*) + \beta(x^*) = .683$. Under the assumption that $2C / K = .3$, this test satisfies the boundary condition (13), as $\alpha(x^*) + \beta(x^*) = .683 < 1 - .3 = .7$

Figure 10 shows where the $LR(x^*) = 1$ test and the fixed $\alpha = .05$ NHST lie on the production possibilities curve under H_i^c (where $p_i^c = .375$) when $N = 10$. The fixed $\alpha = .05$ NHST is located on the production possibilities curve in the region closest to the dashed horizontal line labeled $\alpha = .05$. As discussed, this rule rejects the null hypothe-

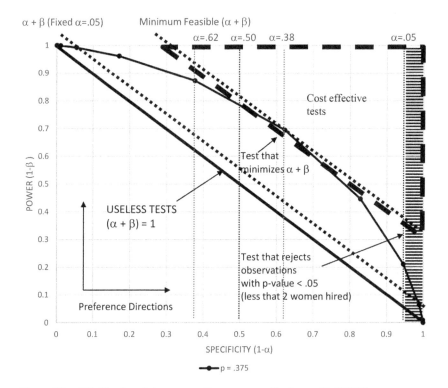

Figure 10. $LR(x^*) = 1$, minimum $\alpha + \beta$ test, versus fixed $\alpha = .05$, NHST

sis when fewer than two women are hired and generates a sum of type I and type II error rates $(\alpha(x^C) + \beta(x^C))$ close to 1, the measure of a noninformative or useless test. In contrast, the LR$(x^*) = 1$ test that lies on the production possibilities curve and minimizes the sum of the error rates $(\alpha(x^*) + \beta(x^*))$ produces a lower total error cost rate equal to .6827; this test lies on an $(\alpha + \beta)$ line with a lower total error rate, and it lies within the cost-effective range.

5.2. Alpha, Beta, and the Relevant Alternative Hypothesis

The properties of the LR$(x^*) = 1$ test depend on the specified alternative hypothesis and can generate levels of α that are less than, greater than, or equal to .05. To illustrate this point, consider alternative hypothesis d (H$_1^d$), the hypothesis that the firm does not hire women, so that $p_1^d = 0$. Figure 11 shows distributions of the number of women hired for both the null and alternative hypotheses (H$_1^d$) on the same graph. A fixed $\alpha = .05$ NHST (which rejects the null when fewer than two women are hired) produces a type I error rate of .0107. Because the distribution under the alternative hypothesis (H$_1^d$) has all of its mass at 0, the probability that two or more women would be hired under H$_1^d$ is 0. Thus, this test has a type II error rate of 0. Although the fixed $\alpha = .05$ NHST produces low type I and no type II errors, a superior test exists, one that lowers type I error without producing type II error. This is the test that rejects the null hypothesis when no women are hired. Compared with the fixed α test, this test does not increase β, but it does reduce α by .01.

Figure 12 illustrates the LR$(x^*) = 1$ test that minimizes $\alpha + \beta$ for all the three alternative hypotheses contained in table 1. In addition to the production possibility curve for alternative hypothesis H$_1^c$ depicted in figure 9, figure 12 also contains the production possibility curve for the other two alternative hypotheses listed in table 1, H$_1^b$ (the firm does not hire women with children) and H$_1^d$ (the firm does not hire women). The LR$(x^*) = 1$ test that minimizes $\alpha + \beta$ for H$_1^d$ has high power and high specificity and is a near-perfect test that lies in the upper right corner of figure 12. The LR$(x^*) = 1$ test that minimizes $\alpha + \beta$ for H$_1^b$, in contrast, is not cost-effective. For example, the LR$(x^*) = 1$ test that minimizes $\alpha + \beta$ under H$_1^b$ has the same $\alpha(x^*) = .377$ as the test that minimizes $\alpha + \beta$ under H$_1^c$. However, the test has a lower power, and thus a higher β. This is because the test under H$_1^b$ is attempting to discern between two hypotheses that are much closer to each other ($p_0 = .5$ vs. $p_1^b = .444$, a difference of just .056) than the test under H$_1^c$ ($p_0 = .5$ vs. $p_1^c = .375$, a difference of .125). Thus, for tests of equal significance, H$_1^b$ will have lower power than H$_1^c$.

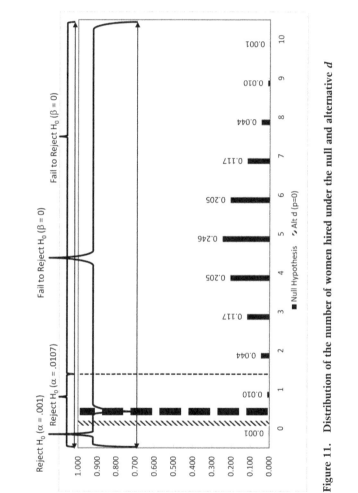

Figure 11.   Distribution of the number of women hired under the null and alternative d

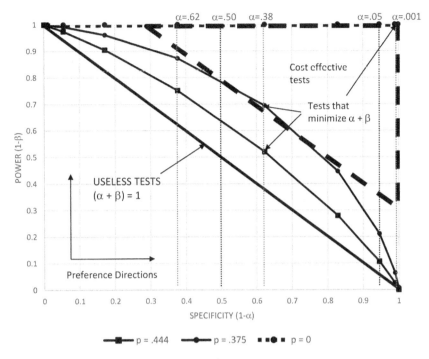

Figure 12.   Alternative hypotheses and the nature of the $\alpha + \beta$ minimizing test

The LR$(x^*) = 1$ tests under H$_1^b$, H$_1^c$, and H$_1^d$ produce type I error rates of $\alpha(x^*) = .38$, .62, and less than .001 respectively.

5.3. Alpha, Beta, and Sample Size

The rate of the errors α and β are affected by the sample size N, which in turn determines the standard deviation of the underlying distributions of the null and alternative hypotheses. For a fixed α NHST test, a higher N will result in greater power (a lower β), but—by design—no change in α. Figure 13 illustrates the production possibilities curve of the LR$(x^*) = 1$ test for H$_1^c$ for different levels of N. In addition to the production possibilities curve for $N = 10$ illustrated earlier, figure 13 provides the production possibilities curve for $N = 100$ and $N = 1,000$. As just shown, the fixed $\alpha = .05$ NHST for H$_1^c$ and $N = 10$ yields error rates $\alpha(x^C) = .0107$ and $\beta(x^C) = .9363$. When $N = 100$, $\alpha(x^C) = .04$ and $\beta(x^C) = .204$ and when $N = 1,000$, $\alpha(x^C) = .047$ and $\beta(x^C) = .0001$.

For the LR$(x^*) = 1$ tests, the minimum α and β decrease as N increases. Although the minimum $\alpha + \beta$ test for H$_1^c$ with $N = 10$ yields error rates $\alpha(x^*) = .377$ and $\beta(x^*) = .306$, the error rates fall to $\alpha(x^*) =$

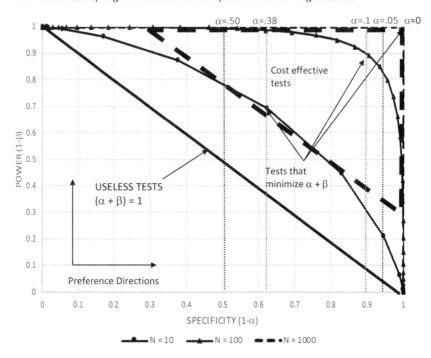

Figure 13.   Number of observations and the nature of the $\alpha + \beta$ minimizing test

.097 and a $\beta(x^*) = .108$ when $N = 100$, and $\alpha(x^*) = .00003$ and a $\beta(x^*) = .00004$ when $N = 1,000$. Notice that for the class of tests that minimizes $(\alpha + \beta)$, both error rates fall as the sample size increases. This pattern contrasts starkly to the practice of holding the type I error rate fixed as the sample size increases; that practice will not emerge as an optimal one unless the test designer has lexicographic preferences over the two types of errors (for an early instance of this point, see Arrow 1960).

The relationship between α, β, and N can be further illustrated by considering the normal approximations to the null and alternative distributions as N varies. Table 7 lists the mean and standard deviation of the null and alternative distribution, H_1^c of x for $N = 10, 100$, and 1,000. Table 7 also lists the critical values x^C for a one-tailed $\alpha = .05$ NHST, and the critical value x^* for the $LR(x^*) = 1$ test that minimizes $\alpha + \beta$.

Figure 14A depicts the normal approximation to the null distribution $f(x|H_0)$ and alternative distribution $f(x|H_1^c)$ for $N = 10$. The $\alpha = .05$ one-tailed critical value for this distribution is $x^C = 2.40$, and the power of a test that rejects H_0 when $x < x^C$ equals $1 - \beta = .189$. Thus, as demonstrated previously, fixing the significance level at $\alpha = .05$ results in a high type II error rate $(\beta(x^C) = .811)$.

Table 7. Distribution Properties and N Using Normal Approximation, with H_1^c as Alternative Hypothesis

	NULL HYPOTHESIS			ALTERNATIVE HYPOTHESIS		
N	Mean	SD	x^c	Mean	SD	x^*
10	5	1.58	2.40	3.75	1.53	4.43
100	50	5	41.78	37.5	4.84	43.71
1,000	500	15.81	473.99	375	15.31	436.50

Increasing the critical value for rejection of the null hypothesis can increase the power of the test by more than it reduces specificity and lower the sum of the error rates. The $LR(x^*) = 1$ test that minimizes $\alpha + \beta$ is the test that rejects H_0 when $x < x^* = 4.43$. Figure 14A illustrates the effect on the type I and type II errors of moving from the $\alpha = .05$ significance level cutoff of $x^c = 2.40$ to $x^* = 4.43$. The increase in the type I error rate $(\Delta\alpha = .309)$ is more than offset by the decrease in the type II error rate $(\Delta\beta = -.482)$.[52]

However, because of the large overlap between the null and alternative distributions, any test—even the test $LR(x^*) = 1$ that minimizes $\alpha + \beta$—will have a high total error rate. As a result, even the $LR(x^*) = 1$ test that rejects H_0 for values of $x < x^* = 4.43$ produces type I and type II error rates that are both over .3, and, as we have seen, the total error rate is just under .7 $(\alpha(x^*) + \beta(x^*) = .688)$.[53]

The properties of the normal approximations to the null and alternative sampling distributions when $N = 100$ are depicted in figure 14B. When $N = 100$, the means of the null and alternative sampling distributions are 2.5 SD apart, reducing the overlap between the two distributions. As a result, the power associated with the fixed $\alpha = .05$ test exceeds .8. The type I and type II errors under the $LR(x^*) = 1$ test are smaller, with both approximately equal to .10.[54]

[52] Because the null and alternative distributions have different standard deviations, the test that minimizes $\alpha + \beta$ will not generally equalize the type I and type II error rates (see Meyerson and Meyerson 2010, advocating a test where $\alpha = \beta$).

[53] These error rates are based on the normal approximation and thus differ slightly from the rates based on the binomial probabilities just reported.

[54] The effect of increasing N can also be seen by examining the standardized test statistic Z discussed in n. 48. For a binomial sampling distribution for counts, the normal test statistic is $Z = \sqrt{N}[(p - p_0)/\sqrt{p_0(1 - p_0)}]$. This expression shows that increasing N will increase Z for any given difference $p - p_0$. As a result, for large N, even small differences from the null probability p_0 will be statistically significant at "standard" fixed levels of α (e.g., .05)

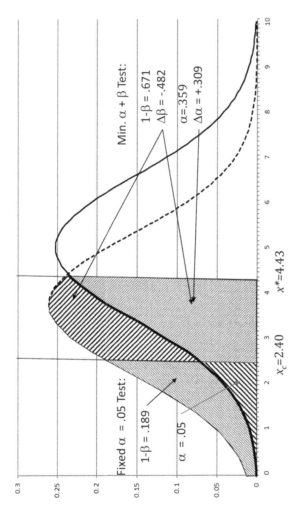

Min. α + β Test:

1-β = .671
Δβ = -.482

α=.359
Δα = +.309

Fixed α = .05 Test:

1-β = .189

α = .05

x_c=2.40 x^*=4.43

Figure 14. Null and alternative distribution H$_i$: (A) N = 10; (B) N = 100; (C) N = 1,000

46

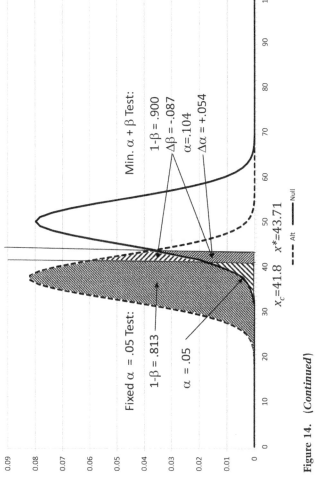

Figure 14. (*Continued*)

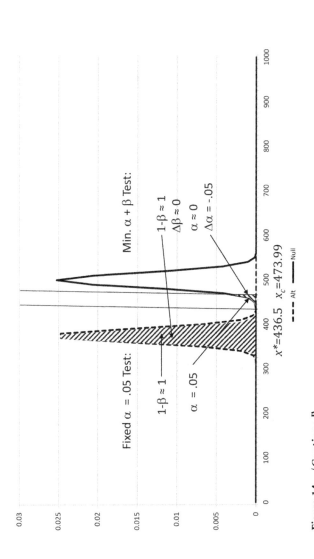

Figure 14. (*Continued*)

Finally, figure 14C shows the normal approximations to the null and alternative sampling distributions when N =1,000. The means of the distributions are more than 7 SD apart, and overlap of the distributions is minute. The fixed α = .05 NHST produces a test with near-perfect power. By design, this test still has α = .05, so total error probability is always at least .05. By contrast, the LR(x^*) = 1 test, which lowers the critical value from x^C to x^*, only negligibly reduces power even as it reduces the type I error rate from .05 nearly to 0. The result is a near-perfect test, with α and β both approximately equal to 0. This example shows that when sample size is large, total error costs can be reduced below what the fixed α test delivers, precisely because such a test fixes α at a positive level.

5.4. Relationship of the Mathematical Representation of the Preponderance Standard to the Significance Level

Under the preponderance standard, a court should find for the plaintiff when evidence supporting the plaintiffs' case is more likely than the evidence that supports the defendant's case. Under the assumption of equal error costs, the standard of proof threshold from the preponderance standard is the LR(x^*) = π test given in equation (10).

The prior sections have established that the fixed α = .05 NHST is generally not the same as the LR(x^*) = π preponderance test. This is true in general for any fixed α NHST test. When a specific alternative is specified, it is not true that the preponderance standard requires a significance level α = .50 (Cohen 1985, 415–16).[55] Based on a one-tailed test, such an α = .50 test would require that the null hypothesis be rejected when the outcome is below the mean of the null distribution or

$$\mu_0 = Np_0, \text{ or } \alpha = \int_{-\infty}^{Np_0} f(x|H_0)dx = F(Np_0) = .5. \quad (15)$$

Figure 15 depicts the nonequivalence of the preponderance standard and fixed α NHST when N = 100. From condition (15), the threshold for the fixed α = .50 null hypothesis is determined by the point where the null distribution function $F(x|H_0)$ intersects the horizontal line at .5. This yields a critical value $x^C = \mu_0 = Np_0 = 50$. In contrast, from equation (11), the threshold x^* for the preponderance standard with diffuse priors requires that the trier of fact finds for the plaintiff when LR = $[f(x|H_1) / f(x|H_0)] > LR(x^*)$ = 1. This condition holds when $x < x^*$. The preponderance standard threshold is determined

[55] See also the text in n. 5, presenting examples of plaintiff's experts arguing for use of a 50% significance level.

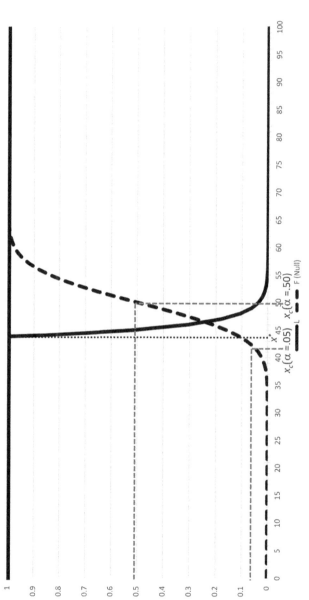

Figure 15. Distribution function, preponderance standard, and fixed α tests

by the point where the likelihood ratio intersects the horizontal line at 1.0. This criterion yields a critical value $x^* = 43.71 < 50$. Thus, $x^* \neq x^C = \mu_0 = Np_0$.

To provide an alternative view of this point, figure 16 depicts the critical thresholds from the fixed $\alpha = .05$ NHST, the $LR(x^*) = 1$ test, and the fixed $\alpha = .50$ NHST, all based on normal approximations to the null and H_1^c distributions when $N = 100$. As was demonstrated earlier when $\pi = \omega = 1$, the preponderance threshold is identical to the $LR(x^*) = 1$ threshold. It does not coincide with the fixed $\alpha = .05$ threshold, which could lie to the left or right of the former. In figure 16's particular example, the $\alpha = .05$ threshold lies to the left of the $LR^* = 1$ threshold. In this example, the preponderance threshold also does not generally coincide with the $\alpha = .50$ threshold; in the example depicted in figure 16, the $\alpha = .50$ test would increase the total error cost rate $\alpha + \beta$ relative to the preponderance standard, raising the type I error rate by .396 and reducing type II error rates by .095.

In fact, in the setting considered in this article, the preponderance standard and the fixed $\alpha = .50$ test are the same test only if the null and alternative distributions are identical (or in the limit as the alternative hypothesis approaches the null hypothesis). This article has fo-

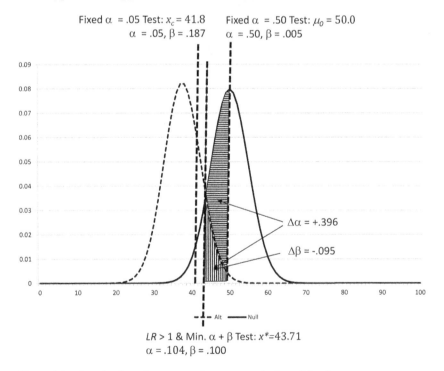

Figure 16.   Density function, preponderance standard, and fixed α tests

cused on the case of choosing between two simple hypotheses. Interesting instances of that case always involve distinct null and alternative hypotheses. Accordingly, the distinctiveness of the preponderance standard and the fixed α = .50 test hinges on the assumption that a particular alternative hypothesis can be specified.[56]

In the Title VII context, it is reasonable to think that the relevant null hypothesis might be simple. An employer-defendant might insist that it favors no group in its hiring practices, because a finding that it favors today's plaintiff from one group might be issue-preclusive in a suit brought by tomorrow's plaintiff from another group. That implies a specific null hypothesis—that the employer's practices yield the same hiring rate for all groups. It is less clear when the plaintiff-applicant is likely to allege a simple alternative hypothesis, as we have assumed throughout this article; plaintiff-applicants can win by showing many possible degrees of disparate impact.

When it is not possible to specify simple hypotheses for both parties' positions, the analysis in this article must be generalized to fit composite hypotheses. Two of us have carried out that generalization in work related to this article that examines thresholds for the legal sufficiency of statistical evidence (Gelbach and Kobayashi 2018). An important result of that generalization is that there are important circumstances under which the preponderance standard corresponds either exactly or approximately to the fixed α = .50 test. This caveat is important to remember in practice.[57]

5.5. Preliminary versus Final Adjudication

Finally, the analysis can be used to model other legal thresholds. Many of the discussion of burdens of proof in the law and economics literature focus on the standard applicable to final adjudication. However, as previously noted, the same standards are sometimes applied

---

[56] Cohen (1985, 415–16) argues that the preponderance standard yields the same critical threshold as the α = .50 threshold. Setting α = .50 results in a cutoff at the mean of the null distribution, which is consistent with rejecting the null hypothesis when the proportion of females hired $p = x/N$ is less than .5, which Cohen equates with the absolute probability preponderance standard. But this $p = x/N < .5$ is not the preponderance standard set out in eq. (10) or (11), that is, the standard of rejecting the null hypothesis whenever the likelihood ratio in favor of the alternative hypothesis exceeds 1.

[57] For further analysis of the intersection of black-letter legal doctrines and the theoretical results in Gelbach and Kobayashi (2018), see Gelbach (2018). See also Froeb, Ganglmair, and Tschantz (2016) for their model where parties endogenously construct optimal competing hypotheses based on the evidence.

to adjudicate preliminary issues, such as the burden of production for a prima facie case of discrimination just examined in this article.

For example, the analysis can be applied to the pleading standard applicable to scienter under the Private Securities Litigation Reform Act of 1995 (Pub. L. 104-67, 109 Stat. 737) (PSLRA), as interpreted by *Tellabs* (551 U.S. 308 [2007]). The court in *Tellabs* describes the heightened pleading standard under the PSLRA in the following way: "In order to survive a motion to dismiss . . . a plaintiff must allege facts from which a reasonable person would deem the inference of scienter cogent and at least as compelling as any opposing inference one could draw from the facts alleged."[58]

Letting H_1 denote the plaintiff's hypothesis and H_0 denote the defendant's hypothesis, a natural interpretation of the *Tellabs* standard is that $LR = [f(x|H_1) / f(x|H_0)] > LR(x^{Tellabs}) = 1$. Mathematically, the application of our analytical framework to the *Tellabs* pleading standard would be identical to that used to evaluate the preponderance threshold with diffuse priors.

However, although the formal analysis is the same, the circumstances under which the critical likelihood ratio is applied will likely differ in a preliminary adjudication. Motions to dismiss occur prior to the exchange of information through discovery and thus are likely to be characterized by sampling distributions with less precision (e.g., greater standard errors) than will be the case during a final adjudication postdiscovery.

To illustrate this point, consider again the discrimination example used throughout the article.[59] Suppose that at the time of the motion to dismiss, there is a limited number of relevant observations (e.g., $N = 10$) corresponding to the current round of hiring. Discovery allows the consideration of data associated with prior hiring cycles, so that $N > 10$. Under these circumstances, the preliminary adjudication will involve overlapping sampling distributions depicted in figure 14A where $N = 10$, whereas final adjudication will involve the conditions

---

[58] 551 U.S. at 322.

[59] To be sure, the pleading standard for discrimination cases is different from that for cases covered by the PSLRA. As with other cases for which there is no statutory pleading standard, the standard for discrimination cases is set forth by Rule 8(a)(2) as elaborated by the plausibility standard in *Twombly*, 550 U.S. 544 [2007], and filtered through *Ashcroft v. Iqbal*'s (556 U.S. 662 [2009]) application of Rule 1's edict that the Federal Rules of Civil Procedures govern all civil actions. The Supreme Court has insisted that the plausibility standard is not a probability standard, but many commentators, judges, and lawyers have suggested or acted as if it is difficult to understand how that could be so. This response is surely partly due to the Supreme Court's use of language suggesting that the plaintiff has failed to plead plausibly when an alternative story is at least as compelling as the plaintiff's.

depicted in figures 14B and 14C, where the sampling distributions are more precise and thus distinguishable because N is much larger than 10. In terms of the significance level implied by the $\text{LR}(x^{\text{PS}}) = 1$ critical threshold, application to a sampling distribution with $N = 10$ and relatively large standard errors will result in a much higher implied significance level than the application at summary judgment or final adjudication of the $\text{LR}(x^*) = 1$ threshold to sampling distributions with relatively low standard errors (e.g., where $N = 100$ or $N = 1,000$).[60]

6. CONCLUSION

Models of optimal legal decision rules often use loss functions that seek to minimize the sum of error costs and direct costs. In theory, the choice of a statistical cutoff can reflect a similar calculus, but when the parties' positions are captured by simple statistical hypotheses, the standard practice under fixed significance level NHST does not. Thus, it is not surprising that in the simple-hypotheses case, use of a fixed α NHST will not correspond to existing or optimal legal decision rules. This potential for divergence between NHST statistical cutoffs and legal decision rules can inform how to reconcile the tools of statistical inference to be consistent with the applicable legal standard. Our analysis shows how reconciling the two can be achieved by replacing fixed significance levels with likelihood ratio tests.

REFERENCES

Allen, Ronald J. 2003. "The Error of Expected Loss Minimization." *Law, Probability, and Risk* 2:1–7.
Allen, Ronald J., and Michael S. Pardo. 2007. "The Problematic Value of Mathematical Models of Evidence." *Journal of Legal Studies* 36: 107–40.
Allen, Ronald J., and Alex Stein, 2013. "Evidence, Probability, and the Burden of Proof." *Arizona Law Review* 55:557–602.
Arrow, Kenneth J. 1960. "Decision Theory and the Choice of a Level of Significance for the *t*-Test." In *Contributions to Probability and Statistics*, edited by I. Olkin, W. Hoeffding, S. G. Gurye, W. G. Madow, and H. B. Mann, 70–78. Stanford, CA: Stanford University Press.
Blackstone, William. 1765. *Commentaries on the Laws of England*, vol. 4. Oxford: Clarendon.

---

[60] The application of the $\text{LR}^* = 1$ test at the motion to dismiss stage will result in high total error costs $\alpha + \beta$, but such a test will likely be associated with relatively low costs C.

Brav, Alon, and J. B. Heaton. 2015. "Event Studies in Securities Litigation: Low Power, Confounding Effects, and Bias." *Washington University Law Review* 93:583–614.

Cheng, Edward K. 2009. "A Practical Solution to the Reference Class Problem." *Columbia Law Review* 109:2081–105.

Cheng, Edward K. 2013. "Reconceptualizing the Burden of Proof." *Yale Law Journal* 122:1254–79.

Cheng, Edward K., and Michael S. Pardo. 2015. "Accuracy, Optimality, and the Preponderance Standard." *Law, Probability, and Risk* 14:193–212.

Clermont, Kevin M. 2009. "Standards of Proof Revisited." *Vermont Law Review* 33:469–87.

Cohen, Neil B. 1985. "Confidence in Probability: Burdens of Persuasion in a World of Imperfect Knowledge." *New York University Law Review* 60:385–422.

Demougina, Dominique, and Claude Fluet. 2006. "Preponderance of Evidence." *European Economic Review* 50:963–76.

Ehrlich, Isaac, and Richard A. Posner. 1974. "An Economic Analysis of Legal Rulemaking." *Journal of Legal Studies* 3:257–86.

Federal Judicial Center. 2011. *Reference Manual on Scientific Evidence*, 3rd ed. Washington, DC: National Academies.

Fidler, Fiona, Geoff Cumming, Mark Burgman, and Neil Thomason. 2004. "Statistical Reform in Medicine, Psychology and Ecology." *Journal of Socio-Economics* 33:615–30.

Finkelstein, Michael O., and Bruce Levin. 2014. *Statistics for Lawyers*, 3rd ed. New York: Springer.

Fisch, Jill E., Jonah B. Gelbach, and Jonathan Klick. 2018. "The Logic and Limits of Event Studies in Securities Fraud Litigation." *Texas Law Review* 96:553–618.

Fisher, Ronald A. 1966. *The Design of Experiments*, 8th ed. Edinburgh: Oliver & Boyd.

Froeb, Luke M., Bernhard Ganglmair, and Steven Tschantz. 2016. "Adversarial Decision Making: Choosing between Models Constructed by Interested Parties." *Journal of Law and Economics* 59:527–48.

Garaud, Marcel C. 1990. "Legal Standards and Statistical Proof in Title VII Litigation: In Search of a Coherent Disparate Impact Model." *University of Pennsylvania Law Review* 139:455–503.

Gastwirth, Joseph L. 1992. "Statistical Reasoning in the Legal Setting." *American Statistician* 46:55–69.

Gastwirth, Joseph L. 2012. "Statistical Considerations Support the Supreme Court's Decision in *Matrixx Initiatives v. Siracusano*." *Jurimetrics Journal* 52:155–75.

Gelbach, Jonah B. 2018. "A Theory of Statistical Estimation Evidence in Federal Civil Litigation." Unpublished manuscript, University of Pennsylvania Law School.

Gelbach, Jonah B., and Bruce H. Kobayashi. 2018. "Legal Sufficiency of Statistical Evidence." George Mason Legal Studies Research Paper no. LS 18-29. http://dx.doi.org/10.2139/ssrn.3238793.

Hay, Bruce L. and Kathryn E. Spier. 1997. "Burdens of Proof in Civil Litigation: An Economic Perspective." *Journal of Legal Studies* 26:413–31.

Hogg, Robert V., Elliot Tanis, and Dale L. Zimmerman. 2015. *Probability and Statistical Inference*, 9th ed. Boston: Pearson.

Johnson, Phillip, Edward Leamer, and Jeffrey Leitzinger. 2017. "Statistical Significance and Statistical Error in Antitrust Analysis." *Antitrust Law Journal* 81:641–66.

Kaplow, Louis. 1992. "Rules versus Standards: An Economic Analysis." *Duke Law Journal* 42:557–629.

Kaplow, Louis. 2011. "On the Optimal Burden of Proof." *Journal of Political Economy* 119:1104–40.

Kaplow, Louis. 2012. "Burden of Proof." *Yale Law Journal* 121:738–859.

Kaplow, Louis. 2014. "Likelihood Ratio Tests and Legal Decision Rules." *American Law and Economics Review* 16:1–39.

Kaye, David H. 1983. "Statistical Significance and the Burden of Persuasion." *Law and Contemporary Problems* 46:13–23.

King, Allan G. 2007. "'Gross Statistical Disparities' as Evidence of a Pattern and Practice of Discrimination: Statistical versus Legal Significance." *Labor Lawyer* 22:271–92.

Lehmann, E. L. 1993. "The Fisher, Neyman-Person Theories of Testing Hypotheses: One Theory or Two?" *Journal of the American Statistical Association* 88:1242–49.

Lempert, Richard O. 2009. "The Significance of Statistical Significance: Two Authors Restate an Incontrovertible Caution. Why a Book?" *Law and Social Inquiry* 14:225–52.

Meyerson, Michael I., and William Meyerson. 2010. "Significant Statistics: The Unwitting Policy Making of Mathematically Ignorant Judges." *Pepperdine Law Review* 37:771–846.

Mungan, Murat C. 2011. "A Utilitarian Justification for Heightened Standards of Proof in Criminal Trials." *Journal of Institutional and Theoretical Economics* 167:352–70.

Newman, Jon O. 2006. "Quantifying the Standard of Proof beyond a Reasonable Doubt: A Comment on Three Comments." *Law, Probability, and Risk* 5:267–69.

Neyman, Jerzy, and Egon S. Pearson. 1933. "On the Problem of the Most Efficient Test of Statistical Hypothesis." *Philosophical Transaction of the Royal Society of London—Series A* 231:289–337.

Pardo, Michael S. 2013. "The Nature and Purpose of Evidence Theory." *Vanderbilt Law Review* 66:547–613.

Pardo, Michael S., and Ronald J. Allen. 2008. "Juridical Proof and the Best Explanation." *Law and Philosophy* 27:223–68.

Peresie, Jennifer L. 2009. "Toward a Coherent Test for Disparate Impact Discrimination." *Indiana Law Journal* 84:773–802.

Posner, Richard A. 2003. *Economic Analysis of Law*, 6th ed. New York: Aspen.

Rubinfeld, Daniel L. 1985. "Econometrics in the Courtroom." *Columbia Law Review* 85:1048–97.

Sanchirico, Chris W. 1997. "The Burden of Proof in Civil Litigation: A Simple Model of Mechanism Design." *International Review of Law and Economics* 17:431–47.

Scurich, Nicholas, and Richard S. John. 2017. "Jurors' Presumption of Innocence." *Journal of Legal Studies* 46:187–206.

Stock, James H., and Mark W. Watson. 2011. *Introduction to Econometrics*, 3rd ed. Boston: Pearson.

Wooldridge, Jeffrey M. 2002. *Introductory Econometrics*, 2nd ed. Mason: South-Western.

Ziliak, Stephen T., and Deirdre N. McCloskey. 2008. *The Cult of Statistical Significance: How the Standard Error Costs Us Jobs, Justice, and Lives*. Ann Arbor: University of Michigan Press.

A Comment on Statistical Significance and Standards of Proof

*Michael S. Pardo**

It is a pleasure to have the opportunity to comment on "Error Costs, Legal Standards of Proof, and Statistical Significance" by Michelle M. Burtis, Jonah B. Gelbach, and Bruce H. Kobayashi (2017). The article provides a clear, sophisticated, and persuasive discussion of the relationships between conventional tests of statistical significance and legal standards of proof. Although tests of statistical significance and legal standards of proof are, in theory, each concerned with similar considerations regarding the types and frequency of inferential errors, the article in my view is correct to argue that they are analytically distinct and that one cannot be mapped onto the other in a straightforward manner. Thus, I agree with their general conclusion: "There is no one level of statistical significance that generally corresponds to the legal standard of proof." The article's related discussion of different types of statistical tests is also persuasive. I thus also agree with their general conclusion that likelihood ratio tests (comparing competing explanations supporting each side) map onto legal standards of proof more closely than conventional tests with a fixed significance level.[1]

Despite the fact that courts, litigants, and academics have sometimes argued or assumed that evidence in the form of conventional tests of statistical significance (at the typical .05 level, or at some other level)

* Henry Upson Sims Professor of Law, University of Alabama School of Law.

[1] Burtis et al. (2017) note that "reconciling legal standards of proof and statistical thresholds can be achieved by replacing fixed significance levels with likelihood ratio tests." In addition to the general conclusions, I found nearly all of the analysis to be persuasive, taking issue with only minor details—for example, the assumption that the "presumption of innocence" in criminal cases refers to prior odds of guilt. For a contrary view, see Laudan (2006, 90–109).

Electronically published: December 7, 2018

is necessary or sufficient to satisfy a legal standard of proof, the article illustrates clearly the problems with these arguments and assumptions. Here is the crux of the analysis: conventional tests of statistical significance typically focus on one type of error (false positives) and are less concerned with false negatives. In other words, the thumb is on the scale of not declaring that a relationship exists (e.g., causation or discrimination) unless it is warranted or justified, but there is less concern with failing to declare a relationship when one does, in fact, exist. Legal standards of proof, by contrast, are concerned with both types of errors and their costs. The article demonstrates how likelihood ratio tests that focus on both types of error are likely to improve accuracy and reduce overall error costs compared with tests based on fixed significance levels.[2]

In this comment, my aim is to situate the article's analysis in the academic literature and debates on legal standards of proof (focusing on the "preponderance of the evidence" standard). Here is a brief, somewhat simplified picture of standards of proof and their underlying rationales.[3] Standards of proof focus on the related goals of accuracy and allocating the risk of error between the parties. Common assumptions about the preponderance standard are that it aims at minimizing total errors and allocating the risk of error roughly evenly among civil litigants. These assumptions are justified, in part, by the further assumption that the costs of each type of error will be roughly similar (and thus reducing total errors is likely to reduce to error costs). Moreover, equalizing the risk of error reflects a principle of equality among civil litigants (see Redmayne 1999, 171–74; Solum 2004, 286–89). Asymmetric error costs then justify higher proof standards (e.g., "clear and convincing evidence" and "beyond a reasonable doubt"), which attempt to skew the risk of error away from false positives.

This simple picture gives rise to several distinct theoretical issues that have generated disagreements among evidence scholars. I discuss three such issues as they relate to the analysis in the article.

1. TO WHAT EXTENT ARE THE STANDARDS COMPARATIVE?

Standards of proof are sometimes interpreted as probabilistic thresholds (e.g., > .5) and sometimes as comparative assessments (e.g., a likelihood ratio > 1). These interpretations are not the same, and they im-

---

[2] Burtis et al. (2017) illustrate the differences between the tests with an employment-discrimination example. Their analysis of the example should be required reading for any courts, litigants, or academics arguing that there is a clear relationship between statistical significance and legal standards of proof.

[3] The assumptions in this picture are each contested, but they are nevertheless common. For a more detailed discussion, see Allen et al. (2016, 803–59).

ply different outcomes. Suppose a plaintiff's theory of what happened is .4 probable and the defendant's alternative theory is .2 probable. Has the plaintiff proven its case by a preponderance of the evidence? The issue concerns what to do with the unknown probability space. Should all the unknown possibilities go against the plaintiff, or should they be divided evenly among the parties? A number of scholars (myself included) have argued, from different perspectives, that a comparative account better explains the legal standards and better fits with their assumed goals regarding accuracy and the risk of error (see, e.g., Pardo and Allen 2008; Cheng 2013; Clermont 2013, 149). Although the article focuses on general defense explanations (e.g., "no discrimination"), the likelihood ratio framework appears to likewise embrace a comparative interpretation of legal standards. One question the article leaves open, however, is how the analysis would change in a situation in which the plaintiff and the defendant are each offering more specific, alternative explanations. In other words, suppose the defendant's explanation is not the null hypothesis (as the article assumes) but instead involves a more specific explanation for the actions. This relates to the distinction that the article raises between simple and composite explanations (Burtis et al. 2017), but not necessarily. Neither side may be offering a composite of alternatives—there may just be two simple theories that do not fill the entire space of possibilities.

2. WHAT ARE THE CRITERIA THAT UNDERLIE THE STANDARDS?

There is substantial debate on whether the thresholds employed by legal standards of proof are probabilistic thresholds or whether they depend on other criteria (e.g., explanatory threshold; see Pardo and Allen 2008; Allen and Pardo, forthcoming). The article assumes they are probabilistic thresholds of some sort (expressed by either fixed probability thresholds or likelihood ratios), but there is a wrinkle with this assumption, with potentially deep consequences. Legal standards of proof apply to individual elements of claims, not to claims as a whole, so even proving a plaintiff's claim on particular elements may create suboptimal results in terms of errors and errors costs (see Allen and Jehl 2003; Cohen 1977, 58–67). For example, in a two-element claim, A and B, a plaintiff will win under the preponderance standard by proving each element to .6. But if A and B are probabilistically independent, then the plaintiff's claim is only .36 probable. The effect gets worse with more elements.[4] Once again, this is related to—but not quite the same as—

---

[4] Probabilistic dependence among elements creates similar problems (see Allen and Pardo, forthcoming). The conjunction effect also applies to comparative probabi-

the issue of simple versus composite explanations that the authors note (Burtis et al. 2017). Even simple hypotheses offered by a party may contain multiple legal elements (e.g., "I suffered an adverse employment action because of race" or "The defendant's product caused my injuries"). In sum, the analysis in the article applies most clearly to legal disputes that involve one legal element and one contested factual issue.

3. WHAT IS THE RELATIONSHIP BETWEEN ITEMS OF EVIDENCE AND STANDARDS OF PROOF?

More generally, the article well illustrates the need to keep separate—as a conceptual matter—evidence, on one hand, and the standard of proof, on the other. The different types of statistical tests that are examined (those based on fixed significance levels and likelihood ratios) are essentially different types of evidence, and the article provides compelling reasons why the tests are likely to differ in terms of their probative value in proving contested factual issues. As a general matter, the relationship between *any* item of evidence and the standard of proof is complex, and the probative value of evidence will be defeasible (depending on the other evidence, the specific context, and the contrasting claims and arguments of the parties). This is so for statistical tests regarding discrimination, for relative-risk analysis in proving causation in toxic-tort cases under the preponderance standard, and for random-match probabilities in proving identity in criminal cases under the beyond a reasonable doubt standard, to name just a few vexing examples. This is also true for eyewitness testimony, confessions, or any other nonstatistical evidence. Thus, one lesson to take from the article's analysis is that various doctrinal rules of thumb (e.g., the 80% rule in measuring disparate impact; Burtis et al. 2017) or requiring a relative risk of ≥ 2.0 in tort cases[5]), or various presumptions that shift a burden of production or persuasion based on particular items of evidence (see Allen et al. 2016, 821–35, 857–59), will always be imperfect guides to legal standards of proof rather than capturing something essential about the relationship between the evidence and the standard of proof.

---

listic standards. For example, suppose that in a two-element claim the plaintiff proves one to .9 and the other to .4, and the probability of the defendant's alternative theory on the elements is .1 and .6. The plaintiff will lose despite offering a theory that is six times more likely than the alternative (.36 vs. .06).

[5] According to Gold (2011), "courts have equated more than a doubling of relative risk in an exposed group to a more-likely-than-not probability of causation in an exposed individual plaintiff" (1523).

REFERENCES

Allen, Ronald J., and Sarah A. Jehl. 2003. "Burdens of Persuasion in Civil Cases: Algorithms vs. Explanations." *Michigan State Law Review* 2003:893–944.

Allen, Ronald J., and Michael S. Pardo. Forthcoming. "Relative Plausibility and Its Critics." *International Journal of Evidence and Proof.*

Allen, Ronald J., Eleanor Swift, David S. Schwartz, Michael S. Pardo, and Alex Stein. 2016. *An Analytical Approach to Evidence: Text, Problems and Cases,* 6th ed. New York: Wolters Kluwer.

Burtis, Michelle M., Jonah B. Gelbach, and Bruce H. Kobayashi. 2017. "Error Costs, Legal Standards of Proof, and Statistical Significance." *Supreme Court Economic Review* 25:1–58.

Cheng, Edward K. 2013. "Reconceptualizing the Burden of Proof." *Yale Law Journal* 122:1254–79.

Clermont, Kevin M. 2013. *Standards of Decision in Law.* Durham, NC: Carolina Academic.

Cohen, L. Jonathan. 1977. *The Probable and the Provable.* Oxford: Clarendon.

Gold, Steve C. 2011. "The 'Reshapement' of the False Negative Asymmetry in Toxic Tort Causation." *William Mitchell Law Review* 37: 1507–81.

Laudan, Larry. 2006. *Truth, Error, and Criminal Law: An Essay in Legal Epistemology.* Cambridge: Cambridge University Press.

Pardo, Michael S., and Ronald J. Allen. 2008. "Juridical Proof and the Best Explanation." *Law and Philosophy* 27:223–68.

Redmayne, Mike. 1999. "Standards of Proof in Civil Litigation." *Modern Law Review* 62:167–95.

Solum, Lawrence B. 2004. "Procedural Justice." *Southern California Law Review* 78:181–321.

Crime and Punishment under Evidentiary Uncertainty: Laboratory Evidence

Florian Baumann[*]
Tim Friehe[†]

We use experimental data to investigate how potential viola-tors and third-party punishers choose at different levels of evi-dentiary uncertainty. Between subjects, we compare decision making for various harm and sanction levels. We find that choices depend on the extent of evidentiary uncertainty. In our data, individual punishment behavior is significantly in-fluenced by neither the level of harm nor the severity of the sanction. This is aligned with legal requirements regarding the standard of proof but does not confirm predictions from eco-nomic models. Potential violators' choices depend on the level of harm, but higher sanctions do not deter the norm violation.

* University of Bonn, Center for Advanced Studies in Law and Economics. Email: fbaumann@uni-bonn.de. Tel.: +49 228 735892; Fax: +49 228 739111.

† University of Marburg, Public Economics Group, Am Plan 2, 35037 Marburg, Ger-many. CESifo, Munich, Germany. EconomiX, Paris. Email: tim.friehe@uni-marburg.de. Tel.: +49 64212821703; Fax: +49 64212824852. JEL Classification: K42, D81, C91. We thank James Andreoni, Brandon Brice, Dominique Demougin, Eberhard Feess, Michael Kurschilgen, Hannah Schildberg-Hörisch, Avraham Tabbach, and participants of the Su-preme Court Economic Review Roundtable, the 2015 German Law and Economics As-sociation meeting, the 2015 European Association of Law and Economics meeting, and the 2015 workshop on "Public Law Enforcement and Deterrence Policies" at the Uni-versity Paris Ouest Nanterre for their highly appreciated comments on earlier versions of this article. We are grateful to Lisa V. Bruttel for her cooperation in designing and im-plementing the experiment and to an anonymous reviewer for helpful suggestions.

Electronically published: December 6, 2018

1. INTRODUCTION

1.1. Motivation and Main Results

When deciding whether to convict a criminal suspect, legal decision makers require proof beyond a reasonable doubt. The famous ratio first formulated by Blackstone (1769)—better that 10 guilty defendants escape than that one innocent suffer—is often referred to in this context (see, e.g., Epps 2015). This standard of proof does not vary with the specific aspects of the case; rather, it is solely concerned with the quality of the evidence. For example, jury instructions in New York State refer to the absence of any reasonable doubt concerning the existence of any element of the crime and the defendant's identity as the person who committed the crime (New York State Unified Court System 2015) without asking jurors to view the quality of the evidence in light of the circumstances of the case, including the severity of the criminal act and the punishment applied in the event of a conviction.[1] However, from an economic point of view, it might make sense for the evidence required by a legal decision maker for the conviction of a criminal defendant to be tailored to the case at hand (e.g., such tailoring may reduce the expected costs of legal errors from wrongful convictions or acquittals; Andreoni 1991).

We analyze experimental data to explore the interaction between evidentiary uncertainty and the choices of potential violators and third-party punishers when the aspects of the case (i.e., the harm and sanction levels) are varied. In so doing, we respond to Miceli (2009), who notes the lack of evidence on how (legal) decision makers actually interpret reasonable doubt—as more closely aligned either with the legal understanding (as exemplified by the New York jury instructions) or with the economic perspective based on the minimization of legal error costs (described next). In our experiment, player A may take points from player B, who suffers harm as a result. Player A's choice sends a noisy signal to player C, who can then decide to punish player A under evidentiary uncertainty. We consider two sanction levels and two harm levels in a between-subject design. In addition, we distinguish between different extents of evidentiary uncertainty presented to all subjects. We are interested in the implications of evidentiary uncertainty and the aspects of the case (harm and sanction levels) for the punishment decision, the point-taking choice, and the likelihood of legal errors. By relying on experimental data, we can control other influences apart from the harm and sanction levels and directly determine the extent of evidentiary un-

---

[1] This independence of the standard of proof from the aspects of the case is also explicated in criminal law textbooks such as Pollock (2012).

certainty. In addition, we can unambiguously identify the third-party punisher's choice as correct or erroneous.

To predict how the choices of legal decision makers and potential violators are influenced by the extent of evidentiary uncertainty, the level of harm implied by the norm violation, and the fixed level of the sanction, we build upon Andreoni (1991) and Feess et al. (2015). For a given potential violator's behavior, the optimal standard of proof for an error cost-minimizing legal decision maker is increasing in the sanction level and decreasing in the harm level. This results from the assumption that a higher sanction increases the decision maker's intrinsic costs arising from wrongful convictions (i.e., a legal error of type I), whereas higher levels of harm make wrongful acquittals (i.e., a legal error of type II) more costly. As a result of the implied change in the standard of proof, the probability of wrongful convictions should decrease in the sanction level and increase in the harm level, whereas the probability of wrongful acquittals should increase in the sanction level and decrease in the harm level. A reduction in the extent of evidentiary uncertainty should make punishment more (less) likely when the decision maker receives an incriminating (exonerating) signal, lowering the probability of errors. With respect to potential offenders, we assume that moral costs—which are induced by the norm violation and are increasing in the harm level—are an important factor in the choice of whether to violate the norm, in addition to the monetary gains and the expected sanction. Taking the legal decision maker's behavior as given, lower evidentiary uncertainty and higher levels of both harm and sanction deter norm violations.[2]

We find that punishment and point-taking decisions respond strongly to variations in the extent of evidentiary uncertainty. A higher signal precision clearly lowers the frequency of norm violations and increases the share of third-party punishers willing to (unwilling to) impose the sanction when the signal received is incriminating (exonerating), all else held equal. At the individual level, neither the level of the sanction nor the level of harm are significant determinants of the punishment probability in our data. This seems to be aligned with the legal understanding of a standard of proof. The results carry over to the probability of legal errors, which in our experiment are significantly lower for more precise signals but are not dependent on either harm or sanction levels. With respect to the norm violation, a high level of harm

---

[2] The equilibrium effects with respect to the quality of evidence and harm and sanction levels are complex due to the simultaneous change in the opposing party's behavior. However, our experimental design allows us to focus on the direct effects of parameter changes in our empirical analysis, as we control for beliefs about the other party's behavior.

reduces the share of offenders, whereas a high level of the sanction has no additional deterrent effect.

Our analysis and results are relevant to a large number of settings, as all adjudicative procedures must deal with the possibility of errors. The issue of interpreting a standard of proof is particularly important when laymen are assigned the task of deciding cases—for example, in criminal jury cases in the United States. Our focus on a third party's decision of whether to impose a fixed sanction is practically relevant in settings in which the court's discretion with regard to the level of the sanction is restricted, as is the case for judicial decision makers in the United States operating under sentencing guidelines (e.g., Miceli 2008; Schanzenbach and Tiller 2007). Standards of proof are imposed in other contexts as well: for promotion and employee discipline in the internal organization of firms, for example, and for the determination of appropriate defect rates for the rejection of a supplier's shipment (Kaplow 2011).

1.2. Related Literature

The theoretical literature on standards of proof is quite extensive (see, e.g., Davis 1994; Friedman and Wickelgren 2006; Kaplow 2011; Lando 2009; Miceli 1990; Mungan 2011; Ognedal 2005; Rizzolli and Saraceno 2013; Rubinfeld and Sappington 1987; Yilankaya 2003). In some treatises (e.g., Rubinfeld and Sappington 1987), the standard of proof and the penalty are both considered policy instruments of the court. The aspect that we revisit using data from the laboratory—namely, how decisions regarding whether to convict are influenced by the level of the sanction and the level of harm in the presence of evidentiary uncertainty—is theoretically analyzed by Andreoni (1991) and the closely related contribution by Feess and Wohlschlegel (2009). The latter establish, inter alia, that the deterrence-maximizing sanction might be increasing with the quality of the legal system (quality of information).[3]

Empirically, the effect of evidentiary uncertainty has been studied in voluntary contribution mechanism (VCM) experiments (Ambrus and Greiner 2012; Grechenig, Nicklisch, and Thöni 2010). In contrast to our setup, the individuals who decide on punishment in these experiments usually take part in the VCM as well. For example,

---

[3] There is also literature specifically focusing on the standard of proof in civil law, a context in which legal errors are not as critical as in criminal law. For example, Demougin and Fluet (2006) analyze the "preponderance of the evidence" standard, determining that this standard of proof should not take into account the aspects of the case. Zamir and Ritov (2012) scrutinize the same standard from a behavioral perspective.

Grechenig et al. (2010) find that people punish extensively despite evidentiary uncertainty and that a deterioration in evidentiary quality sometimes even increases punishment. This is at odds with our results for third-party punishment. Obviously, third-party punishment is more relevant to our research interest than peer punishment. Rizzolli and Stanca (2012) consider a take game, investigating how exogenously imposed legal errors influence deterrence (i.e., how errors influence potential offenders), abstracting from the source and the severity of legal errors. Sonnemans and van Dijk (2012) are interested in judicial decisions when there is a possibility of legal error. In their design, subjects were asked to identify the correct decision in 30 abstract cases based on a probability of guilt fixed at one-half and the outcome of an investigation (incriminating, exonerating, or neutral). The authors thereby examine how subjects process the information available and how they arrive at verdicts, finding that a considerable number of people use the information provided rationally but may not acquire the optimal amount of information. Our analysis is complementary, in that we consider how the standard of proof required for conviction is influenced by the aspects of the case at hand (i.e., the level of harm and the level of the sanction). However, our approach also introduces several key differences in experimental design, as judicial decision makers in our setting decide without preset priors and with the knowledge that their verdict has payoff consequences for other experimental subjects.[4] In another line of inquiry, Lyons, Menzies, and Zizzo (2012) actually present subjects with six standards of proof (i.e., six different wordings) and establish that decision makers who must determine merger regulation under evidentiary uncertainty about a merger's welfare repercussions indeed respond to these differences in proof standards.

Most closely linked to our research question about how evidentiary uncertainty interacts with sanction and harm levels in relation to the standard of proof is the study by Feess et al. (2015). In fact, Feess et al. and the present work are the only contributions in which the risk of legal errors depends endogenously on the behavior of potential violators—practically speaking, the most relevant scenario. Our article is complementary to Feess et al. due to important differences in experimental design. One crucial difference is that Feess et al. consider within-subject variation with regard to the level of the sanction, which may draw subjects' attention to this key variable; they also do not consider

---

[4] Van Dijk, Sonnemans, and Bauw (2014) consider the distinction between individual decision makers and groups with respect to judicial error, finding that group decisions tend to reduce the occurrence of legal errors.

different harm levels. In addition, our design allows for greater variety with respect to the extent of evidentiary uncertainty. By making use of the strategy method, Feess et al. focus on the distinction between the direct and total effects of parameter changes on the choices of potential violators and third-party punishers, whereas we use incentivized belief statements to identify partial effects.

1.3. Outline

The remainder of this article is organized as follows. Section 2 explains the theoretical background of our experiment and the behavioral predictions to be considered in our analysis of the experimental data. Section 3 presents the design and implementation of our experiment. Section 4 describes our empirical results. Section 5 concludes.

2. THEORETICAL BACKGROUND AND BEHAVIORAL PREDICTIONS

To derive our behavioral predictions, we build on Andreoni (1991) and Feess et al. (2015) by considering a game in which a potential violator first determines whether to offend and a legal decision maker subsequently decides whether to impose a predetermined sanction on the potential violator. Evidentiary uncertainty prevails because the legal decision maker obtains only a noisy signal about the potential violator's decision.

In our analysis of this game, we consider the decision problems of the potential violator and the legal decision maker for given beliefs about other players' behavior and how their choices are influenced by our key variables (i.e., the level of harm imposed by an offense, the level of the sanction, and the extent of evidentiary uncertainty). We choose not to describe the Bayes-Nash equilibrium because the regression exercises in our empirical analysis consider the partial effect of a parameter change holding the other party's behavior fixed by conditioning on beliefs.

2.1. Legal Decision Makers

Legal decision makers must decide whether to punish a suspect with a predetermined sanction under evidentiary uncertainty. The decision maker's utility arising from the correct punishment of a guilty suspect or the correct acquittal of an innocent suspect is normalized to zero. In contrast, legal decision makers face expected disutility from wrongful convictions or wrongful acquittals. Sanctioning an innocent suspect (i.e., making a type I error) results in a disutility amounting to αs, which is increasing in the level of the sanction s imposed on the suspect ($\alpha > 0$). Not sanctioning a guilty suspect (i.e., making a type II error) is associated with a disutility of βh, which is increasing in the level of harm h that the offender imposes on society ($\beta > 0$). Let μ denote the relative importance of type I errors (i.e., $\mu = \alpha / \beta$). Without loss of generality, we can linearly transform the legal decision maker's utility function using the factor $1 / \beta$ to arrive at a specification in which the disutility of a type I error amounts to $c_I = \mu s$ and the disutility of a type II error equals $c_{II} = h$.[5] For the population of legal decision makers, we assume that the parameter μ (indicating the relative importance of a type I error) is distributed on $[\underline{\mu}, \bar{\mu}]$ according to the cumulative distribution function $F(\mu)$.

Before hearing the evidence, the legal decision maker has a prior amounting to q that the suspect is guilty. Hearing the evidence during the trial transmits an informative but noisy signal θ, $\theta \in \{b, w\}$, to the legal decision maker. The signal b (w) indicates guilt (innocence) and is correct with probability $r \in [1/2, 1]$. According to Bayesian updating, the legal decision maker's prior and the signal θ result in a probability of guilt equal to

$$p(g|b, q, r) = p_b = \frac{qr}{qr + (1 - q)(1 - r)} \tag{1}$$

and

$$p(g|w, q, r) = p_w = \frac{q(1 - r)}{q(1 - r) + (1 - q)r} \tag{2}$$

for the signals b and w, respectively. The probability of guilt is contingent on the signal received, the decision maker's prior, and the signal precision. From the informativeness of the signal when $r > 1/2$, it follows that $p_b > p_w$ and that an increase in the signal's precision increases the difference between the updated probabilities of guilt (i.e., $\partial p_b/\partial_r > 0 > \partial p_w/\partial r$). Circumstances in which the legal decision maker has a higher prior q are associated with higher updated guilt probabilities.

The legal decision maker chooses between punishing with a predetermined sanction and acquitting. Punishing the suspect after having received signal θ implies expected error costs for the decision maker of $(1 - p_\theta)c_I(\mu,s)$; acquitting the suspect implies expected error costs equal to $p_\theta c_{II}(h)$. The comparison of expected error costs leads to a level of

[5] Without changing our results qualitatively, we could alternatively assume that the decision maker's disutility from a type II error is equal to net social harm (i.e., gross social harm less the violator's benefit).

μ indicating the type of the indifferent legal decision maker that can be expressed as

$$\mu_\theta(h, s, q, r) = \frac{p_\theta}{1 - p_\theta} \frac{h}{s}, \tag{3}$$

where

$$\frac{p_b}{1 - p_b} = \frac{q}{1 - q} \frac{r}{1 - r}; \quad \frac{p_w}{1 - p_w} = \frac{q}{1 - q} \frac{1 - r}{r}. \tag{4}$$

Accordingly, (no) punishment is chosen when $(\mu > \mu_\theta) \mu \le \mu_\theta$.[6] The share of decision makers who impose the sanction based on the evidence θ is given by $F(\mu_\theta)$. Obviously, the signal b increases the probability of punishment such that $F(\mu_b) > F(\mu_w)$ when $r > 1/2$ (i.e., when the signal is informative). For a given legal decision maker's prior q, a higher level of harm increases μ_θ, a higher level of the sanction decreases the critical level of the cost parameter, and a higher precision increases (decreases) μ_θ when $\theta = b$ ($\theta = w$). Moreover, the level of μ_θ is increasing in the level of the decision maker's prior about the suspect's participation in norm violations, where the critical value in the event of signal b, μ_b, increases at a faster rate than the critical value in the event of signal w, μ_w.

To conclude the analysis for the legal decision maker, we take the error probabilities into account. An error of type I occurs if an innocent potential violator is sanctioned. Contingent on the potential offender being innocent, a type I error takes place with probability

$$E_I(h, s, q, r) = (1 - r)F(\mu_b) + rF(\mu_w), \tag{5}$$

where the first (second) term indicates that signal b (w) was received when the potential offender did not offend. From our argumentation with respect to the threshold levels, we deduce that $\partial E_I / \partial_h > 0$, $\partial E_I / \partial s < 0$, and $\partial E_I / \partial q > 0$. The change in the error probability with respect to the signal precision follows from

$$\frac{\partial E_I}{\partial r} = -[F(\mu_b) - F(\mu_w)] + \frac{(1 - r)f(\mu_b)\mu_b - rf(\mu_w)\mu_w}{r(1 - r)} \frac{h}{s}. \tag{6}$$

The direct effect of a higher signal precision is to lower the probability of a type I error, as signal b (w) becomes less (more) likely for an inno-

---

[6] The type of the indifferent legal decision maker in eq. (3) is well defined only when $q \in (0,1)$ and $r \in (1/2,1)$. Our experimental implementation also considers $r = 1$ (i.e., the absence of evidentiary uncertainty) in which case *all* decision makers ought (not) to punish when the signal is b (w).

cent individual. However, the variation in r also changes the punishment probability in the two states, which may amplify or counteract the direct effect.

An error of type II implies that an actual violator is acquitted. Contingent on the individual being guilty, a type II error takes place with probability

$$E_{II}(h, s, q, r) = r(1 - F(\mu_b)) + (1 - r)(1 - F(\mu_w)). \tag{7}$$

We conclude that $\partial E_{II} / \partial h < 0$, $\partial E_{II} / \partial s > 0$ and $\partial E_{II} / \partial q < 0$. The change in the error probability with respect to the signal precision follows from

$$\frac{\partial E_{II}}{\partial r} = -[F(\mu_b) - F(\mu_w)] - \frac{rf(\mu_b)\mu_b - (1 - r)f(\mu_w)\mu_w}{r(1 - r)} \frac{h}{s}. \tag{8}$$

When the signal becomes more informative, a violation will be signaled more (less) often with b (w). The difference between punishment probabilities implies that the direct effect of higher signal precision lowers the probability of a type II error. In principal, the variation in the critical levels allows for a countervailing effect. However, when F is close to a uniform distribution, the overall effect is unambiguously negative.

2.2. Potential Violator

We now turn to the potential violator's choice between violating and not violating in the initial stage of the game. The expected payoff from violating is the gain x less the expected sanction applying to offenders and the moral costs vh, which we assume to be increasing in harm h. Among potential violators, the moral cost parameter is distributed on $[\underline{v}, \bar{v}]$ according to the cumulative distribution function $G(v)$. The expected cost of the decision to not violate the norm is the expected sanction mistakenly imposed on nonoffenders. With regard to the punishment probabilities, potential violators form beliefs about the behavior of the legal decision makers. Denoting the potential violator's belief about the share of legal decision makers who punish upon receiving the signal θ as m_θ, the expected punishment probability applying to violators (nonviolators) is given by $m_b r + m_w (1 - r) (m_b (1 - r) + m_w r)$, as offending invokes signal b with probability r and signal w with probability $(1 - r)$. We assume that $m_b \geq m_w$ due to the informativeness of the signal. A potential offender with a moral cost parameter v thus prefers to violate the norm when

$$x - vh - (m_b r + m_w(1 - r))s \geq -(m_b(1 - r) + m_w r)s. \tag{9}$$

This leads to a critical level for the moral cost parameter that can be expressed as

$$\nu_c(s, m_b - m_w, r) = \frac{x - (2r - 1)[m_b - m_w]s}{h}, \tag{10}$$

which is equal to the criminal gain less the implied increase in the expected sanction due to the violation (when the signal is informative, that is, when $r > 1/2$) divided by the harm level. A higher level of the sanction, greater signal precision, and a higher harm level all lower the level of ν_c (signifying deterrence) for fixed beliefs about legal decision makers' punishment behavior. An increase in the difference $\Delta = m_b - m_w$ reduces the share of potential offenders willing to violate the norm. The share of potential offenders who decide to violate the norm is given by $G[\nu_c(h, s, \Delta, r)]$.

2.3. Summary

We summarize the effects that we have just described in table 1. With respect to error probabilities, the direct effect of a more precise signal argues for a reduction in error probabilities; however, an indirect effect may counteract the direct effect. We use parentheses to indicate predictions potentially affected by countervailing effects.

Table 1. Behavioral Hypotheses for Given Beliefs

	HARM	SANCTION	TAKING BELIEF	SIGNAL PRECISION	PUN. BELIEF
	h	s	q	r	$m_b - m_w$
Pun. prob. ball b	+	−	+	+	
Pun. prob. ball w	+	−	+	−	
Point-taking prob.	−	−		−	−
Error I prob.	+	−	+	(−)	
Error II prob.	−	+	−	(−)	

Note: Table entries indicate the expected sign of the change in the decisions made and error probabilities due to an increase in the parameters. For error probabilities, the predicted negative sign of the direct effect from an increase in signal precision may be counteracted by indirect effects; this is indicated by parentheses. Pun. = punishment; prob. = probability.

3. EXPERIMENTAL DESIGN, IMPLEMENTATION, AND DATA

3.1. Experimental Design

In our experiment, all subjects were endowed with 20 points and assigned a role (player A, B, or C). The exchange rate for all payoffs was 1 point = 40 Euro cents. The subjects were divided into (anonymous) groups of three, each with a player A, B, and C. In brief, our main experiment included the following three stages (explained in detail next): in stage 1, player A had to decide whether to take points from player B to increase his or her payoff. In stage 2, player C received a noisy signal about player A's choice and then had to decide whether to deduct points from player A; this punishment had no influence on player C's material payoffs.[7] Player B remained passive in stages 1 and 2. In stage 3, beliefs were elicited from all participants about both the point taking and the punishment probabilities.

We considered two treatment dimensions in a between-subjects design (see table 2): the harm h incurred by player A's taking of points from player B could be either high or low, $h \in \{10; 20\}$, and the sanction s that player C could impose on player A could be either high or low, $s \in \{10; 20\}$. Table 2 summarizes the resulting four treatments. For each treatment, the first entry refers to the sanction and the second to the harm level, with L/H indicating low/high, H/L indicating high/low, L/L indicating low/low, and H/H indicating high/high.

With respect to the extent of evidentiary uncertainty, we had all subjects make decisions for six levels of signal precision in a within-subjects approach (as explained next). Each subject participated in one treatment, resulting in a between-subjects approach for the various harm and sanction levels. In the following paragraphs, we describe the three stages of our main experiment in more detail.

In stage 1, player A could take h points from player B to receive x points. The level of player A's gross benefit from taking was fixed at $x = 5$ for all treatments. The level of h represented the external cost of player A's point taking. The level of harm (either 10 or 20) always exceeded player A's private gain by a wide margin, clearly conveying that point taking should be seen as a norm infraction, and a change in the level of h implied a corresponding variation in the net efficiency loss $h - x$. Player A knew that the decision to take points or not from

---

[7] The instructions used neutral terminology. The potential point taking by player A and the potential punishment of player A by player C were referred to as "deductions of points." See app. B, available online, for a translated version of the instructions. In stage 4, payoff composition is determined based on subjects' choices and the outcome of a random mechanism.

Table 2.   Treatments

	TREATMENT	
SANCTION	Low Harm (h = 10)	High Harm (h = 20)
Low (s = 10)	L/L	L/H
High (s = 20)	H/L	H/H

player B would influence the signal received by player C in stage 2 and that player C might punish player A by deducting a commonly known sanction from player A's payoff.[8] The level of the sanction was either low (s = 10) or high (s = 20).

With respect to the signaling technology, in stage 2, player C learned the color of a ball (either black or white) that was randomly drawn from urn BLACK when player A took points from player B and from urn WHITE otherwise.[9] The probability that the draw would be a black ball was (weakly) higher when player A actually took points from player B than when player A did not take points, ensuring that the signal was informative (corresponding to $r \geq 1/2$ in sec. 2). We used six urn compositions (as displayed in table 3), thereby varying the informativeness of the signal received by player C. In all possible urn compositions, both urns contained 10 balls. The signal's precision varied from the perfectly revealing signal of urn composition 10/0—10 black (white) balls and no white (black) balls in urn BLACK (WHITE)—to the totally uninformative signal of urn composition 5/5—5 black and 5 white balls in urn BLACK and in urn WHITE. In addition to the two extreme urn compositions, we used the intermediate urn compositions 9/1, 8/2, 7/3, and 6/4. Referring to our theoretical model, we thus examined the extent of evidentiary uncertainty $r \in \{1; 9/10; 4/5; 7/10; 3/5; 1/2\}$. With these facts in mind, players A indicated their decision for each of the possible urn combinations. Choices by player A were made on one screen showing all scenarios in an order of declining signal quality. This procedure parallels what is done for eliciting risk preferences (e.g., Dohmen et al. 2010) or reservation prices (e.g., Becker, DeGroot, and Marschak 1964) in other circumstances.

In stage 2, player C could punish player A at no personal material cost by subtracting s points from player A's payoff. For some players C, the level of the sanction was low (s = 10), whereas it was high (s = 20) for

---

[8] All participants were fully informed about the signaling technology.
[9] Relating back to our presentation in sec. 2, receiving the information that the ball is black (white) represents the case in which the legal decision maker receives signal b (w).

Table 3.   Urn Compositions

	NUMBER OF BALLS	
COMPOSITION	Urn BLACK	Urn WHITE
10/0	10 black / 0 white	0 black / 10 white
9/1	9 black / 1 white	1 black / 9 white
8/2	8 black / 2 white	2 black / 8 white
7/3	7 black / 3 white	3 black / 7 white
6/4	6 black / 4 white	4 black / 6 white
5/5	5 black / 5 white	5 black / 5 white

others. The level of the sanction always exceeded player A's private gain from point taking (which was fixed at 5 points), such that punishment more than offset any gain from the norm violation. Player C had to decide whether to punish based on the information inferred from the signal about player A's choice (i.e., the color of the ball drawn) and his or her prior about player A's taking decision. To familiarize participants with Bayesian updating (which is required in our design to rationally process the signal), our instructions worked through two examples—one with a prior of $q = 0.2$ and one with a prior of $q = 0.8$—stating the respective ex post probability of point taking for both colors of the ball and each urn composition (see app. B, available online, for the complete instructions).[10] Player C chose between punishment and no punishment contingent on the ball being black or white for all six urn compositions, implying a total of 12 decisions: one decision for every possible combination of ball color (black or white) and urn composition, thereby implementing the strategy method (Selten 1967). Matching the procedure for players A, players C entered their decisions using one screen for both colors of the ball and all urn compositions (presented in an order of descending signal quality).

In stage 3, subjects stated their (incentivized) beliefs regarding how many players A and C in their session but outside their own group took points and assigned punishment for each urn composition (ensuring that their own decisions would not directly affect their statements). Each session consisted of either seven or eight groups. Subjects

---

[10] We ensured understanding by asking a set of control questions; correct solutions were required for the experiment to begin (see online app. B).

earned 4 points for each correct belief.[11] By adding the third stage, we obtained information about the subjects' priors that is critical for understanding their decision making in relation to our theoretical predictions. As stated earlier, players B did not make decisions in stages 1 and 2 but did state their beliefs in stage 3.

3.2. Implementation and Data

In total, 504 subjects (median age: 24 years; 56% female) participated in our experiment at the University of Bonn; the experiment was computerized using zTree (Fischbacher 2007). ORSEE (Greiner 2015) was used for recruitment. Data were collected from June to October 2014. The 504 subjects formed 168 groups. We analyzed data from 55 groups for treatment L/L, 51 for treatment H/L, 32 for treatment L/H, and 30 for treatment H/H.

The experiment was not preceded by any other experiment and concluded with a long questionnaire before which we elicited risk preferences using the procedure proposed by Holt and Laury (2002).[12] Payoffs were assessed in stage 4 as follows: (1) one urn composition was drawn randomly; (2) player A's decision for that composition was implemented, which determined whether urn BLACK or urn WHITE was relevant; and (3) the color of the ball was determined by a random draw according to the composition of the relevant urn (either BLACK or WHITE), and the decision of player C (to either punish or not punish) was implemented. In addition, subjects received payments for correct beliefs in stage 3 and for one randomly selected choice (and possibly lottery draw) of the Holt and Laury procedure. Completing the questionnaire was rewarded with an additional 20 points. On average, participants earned 18.04 Euros for taking part in one of our sessions, which lasted an average of 80 minutes.

4. RESULTS

In this section, we present the results of our experiment. We start with an investigation into the punishment decisions by players C (sec. 4.1) before turning to the taking decisions by players A (sec. 4.2). Finally, in section 4.3, we report on error probabilities.

---

[11] In contrast to Sonnemans and van Dijk (2012), we did not present priors, as it would have been impossible in our design (given that infractions were determined by player A).

[12] More specifically, participants were confronted with 10 choices between a lottery and a certain payoff. Our measure of individual risk aversion is equal to the number of times the certain option was chosen by the subject.

4.1. Punishment Decision

Players C could either impose the predetermined sanction or not. Figures 1 and 2 summarize the shares of players C who punished after a black ball and a white ball were drawn, respectively. For each ball color, we can distinguish 24 constellations according to the four treatments and six urn compositions. In figures 1 and 2, observations are displayed for each urn composition under each of the four treatments (see table 2), showing the share of players C who punished and the corresponding 95% confidence interval (see app. A for the numerical values).

Figures 1 and 2 indicate that the punishment decisions varied with the signal precision (i.e., the urn composition) but that differences between treatments were small. Considering the share of punishers when averaging over the four scenarios, we find that the share of players C who punished when a black (white) ball was drawn increases (decreases) from 30.36% (32.14%) for urn composition 5/5 to 81.55% (10.12%) for urn composition 10/0. Considering instead the share of punishers when averaging over the six urn compositions, we find that treatment H/L produced the lowest share of punishers for both a black and a white ball (55.88% and 15.69%). The highest share of punishers after a black (white) ball was drawn occurs in treatment H/H (L/L), amounting to 65.00% (23.33%) of players C.

Following these descriptive observations, we examine whether players C made their punishment contingent on the signal received (i.e., ball color). For each treatment, we find significant differences between the punishment decision after a black ball was drawn and the punishment decision after a white ball was drawn for the high-precision compositions 8/2, 9/1, and 10/0 ($p < .01$, two-tailed exact McNemar test for each treatment-urn combination).[13] No significant differences are obtained for the low-precision compositions 5/5 and 6/4 ($p < .1$, two-tailed exact McNemar test for each treatment-urn combination); results for the composition 7/3 depend on the treatment.[14] These findings are in line with our theoretical prediction that a sufficiently precise signal is required for noticeable differences in punishment probabilities.

---

[13] Because punishment decisions by player C were made for both ball colors and for each composition within a treatment, we use two-tailed exact McNemar tests for a nonparametric within-subject comparison given the possible outcomes of "punishment" and "no punishment."

[14] For the urn composition 7/3, we obtain significant differences at the 1% level for the treatments L/L and H/L and at the 5% level for treatment H/H. In treatment L/H, the difference is only marginally significant at the 10% level. Again, the results refer to two-tailed exact McNemar tests for each scenario.

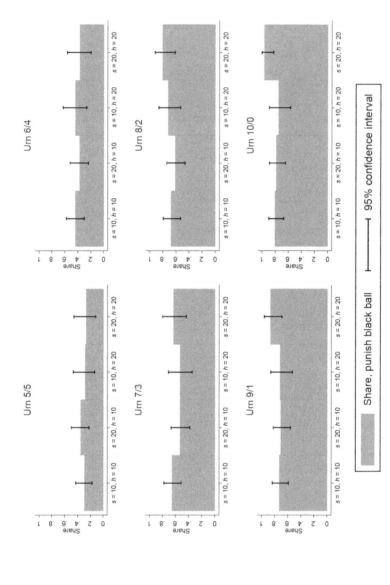

Figure 1. Share of third-party punishers when the ball was black

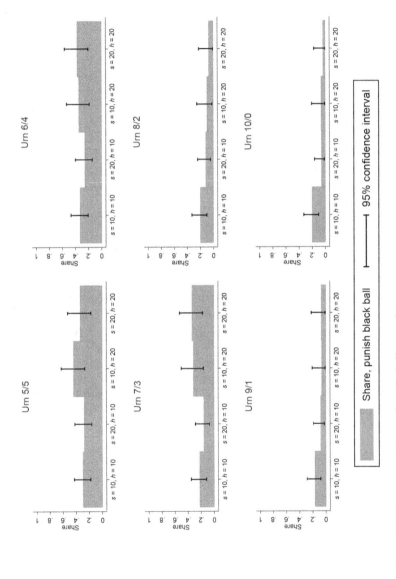

Figure 2. Share of third-party punishers when the ball was white

Next, we compare the punishment shares across signal precision levels, holding the color of the ball drawn and the treatment fixed.[15] When a black ball was drawn, in all but five comparisons we obtain significant differences in the punishment decisions when we consider an improvement in the precision by two balls (e.g., comparing choices for compositions 7/3 and 5/5) ($p < .05$, two-tailed McNemar tests for each treatment and combination of urn compositions).[16] When a white ball was drawn instead, differences between urn compositions are less pronounced. However, for the high-harm treatments L/H and H/H, we find significant differences when comparing the low-precision compositions 5/5, 6/4, and 7/3 with the high-precision compositions 8/2, 9/1, and 10/0 ($p < .05$, two-tailed McNemar tests). With respect to treatment H/L, significant differences result only when comparing choices for composition 5/5 (6/4) with choices for 8/2, 9/1, and 10/0 (9/1 and 10/0) ($p < .05$, two-tailed McNemar tests). In treatment L/L, only the comparison between the decisions for 6/4 and 9/1 reveals significant differences in punishment behavior for a white ball ($p < .05$, two-sided McNemar test).

In summary, our data suggest that players C (i) responded to the signal (black or white ball) when the signal was sufficiently informative and (ii) reacted to variations in signal precision. These findings are consistent with our theoretical predictions. This is interesting because the monetary payoffs for players C were unaffected by their punishment decisions.[17] However, other findings cannot be easily reconciled with our theoretical considerations. In contrast to our predictions, when urn composition 10/0 applied, some players C punished player A even when a white ball was drawn (perfectly revealing that player A did not take points). Moreover, for urn composition 10/0, some players C abstained from punishing player A even when a black ball was drawn (perfectly revealing that player A had taken points).[18] Table 4 summarizes the decisions by players C for composition 10/0. In all treat-

[15] This involves 15 possible comparisons for each treatment and ball color. Urn composition 5/5 can be compared with all the other five compositions, leaving four more comparisons for urn composition 6/4, and so on.

[16] Differences are not significant for the comparison of urn composition 7/3 to 9/1 in treatments L/L and L/H, the comparison of urn compositions 7/3 and 10/0 in treatment L/H, or for the comparison of urn composition 8/2 to 10/0 in treatments L/H and H/H.

[17] We deliberately chose not to incentivize decisions by players C in order to represent the idea of moral error costs.

[18] However, the fact that punishment decisions are not significantly different for black or white balls for the uninformative urn composition 5/5 is fully in line with theory.

Table 4. Punishment Decisions for Urn Composition 10/0

Treatment	Punishment Only for Black Ball	Never Punish	Punishment Only for White Ball	Always Punish	Sum
$s = 10, h = 10$	37	7	4	7	55
$s = 20, h = 10$	38	10	1	2	51
$s = 10, h = 20$	22	8	0	2	32
$s = 20, h = 20$	28	1	0	1	30

ments, the majority of players C indeed punished only after a black ball was drawn. At the same time, we also observe individuals who did not punish player A after either color of the ball was drawn. This may be explained by the fact that ex post punishment had no deterrence benefit in our setting and implied a loss in efficiency.[19]

Turning to a comparison between treatments, nonparametric tests confirm the first intuition from figures 1 and 2 that basically no differences in punishment behavior can be observed across treatments ($p > .1$, Fisher's exact tests for each urn composition and pairwise comparison of treatments). Likewise, aggregating data over urn compositions and applying a Wilcoxon rank sum test on the share of punishers yield no significant difference for either a black or a white ball.

Finally, we analyze the punishment data using probit estimations. Table 5 summarizes results reporting marginal effects. Columns 1 and 2 (cols. 3 and 4) depict the results for the case in which the ball drawn was black (white). Columns 2 and 4 include the beliefs of players C regarding the probability that players A took points from players B, thereby representing the regressions most relevant for our behavioral hypotheses from table 1.[20] All estimates indicate that the signal precision (i.e., the extent of evidentiary uncertainty as represented by the urn composition) was crucial for the punishment decision. Each discrete improvement in signal precision translated into a higher (lower) punishment probability after signal b (w) was received, where the

---

[19] This rationale was cited by many participants in the postexperimental questionnaire. In all, 24 players C chose to never punish player A under any circumstances. However, three of our players C chose to always punish player A.

[20] Summary statistics for beliefs are presented in app. A. With respect to our measure of risk aversion, when considering all players C, we obtain a mean of 6.21, a standard deviation of 1.72, and a minimum (maximum) value of 0 (10), where higher scores indicate higher risk aversion.

Table 5. Probit Regressions for Punishment

	BLACK BALL		WHITE BALL	
	(1)	(2)	(3)	(4)
High fine	.0040	.0067	−.0572	−.0506
	(.08)	(.13)	(−1.33)	(−1.19)
High harm	.0368	.0379	.0066	.0103
	(.68)	(.71)	(.15)	(.24)
Urn 6/4	.1008**	.1037**	−.0059	.0041
	(3.67)	(3.76)	(−.26)	(.17)
Urn 7/3	.2855**	.2919**	−.0834**	−.0641+
	(7.74)	(7.82)	(−2.60)	(−1.90)
Urn 8/2	.3810**	.3904**	−.1909**	−.1668**
	(9.25)	(9.34)	(−4.96)	(−4.03)
Urn 9/1	.4402**	.4516**	−.2207**	−.1951**
	(10.11)	(10.18)	(−5.42)	(−4.46)
Urn 10/0	.5114**	.5223**	−.2213**	−.1952**
	(12.16)	(12.13)	(−5.44)	(−4.54)
Risk aversion	−.0136	−.0137	.0049	.0049
	(−.85)	(−.85)	(.41)	(.41)
Belief point taking (q)		.0506		.1137+
		(.75)		(1.87)
Pseudo-R^2	.1073	.1084	.0625	.0729
No. of obs.	1,008	1,008	1,008	1,008

Note: Marginal effects; z values in parentheses. Standard errors clustered at the individual level. The reference category for the urn composition is urn composition 5/5. The dummy variable high fine is equal to 1 when $s = 20$ and equal to 0 when $s = 10$, and high harm is equal to 1 for $h = 20$ and equal to 0 for $h = 10$. Risk aversion is a variable equal to the number of times a subject chose the certain payoff in the Holt and Laury procedure ranging from 0 to 10. Belief point taking reflects a player C's expectation about the share of players A from the other groups in the session that take points. Cols. 2 and 4 include the beliefs of players C regarding the probability that players A took points from players B, thereby representing the regressions most relevant for our behavioral hypotheses from table 8. obs. = observations.
+$p < .10$.
*$p < .05$.
**$p < .01$.

significance level refers to a comparison to urn composition 5/5.[21] This is fully in line with our argumentation in section 2 and the preceding findings. The coefficients for the dummy variables of high fine (equal to 1 when $s = 20$ and equal to 0 when $s = 10$) and high harm (equal to 1 for $h = 20$ and equal to 0 for $h = 10$) are not significantly different from zero. This result mirrors the insignificant differences in probabilities across treatments observed in the data. With respect to the influence of player C's beliefs about the frequency of point taking, we find that players C who believe that many players A took points were (weakly) more likely to punish even after a white ball was drawn, whereas the effect is not significant for the punishment probability after a black ball was drawn.[22] The coefficient for our measure of individual risk aversion is not statistically significant.

In summary, our data do not support the prediction that the punishment probability will increase with the level of harm and decrease with the level of the sanction. It is important to note that the behavior of players C is thereby completely in accordance with the legal concept of proof beyond a reasonable doubt. This legal understanding emphasizes that evidentiary quality alone, and no further aspects of the case (e.g., the harm level) should influence the verdict (and thus punishment).

4.2. Point-Taking Probability

Another key question is how potential violators behave under evidentiary uncertainty. Rizzolli and Stanca (2012) study this issue for exogenously specified error probabilities. Figure 3 summarizes the taking decisions by players A in our experiment with *endogenously* determined error probabilities. Figure 3 displays the share of players A who took points from player B for each of the 24 possible combinations of treatment and urn composition (see app. A for the numerical values).

Figure 3 illustrates that in all treatments, the share of players A who took points from players B decreases when the signal precision increases. Averaging over all treatments, the share of players A who

---

[21] For a black ball, the increase in the punishment probability when the signal precision increases is statistically significant for any two urn compositions. For a white ball, differences are significant when comparing a low-precision urn composition (5/5, 6/4, or 7/3) with a high-precision composition (8/2, 9/1, or 10/0).

[22] A comparison of the results in cols. 3 and 4 indicates that the incorporation of the weakly significant belief about point taking slightly reduces the coefficients for the signal precision. This is due to the negative correlation between beliefs about point taking and signal precision.

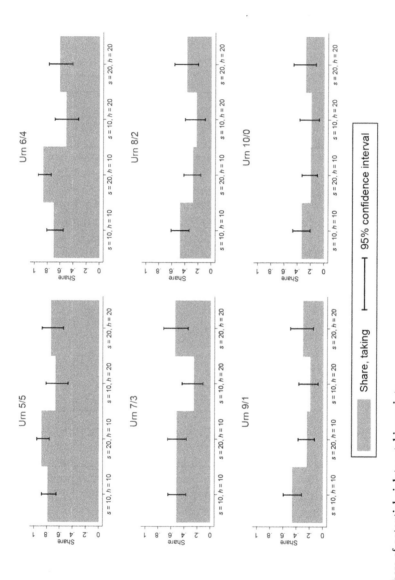

Figure 3. Share of potential violators taking points

took points from players B decreases from 77.98% for composition 5/5 to 25.00% for composition 10/0. When comparing choices across treatments, the findings are more complex. Averaging over all urn compositions, the share of players A who took points is highest in treatment L/L (reaching a level of 53.94%). The minimum share (with a value of 33.33%) occurs in treatment L/H, compared with 49.35% (46.67%) in treatment H/L (H/H). When considering single urn compositions, for all urn compositions the share of takers is lowest in treatment L/Hs and highest in either treatment L/L or H/L (except for urn composition 7/10, for which the share is maximal in treatment H/H at 53.33 %, although this is only slightly higher than the shares in treatment L/L [50.91%] and H/L [50.98%]). Comparing the two low-harm treatments, we note that the share of players A who took points is higher for the high (low) sanction when low (high) levels of signal precision apply.

Following these descriptive observations, we now study potential differences in more detail. First, we compare the taking choices for different signal precision levels and a fixed treatment. For the most part, in both low-harm treatments, taking choices are significantly different across urn compositions ($p < .05$, two-tailed exact McNemar tests); this holds for 11 of the 15 possible comparisons. Considering only signal improvements signified by a difference of at least two balls, choices are significantly different in 8 of the 10 comparisons for the low-harm treatments.[23] In treatment L/H, significant differences emerge when comparing choices for the low-precision compositions 5/5 and 6/4 with those for the compositions 7/3, 8/2, 9/1, and 10/0 ($p < .05$, two-tailed exact McNemar tests). Choices across high-precision urn compositions are not significantly different.[24] In treatment H/H, differences in taking choices are statistically significant between the low-precision urn compositions 5/5 and 6/4 and the high-precision urn compositions 8/2, 9/1, and 10/0. Furthermore, significant differences are obtained when comparing choices for urn composition 7/3 and urn composition 9/1 or 10/0, as well as for a comparison between urn compositions 9/1 and 10/0. In summary, higher levels of signal precision seem to deter point taking, which is in line with our theoretical considerations.

We now turn to a comparison of taking choices across treatments. The different treatments are more crucial for the taking decision than was the case for the punishment decisions previously discussed

---

[23] The differences are not significant in treatment L/L when comparing urn compositions 7/3 and 9/1, or in treatment H/L when comparing compositions 8/2 and 10/0 ($p < .1$, two-tailed exact McNemar tests).

[24] Note that the relatively lower number of observations in the high-harm treatments may affect this result.

(although they are trumped by the differences induced by different levels of signal precision). First, we note that choices for urn composition 10/0 are not significantly different across treatments ($p < .1$, Fisher's exact tests for each treatment combination). For the perfectly revealing signal in urn composition 10/0, we would in theory expect no point takers in any treatment, given that players C punish norm violators (and only norm violators). Thus, the lack of differences is, in this sense, consistent with theory. However, in the experiment, point taking did not disappear for urn composition 10/0 (the taking rate ranges from 18.75% for treatment L/H to 32.73% for treatment L/L), and punishment of norm violators (and only norm violators) was also not assured. Next, we consider treatment L/H, which yields the lowest share of point takers for every urn composition. Comparing choices with those in treatment L/L (H/L), we find significant differences for the relatively high-precision (low-precision) urn compositions 7/3, 8/2 and 9/1 (5/5, 6/4, and 7/3). Choices in treatment L/H are significantly different from those in treatment H/H only for composition 7/3 (all statements refer to $p < .05$, Fisher's exact tests between treatments for a given urn composition). Likewise, a significant difference between taking choices in treatments H/L and H/H results only for composition 6/4. Of interest, when comparing taking decisions across the low-harm treatments L/L and H/L, we obtain more pronounced differences. Taking occurs significantly more often for the high (low) sanction for the low-precision urn composition 6/4 (the high-precision urn compositions 8/2 and 9/1).

When we aggregate taking data for each treatment over the six urn compositions to apply a Wilcoxon rank sum test to the average point-taking rates at the subject level, we find that taking in treatment L/H differs significantly from taking in both low-harm treatments L/L and H/L ($p < .01$, Wilcoxon rank sum test). The significant differences to the high-harm treatment L/H seem consistent with our assumption about moral costs increasing with the level of social harm (but note that there is no significant difference to the other high-harm treatment H/H). Regarding the level of the sanction, a comparison of treatments L/L and H/L indicates that the standard deterrent effect seems to be dependent on a relatively high signal precision. However, a comparison of the high-harm treatments L/H and H/H does not support the standard deterrent effect of higher sanctions for any level of signal precision.

To control for different factors simultaneously, we again turn to probit regressions (see table 6 for marginal effects). We refer to the two leftmost columns in table 6, which are based on all urn compositions. Higher signal precision deters point taking (as foreseen in our predictions and argued in contributions such as Polinsky and Shavell

2007).[25] One key issue in the literature on law enforcement is the deterrent effect of the expected sanction (e.g., Levitt and Miles 2007). In our data, we do not find that the higher sanction produces additional deterrence. This concurs with recent empirical evidence for Germany (Entorf and Spengler 2015), for example, but contrasts with experimental findings by Friesen (2012), who used fixed detection probabilities. In view of our finding that only precise urn compositions in the low-harm treatments produced deterrent effects, this lack of a significant effect is not surprising. With respect to the expected punishment probability, our results are consistent with our predictions. Expecting a higher punishment probability after a white ball is drawn (and thus a smaller $m_b - m_w$) increases point taking. For the subjects' beliefs about the punishment probability after a black ball is drawn, the effect is not significantly different from zero.[26] In accordance with our theoretical predictions, a higher harm level significantly (weakly) reduces point taking. The coefficient of our measure of risk aversion is negative and marginally significant.[27]

Motivated by the possibility of interaction effects suggested by figure 3, we also estimate probit models for low-precision and high-precision signal observations separately (where low-precision signal observations include compositions 5/5, 6/4, and 7/3, and high-precision signal observations include compositions 8/2, 9/1, and 10/0; see cols. 3–6 in table 6). We find that the deterrent effect of a high harm level is relevant only for the low-precision urn compositions. This result may indicate that the moral costs assumed in section 2 are especially relevant when the signal is relatively imprecise, as subjects recognize that they may not be held responsible by a third party. With respect to the level of the sanction, we find a positive coefficient for low levels of signal precision. A possible explanation for the positive effect of the sanction level on point taking may proceed as follows: players A may expect that their actual decisions have little relevance to whether they will be punished, and thus they may feel more entitled to take the 5 points from player B to make up for the punishment by players C if the sanction is high. Finally, we observe that the beliefs of players A about the punishment decisions by players C seem to be of particular importance for high-precision

[25] The differences between coefficients are significant when comparing any two urn compositions except for comparisons between the high-precision compositions 8/2, 9/1, and 10/0.

[26] Note that beliefs about punishment for a black and a white ball are strongly correlated with signal precision. Accordingly, coefficients for the urn compositions are somewhat lower in col. 2 compared with col. 1 in table 6.

[27] When considering all players A with regard to risk aversion, the mean is 6.14, the standard deviation 1.73, and the minimum (maximum) value equal to 0 (10).

Table 6. Probit Regressions for Point Taking

POINT TAKING

	All Urns		Low-Precision Signal		High-Precision Signal	
	(1)	(2)	(3)	(4)	(5)	(6)
High fine	.0436	.0414	.1366**	.1427***	-.0505	-.0355
	(.85)	(.81)	(2.50)	(2.66)	(-.76)	(-.54)
High harm	-.1046*	-.0983+	-.1426**	-.1307*	-.0618	-.0732
	(-1.99)	(-1.88)	(-2.60)	(-2.36)	(-.90)	(-1.07)
Urn 6/4	-.0889**	-.0826**	-.0880**	-.1004**		
	(-3.38)	(-3.01)	(-3.36)	(-3.81)		
Urn 7/3	-.3166**	-.2938**	-.3162**	-.3482**		
	(-7.49)	(-6.51)	(-7.47)	(-7.34)		
Urn 8/2	-.4348**	-.3830**				
	(-9.48)	(-6.80)				
Urn 9/1	-.4704**	-.4025**			-.0359*	.0055
	(-10.58)	(-6.43)			(-2.49)	(.28)

90

	(1)	(2)	(3)	(4)	(5)	(6)
Urn 10/0	-.5294**	-.4420**			-.0950**	-.0130
	(-12.10)	(-6.46)			(-3.89)	(-.38)
Risk aversion	-0.320+	-.0318+	-.0327+	-.0359+	-.0311	-.0233
	(-1.90)	(-1.90)	(-1.73)	(-1.94)	(-1.62)	(-1.16)
Belief punish black		-.0407		.1865+		-.2593**
		(-.41)		(1.75)		(-2.11)
Belief punish white		.2177*		.0620		.2853**
		(2.38)		(.55)		(2.58)
Pseudo-R^2	.1400	.1518	.1055	.1192	.0279	.0650
No. of obs.	1,008	1,008	504	504	504	504

Note: Marginal effects; z values in parentheses. Standard errors clustered at the individual level. In cols. 3 and 4, only obs. for compositions 5/5, 6/4, and 7/3 are included. In cols. 5 and 6, only obs. for compositions 8/2, 9/1, and 10/0 are included. The reference category for the urn composition is composition 5/5 for cols. 1–4 and composition 8/2 for cols. 5 and 6. The dummy variable high fine is equal to 1 when $s = 20$ and equal to 0 when $s = 10$, and high harm is equal to 1 for $h = 10$ and equal to 0 for $h = 10$. Risk aversion is a variable equal to the number of times a subject chose the certain payoff in the Holt and Laury procedure, ranging from 0 to 10. Belief punish black (white) reflects player A's expectations about the share of players C from the other groups that punishes players A after a black (white) ball is drawn. obs. = observations.

+ $p < .10$.
* $p < .05$.
** $p < .01$.

91

signals, whereas the risk aversion measure is not significant when considering this subsample.

4.3. Error Probabilities

We now turn to the question of how error probabilities were affected by variations in the level of harm, the level of the sanction, and the extent of evidentiary uncertainty. To this end, we describe the error probabilities that we analyze in the following regression exercise. In equations (5) and (7) in section 2, we explained the error probabilities for the population of legal decision makers. Now, instead of using the probability of punishing that resulted for the population of legal decision makers, $1 - F(\mu_\theta)$, or of not punishing, $(F(\mu_\theta))$, we use the actual choices of players C at the individual level and calculate error probabilities contingent on the taking choice made by player A. That is, we calculate the probability E_{II} (E_I) of a type II (I) error when player A in fact chose to take (not take) points. Denoting by ϕ_θ the decision by player C of whether to punish $(\phi_\theta = 1)$ or not $(\phi_\theta = 0)$ after observing a black ball $(\theta = b)$ or a white ball $(\theta = w)$, we have

$$E_I = r\phi_w + (1 - r)\phi_b \text{ or } E_{II} = r(1 - \phi_b) + (1 - r)(1 - \phi_w)$$

for a given level of evidentiary uncertainty r (of which there are six in our design). In our data, players A took points in 477 of 1,008 choices, resulting in 531 observations for probabilities of a type I error and 477 observations for probabilities of a type II error.

Given our result that punishment was more likely after a black ball was drawn than after a white ball was drawn when the signal was sufficiently informative (see sec. 4.1), we expect the direct effect of a higher signal precision level to be negative for both kinds of errors (as described in our model in sec. 2). Indirect effects via the induced change in the probability of punishment for a black and a white ball might counter the direct effect. With respect to comparisons between treatments, we expect to see little variation in light of the fact that punishment decisions did not react significantly to variations in the levels of the sanction and harm (in contrast to the theoretical prediction). Finally, given that beliefs about point taking had a marginally significant effect on the punishment decision after a white ball was drawn, beliefs may also affect error probabilities (reducing [increasing] the probability of a type II [I] error).

Figures 4 and 5 display the average probabilities and the corresponding 95% confidence interval of a type I error (fig. 4) or type II (fig. 5) given no point taking (point taking) by player A.[28] As expected, differences

---

[28] See app. A for a summary of the data.

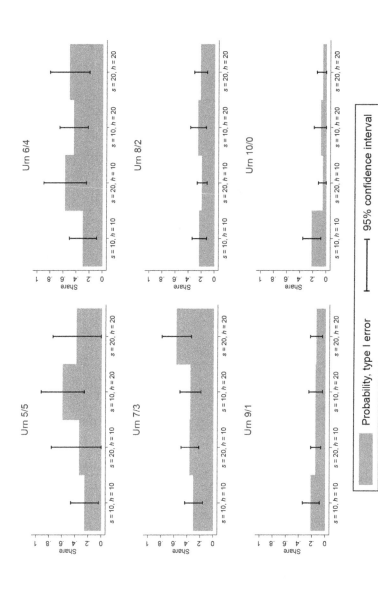

Figure 4. Average probability of a type I error given that player A did not take points

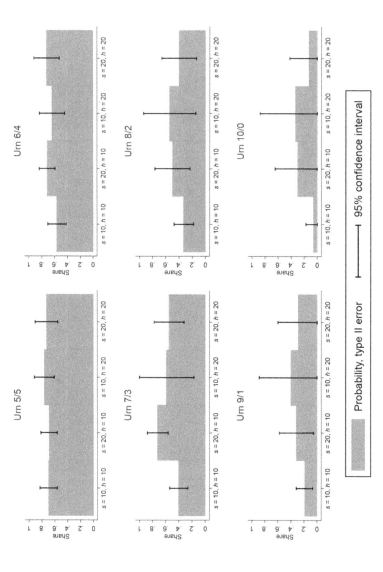

Figure 5. Average probability of a type II error given that player A took points

in error probabilities between various signal precision levels seem more pronounced than between treatments. Averaging over treatments, the probability of a type I error is about 40% for the low-precision compositions (39.19% for 5/5, 42.31% for 6/4, 36.89% for 7/3) and decreases for the more accurate compositions with increasing signal precision (21.63% for 8/2, 15.69% for 9/1, 10.32% for 10/0). The probability of a type II error declines steadily with signal precision from 70.99% for composition 5/5 to 16.67% for composition 10/0. Averaging over urn compositions, treatment L/H is characterized by the lowest probability of a type I error (18.90%) and the highest probability of a type II error (62.91%).[29] The probability of a type I error is nearly the same for the other three treatments, with the highest average probability being observed for treatment L/H at 26.41%. The average probability of a type II error is lowest in treatment L/L (43.26%). However, as the figures convey, for some urn composition-treatment pairs, confidence intervals for error probabilities are quite large because some of the cells include only a very small number of observations.[30] Comparing the two error types, type II errors are on average more likely to occur than type I errors; however, for the most part, the difference is not statistically significant in individual composition-treatment comparisons.[31]

In table 7, we present results from simple ordinary least squares regressions (with standard errors clustered at the group level) for the probabilities of type I and type II errors.[32] The results confirm our expectations: a more precise signal significantly reduces error probabilities (the effect being more pronounced for type II errors), and neither the harm level nor the sanction level significantly affects error probabilities. In our data, a stronger belief that players A have taken points results in a significant increase in the probability of a type I error but does not significantly affect the probability of a type II error. As is true for punishment, in our data, error probabilities are not significantly influenced by the individual degree of risk aversion.

[29] The observed average probability of a type II error is only slightly lower in treatment H/L, amounting to 61.09%.

[30] With a low-precision signal, a relatively large share of players A took points, resulting in only a few observations for the probability of a type I error. With a high-precision signal, a relatively low share of players A took points, resulting in only a few observations for the probability of a type II error.

[31] Significant differences between the error probabilities emerge only in treatment L/L for 5/5 and 6/4, as well as in treatment L/H for 7/3 and 8/2 ($p < .05$, two-sided t-tests).

[32] We abstain from presenting the results from nonparametric tests because they do not yield additional insights, especially given the detailed analysis with respect to punishment decisions in sec. 4.1. In addition to ordinary least squares regressions, we used tobit and fractional probit models as robustness checks. The qualitative results are similar; therefore, we refrain from reporting these results here.

Table 7. Ordinary Least Squares Regressions for Probabilities of Errors of Types I and II

	PROB. ERROR TYPE I		PROB. ERROR TYPE II	
	(1)	(2)	(3)	(4)
High fine	−.0098	−.0005	.0886	.0896
	(−.22)	(−.01)	(1.38)	(1.39)
High damage	.0227	.0136	.0270	.0308
	(.50)	(.31)	(.39)	(.45)
Urn 6/4	.0308	.0399	−.0565⁺	−.0546⁺
	(.58)	(.74)	(−1.94)	(−1.82)
Urn 7/3	−.0203	−.0046	−.1568**	−.1530**
	(−.32)	(−.07)	(−3.30)	(−3.14)
Urn 8/2	−.1725*	−.1541*	−.2935**	−.2868**
	(−2.61)	(−2.30)	(−5.35)	(−4.81)
Urn 9/1	−.2319**	−.2073**	−.4403**	−.4315**
	(−3.38)	(−2.98)	(−8.01)	(−7.21)
Urn 10/0	−.2853**	−.2554**	−.5394**	−.5320**
	(−3.93)	(−3.49)	(−8.48)	(−7.93)
Risk aversion	.0152	.0147	.0278	.0277
	(1.10)	(1.11)	(1.56)	(1.55)
		.1472*		.0269
Belief point taking (q)		(2.51)		(.32)
Constant	.2910*	.2006⁺	.4823**	.4636**
	(2.55)	(1.67)	(3.70)	(3.31)
R^2	.1207	.1449	.1874	.1879
No. of obs.	531	531	477	477

Note: Marginal effects; t values in parentheses. Standard errors are clustered at the group level. The reference category for the urn composition is urn composition 5/5. The dummy variable high fine is equal to 1 when $s = 20$ and equal to 0 when $s = 10$, and high harm is equal to 1 for $h = 20$ and equal to 0 for $h = 10$. Risk aversion is a variable equal to the number of times a subject chose the certain payoff in the Holt and Laury procedure, ranging from 0 to 10. Belief point taking reflects the number of players A from the other groups that a player C expects to take points. Cols. 2 and 4 include the beliefs of players C regarding the probability that players A took points from players B, thereby representing the regressions most relevant for our behavioral hypotheses from table 8. Prob. = probability; obs. = observations.
⁺$p < .10$.
*$p < .05$.
**$p < .01$.

4.4. Summary

In this section, we briefly summarize how our results match up with the predictions derived in section 2. For this purpose, we reproduce table 1 using the notation from our theory section (table 8). The second entry in each cell refers to the experimental results previously described in detail, where 0 indicates that the parameter in question did not have an influence on the dependent variable at conventional levels of statistical significance.

In summary, our theoretical predictions for the precision of the signal (r) are supported by our empirical results. A higher signal precision makes punishment more (less) likely when the legal decision maker obtains incriminating (exonerating) evidence, thereby contributing to deterrence. Turning to the other main variables of interest, the harm and sanction levels, our results indicate that higher harm levels deter violations (possibly contingent on a low-precision signal). Our results are consistent with moral concerns as an important driver of norm compliance. For example, Schildberg-Hörisch and Strassmair (2012) described experimental results indicating that some potential offenders have social preferences. With respect to the punishment probabilities, our data cannot confirm a statistically significant effect (at conventional levels) from variation in the harm levels; the same is true for the error probabilities. On average, a higher sanction level does not significantly change the individual punishment probability in our data.

With regard to beliefs, our data support the hypothesis that deterrence is weakened when potential violators expect to be punished

Table 8. **Behavioral Hypotheses for Given Beliefs**

	HARM	SANCTION	TAKING BELIEF	SIGNAL PRECISION	PUN. BELIEF
	h	s	q	r	$m_b - m_w$
Pun. prob. ball b	+/0	−/0	+/0	+/+	
Pun. prob. ball w	+/0	−/0	+/+	−/−	
Point-taking prob.	−/−	−/0		−/−	−/−
Error I prob.	+/0	−/0	+/+	(−)/−	
Error II prob.	−/0	+/0	−/0	(−)/−	

Note: The first entry in each cell indicates the expected sign of the changes in decisions and error probabilities resulting from an increase in the parameters. The second entry summarizes the results of the empirical analysis, where 0 indicates a nonsignificant effect. Pun. = punishment; prob. = probability.

even in the event of signal w (i.e., a white ball). We do not find that a higher expected share of violators (q) increases the punishment probability after signal b is received. For the favorable signal w, we find a (weakly) significant positive effect in terms of the influence of beliefs on the punishment probability, which translates into a higher probability of type I errors.

5. CONCLUSION

This article considers the responses of potential offenders and third-party punishers to evidentiary uncertainty and how responses are moderated by the facts of the case, namely, the level of the sanction and the level of harm. We rely on data from a laboratory experiment with a 2×2 between-subject design with respect to the level of the sanction and the level of harm; varying extents of evidentiary uncertainty were presented to all subjects.

In our experiment, third-party punishers responded strongly to the quality of the evidence. This is reassuring and contradicts some results obtained for peer punishment (Grechenig et al. 2010). In our experiment, the standard of proof used by third parties was not significantly related to the level of either the sanction or the harm and is thereby compliant with a fixed legal standard. Furthermore, the probabilities of false convictions and false acquittals do not change significantly with the levels of sanction or harm in our data. In line with our predictions, potential violators strongly responded to the quality of the evidence. Moreover, we find that the probability of point taking decreases in the level of harm imposed by a violation, especially when the quality of the evidence is weak, but a high sanction level does not lead to additional deterrence.

The standard of proof actually applied by individuals who assume the position of judicial decision makers is crucial in a number of settings. Understanding how it is derived and how it changes under varying circumstances is thus of great practical importance. This study makes a contribution to this field of inquiry but has certain limitations. Our participants were students (including law students), raising the possibility that professionals would decide differently (although the results of Sonnemans and van Dijk [2012] do not point in this direction). Moreover, we consider a 2×2 design with respect to sanction and harm levels; it should be noted that different behavior could result with other combinations of harm and sanction levels. Overall, however, our research provides some initial results on an important real-world issue that we hope will motivate further investigations.

APPENDIX A

Statistics

Share of Players C Choosing Punishment and Players A Choosing Point Taking. The first (second) entry in each cell in table A1 refers to the share of players C choosing punishment for a black (white) ball. The third entry in each cell refers to the corresponding share of players A taking points.

Beliefs. The first (second) entry in each cell in table A2 refers to the belief of players A regarding the share of players C choosing punishment for a black (white) ball. The third entry in each cell refers to the corresponding belief of players C about the share of players A taking points. Note again that the belief was elicited by asking for the respective behavior of players A and C in the same session but not in the same group.

Error Probabilities. The first (second) entry in each cell in table A3 refers to the average probability of an error of type I (II) given that player A chose not to take points (to take points). The number of observations upon which entries are based is given in parentheses.

Table A1. Share of Players C Choosing Punishment and Players A Choosing Point Taking

URN COMPOSITION	L/L	H/L	L/H	H/H	AVERAGE
5/5	29.09	35.29	28.13	26.67	30.36
	29.09	27.45	43.75	33.33	32.14
	78.18	88.24	65.63	73.33	77.98
6/4	43.64	37.25	43.75	36.67	40.48
	32.73	25.49	34.38	36.67	31.55
	69.09	86.27	50.00	60.00	69.05
7/3	65.45	52.94	53.13	63.33	58.93
	21.82	15.69	31.25	33.33	23.81
	50.91	50.98	25.00	53.33	46.43
8/2	67.27	60.78	71.88	80.00	68.45
	20.00	11.76	9.38	6.67	13.10
	47.27	27.45	21.88	36.67	34.52

TREATMENT spans L/L, H/L, L/H, H/H columns.

Table A1 *(continued)*

URN COMPOSITION	L/L	H/L	L/H	H/H	AVERAGE
			TREATMENT		
9/1	72.73	70.59	71.88	86.67	74.40
	16.36	7.84	6.25	6.67	10.12
	45.45	23.53	18.75	30.00	30.95
10/0	80.00	78.43	75.00	96.67	81.55
	20.00	5.88	6.25	3.33	10.12
	32.73	19.61	18.75	26.67	25.00
Average	59.70	55.88	57.29	65.00	
	23.33	15.69	21.88	20.00	
	53.94	49.35	33.33	46.67	

Note: First entry is the share of players C punishing for a black ball; second entry is the share of players C punishing for a white ball; third entry is the share of players A taking points.

Table A2. Beliefs by Players A about the Share of Players C Choosing Punishment and Beliefs by Players C about Players A Choosing Point Taking

URN COMPOSITION	L/L	H/L	L/H	H/H	AVERAGE
			TREATMENT		
5/5	44.07	43.46	42.41	36.38	42.20
	42.68	51.49	42.86	36.76	44.33
	68.83	68.58	60.71	57.43	65.17
6/4	52.64	50.23	51.79	48.48	51.00
	41.13	45.89	36.16	37.14	40.92
	63.77	58.17	58.93	50.10	58.70
7/3	65.97	61.06	59.38	58.10	61.82
	36.88	39.12	29.46	34.19	35.67
	53.81	54.72	53.57	43.90	52.27
8/2	75.58	76.19	65.18	75.81	73.83
	26.97	27.08	24.11	24.86	26.08
	44.85	50.00	55.80	36.57	47.02

Table A2 *(continued)*

URN COMPOSITION	L/L	H/L	L/H	H/H	AVERAGE
			TREATMENT		
9/1	84.37	85.53	77.23	84.48	83.38
	21.86	17.93	21.43	19.33	20.13
	39.09	44.21	56.70	29.14	42.22
10/0	89.13	91.88	83.04	94.86	89.83
	12.34	11.11	15.18	7.05	11.56
	39.52	37.72	58.48	32.67	41.36
Average	68.63	68.06	63.17	66.35	
	30.31	32.10	28.20	26.56	
	51.65	52.23	57.37	41.63	

Note: First entry is the beliefs of players A about the share of players C punishing for a black ball; second entry is the beliefs of players A about the share of players C punishing for a white ball; third entry is the beliefs of players C about the share of players A taking points.

Table A3. Probability of Errors of Types I and II

URN COMPOSITION	L/L	H/L	L/H	H/H	AVERAGE
			TREATMENT		
5/5	25.00 (12)	33.33 (6)	59.09 (11)	37.50 (8)	39.19 (37)
	69.77 (43)	68.89 (45)	76.19 (21)	72.73 (22)	70.99 (131)
6/4	29.41 (17)	57.14 (7)	43.75 (16)	50.00 (12)	42.31 (52)
	56.32 (38)	71.36 (44)	63.75 (16)	72.22 (18)	65.52 (116)
7/3	29.63 (27)	35.60 (25)	35.00 (24)	56.43 (14)	36.89 (90)
	40.00 (28)	72.31 (26)	58.75 (8)	55.00 (16)	55.77 (78)
8/2	22.76 (29)	18.92 (37)	24.80 (25)	21.05 (19)	21.63 (110)
	33.08 (26)	50.00 (14)	54.29 (7)	40.00 (11)	41.03 (58)
9/1	21.00 (30)	13.85 (39)	14.23 (26)	13.33 (21)	15.69 (116)
	19.20 (25)	31.67 (12)	40.00 (6)	28.89 (9)	26.15 (52)
10/0	21.62 (37)	4.88 (41)	7.69 (26)	4.55 (22)	10.32 (126)
	5.56 (18)	30.00 (10)	33.33 (6)	12.50 (8)	16.67 (42)

Table A3   *(continued)*

| URN COMPOSITION | TREATMENT | | | | AVERAGE |
	L/L	H/L	L/H	H/H	
Average	24.28 (152)	18.90 (155)	26.41 (128)	25.73 (96)	
	43.26 (178)	62.91 (151)	61.09 (64)	54.52 (84)	

Note: First entry is the average probability of an error of type I given no point taking by player A. Second entry is the average probability of an error of type II given no point taking by player A. Number of observations is in parentheses.

REFERENCES

Ambrus, Attila, and Ben Greiner. 2012. "Imperfect Public Monitoring with Costly Punishment? An Experimental Study." *American Economic Review* 102:3317–32.

Andreoni, James. 1991. "Reasonable Doubt and the Optimal Magnitude of Fines: Should the Penalty Fit the Crime?" *RAND Journal of Economics* 22:385–95.

Becker, Gordon M., Morris H. DeGroot, and Jacob Marschak. 1964. "Measuring Utility by a Single-Response Sequential Method." *Systems Research and Behavioral Science* 9:226–32.

Blackstone, William. 1769. *Commentaries on the Laws of England,* vol. 4. Oxford: Clarendon.

Davis, Michael L. 1994. "The Value of Truth and the Optimal Standard of Proof in Legal Disputes." *Journal of Law, Economics, and Organization* 10:343–59.

Demougin, Dominique, and Claude Fluet. 2006. "Preponderance of the Evidence." *European Economic Review* 50:963–76.

Dohmen, Thomas, Armin Falk, David Huffman, and Uwe Sunde. 2010. "Are Risk Aversion and Impatience Related to Cognitive Ability?" *American Economic Review* 100:1238–60.

Entorf, Horst, and Hannes Spengler. 2015. "Crime, Prosecutors, and the Certainty of Conviction." *European Journal of Law and Economics* 39:167–201.

Epps, Daniel. 2015. "The Consequences of Error in Criminal Justice." *Harvard Law Review* 128:1065–51.

Feess, Eberhard, Hannah Schildberg-Hörisch, Marcus Schramm, and Ansgar Wohlschlegel. 2015. "The Impact of Fine Size and Uncertainty on Punishment and Deterrence: Theory and Evidence from the Laboratory." IZA Discussion Paper no. 9388. Institute of Labor Economics, Bonn.

Feess, Eberhard, and Ansgar Wohlschlegel. 2009. "Why Higher Punishment May Reduce Deterrence." *Economics Letters* 104: 69–71.

Fischbacher, Urs. 2007. "z-Tree: Zurich Toolbox for Ready-Made Economic Experiments." *Experimental Economics* 10:171–78.

Friedman, Ezra, and Abraham L. Wickelgren. 2006. "Bayesian Juries and the Limits to Deterrence." *Journal of Law, Economics, and Organization* 22:70–86.

Friesen, Lana. 2012. "Certainty of Punishment versus Severity of Punishment: An Experimental Investigation." *Southern Economic Journal* 79:399–421.

Grechenig, Kristoffel, Andreas Nicklisch, and Christian Thöni. 2010. "Punishment Despite Reasonable Doubt—A Public Goods Experiment with Sanctions under Uncertainty." *Journal of Empirical Legal Studies* 7:847–67.

Greiner, Ben. 2015. "Subject Pool Recruitment Procedures: Organizing Experiments with ORSEE." *Journal of the Economic Science Association* 1:114–25.

Holt, Charles A., and Susan K. Laury. 2002. "Risk Aversion and Incentive Effects." *American Economic Review* 92:1644–55.

Kaplow, Louis. 2011. "On the Optimal Burden of Proof." *Journal of Political Economy* 119:1104–40.

Lando, Henrik. 2009. "Prevention of Crime and the Optimal Standard of Proof." *Review of Law and Economics* 5:33–52.

Levitt, Steven D., and Thomas J. Miles. 2007. "Empirical Study of Criminal Punishment." In *Handbook of Law and Economics*, vol. 1, edited by A. Mitchell Polinsky and Steven Shavell, 455–95. Amsterdam: Elsevier.

Lyons, Bruce, Gordon D. Menzies, and Daniel J. Zizzo. 2012. "Conflicting Evidence and Decisions by Agency Professionals: An Experimental Test in the Context of Merger Regulation." *Theory and Decision* 73:465–99.

Miceli, Thomas. 1990. "Optimal Prosecution of Defendants Whose Guilt Is Uncertain. *Journal of Law, Economics, and Organization* 6:189–201.

Miceli, Thomas. 2008. "Criminal Sentencing Guidelines and Judicial Discretion." *Contemporary Economic Policy* 26:207–15.

Miceli, Thomas. 2009. "The Economics of Criminal Procedure." In *Criminal Law and Economics*, vol. 3, edited by Nuno Garoupa, 129–44. Cheltenham: Elgar.

Mungan, Murat C. 2011. "A Utilitarian Justification for Heightened Standards of Proof in Criminal Trials." *Journal of Institutional and Theoretical Economics* 167:352–70.

New York State Unified Court System. 2015. "Reasonable Doubt." In *CJI2d Instructions of General Applicability*. Last updated August 12, 2018. http://www.nycourts.gov.

Ognedal, Tone. 2005. "Should the Standard of Proof Be Lowered to Reduce Crime?" *International Review of Law and Economics* 25:45–61.

Polinsky, A. Mitchell, and Steven Shavell. 2007. "The Theory of Public Enforcement of Law." In *Handbook of Law and Economics*, vol. 1, edited by A. Mitchell Polinsky and Steven Shavell, 405–54. Amsterdam: Elsevier.

Pollock, Joycelyn M. 2012. *Criminal Law*. New York: Routledge.

Rizzolli, Matteo, and Margherita Saraceno. 2013. "Better That Ten Guilty Persons Escape: Punishment Costs Explain the Standard of Evidence." *Public Choice* 155:395–411.

Rizzolli, Matteo, and Luca Stanca. 2012. "Judicial Errors and Crime Deterrence: Theory and Experimental Evidence." *Journal of Law and Economics* 55:311–38.

Rubinfeld, Daniel L., and David E. M. Sappington. 1987. "Efficient Awards and Standards of Proof in Judicial Proceedings." *RAND Journal of Economics* 18:308–15.

Schanzenbach, Max M., and Emerson H. Tiller. 2007. "Strategic Judging under the US Sentencing Guidelines: Positive Political Theory and Evidence." *Journal of Law, Economics, and Organization* 23:24–56.

Schildberg-Hörisch, Hannah, and Christina Strassmair. 2012. "An Experimental Test of the Deterrence Hypothesis." *Journal of Law, Economics, and Organization* 28:447–59.

Selten, Reinhard. 1967. "Die Strategiemethode zur Erforschung des eingeschränkt rationalen Verhaltens im Rahmen eines Oligopolexperiments" [The strategic method for research on bounded rationality in an experiment with an oligopolistic framework]. In *Beiträge zur experimentellen Wirtschaftsforschung*, edited by H. Sauermann, 136–68. Tübingen: Mohr.

Sonnemans, Joep, and Frans van Dijk. 2012. "Errors in Judicial Decisions: Experimental Results." *Journal of Law, Economics, and Organization* 28:687–716.

Van Dijk, Frans, Joep Sonnemans, and Eddy Bauw. 2014. "Judicial Error by Groups and Individuals." *Journal of Economic Behavior and Organization* 108:224–35.

Yilankaya, Okan. 2003. "A Model of Evidence Production and Optimal Standard of Proof and Penalty in Criminal Trials." *Canadian Journal of Economics* 35:385–409.

Zamir, Eyal, and Ilana Ritov. 2012. "Loss Aversion, Omission Bias, and the Burden of Proof in Civil Litigation." *Journal of Legal Studies* 41:165–207.

Comment on "Crime and Punishment under Evidentiary Uncertainty: Laboratory Evidence"

*Brandon D. Brice**

1. INTRODUCTION

Kathryn Zeiler and Erica Puccetti (2018) recently provided an extensive review of the legal error experimental literature. Future reviews will not be considered complete without discussing this excellent contribution by Baumann and Friehe (2017). From the experimental design to the theoretical explanations used to create behavioral expectations, this article is thorough and complete in its investigation of important issues in legal error theory.

The article is motivated by Miceli (2009), who explains that there is a lack of evidence regarding how legal decision makers interpret reasonable doubt. Do they typically interpret it with legal understanding, or with economic concerns regarding the costs of legal error minimization? Evidence from this experiment suggests that experimental subjects concern themselves with evidentiary certainty and not minimization of legal error costs.

2. EXPERIMENTAL DESIGN

The experimental design is clean and makes significant strides to address potential concerns that arise in experimental publications. The authors do not use any deception, they provide actual payouts, they allow the actors to make decisions under anonymity, they require test

* Department of Economics and Finance, University of North Carolina, Wilmington. Email: briceb@uncw.edu.

Electronically published: December 6, 2018

rounds to ensure that participants understand the objectives, and they provide full disclosure of information.

In their simple and elegant design: player A takes points from player B and, in doing so, inflicts harm. Player A's choice sends a noisy signal to player C (which is determined by random draws of black or white balls), who decides whether to punish player A. With a between-subject design (groups receive different treatments), two separate sanction levels and two separate harm levels are considered. Evidentiary uncertainty is also varied by assigning different precision levels for the ball selection. Thus, the experimental design allows for an analysis of how changes in harm, sanction level, or evidentiary uncertainty affect punishment decisions while controlling for the other variables. A laboratory setting provides additional control against exogenous factors that would certainly affect these decisions in other environments.

3. THEORETICAL FRAMEWORK

The authors adopt a theoretical framework related to Andreoni (1991) and Feess et al. (2015). This literature explains that to minimize the costs of legal error, the optimal standard of proof for a third-party punisher must consider that larger sanctions increase the intrinsic costs from wrongful convictions for punishers, therefore:

As sanctions ↑ | burden of proof ↑ | wrongful acquittals ↑ while wrongful convictions ↓

As sanctions ↓ | burden of proof ↓ | wrongful acquittals ↓ while wrongful convictions ↑

More harm inflicted by the offenders increases the intrinsic costs from wrongful acquittals for punishers, therefore:

As harm ↑ | burden of proof ↓ | wrongful acquittals ↓ while wrongful convictions ↑

As harm ↓ | burden of proof ↑ | wrongful acquittals ↑ while wrongful convictions ↓

For offenders, moral costs increase and benefits increase as harm increases, and costs increase as sanctions increase. Offenders must weigh these costs and benefits. The authors are not nearly as concerned with the actions of the offenders, however, and are focused on how changes to the levels of harm, sanction, and evidentiary uncertainty affect the decision to punish potential violators.

4. RESULTS

A major concern with any laboratory experiment relates to external validity. Beginning with player A, do the actions of these individuals resemble the actual criminal behavior we would like to analyze in this controlled setting? Having a black ball drawn (representing a shaky signal of guilt to the punisher) in this experiment does not appear to be the same as getting caught stealing. It is more closely related to leaving behind some evidence that may allow authorities to track your actions. Then those authorities may decide not to punish, even if they are certain that a theft of points took place. In fact, this event occurred 19.45% of the time when people stole with 100% certainty (there was no uncertainty in the signal). They may also punish even if a theft of points had not occurred with 100% certainty. This result happened 10.12% of the time when people did not steal, and this emitted a signal with no uncertainty. This is an extreme example of what the literature considers punitive preferences, which, if common for the participants, would bias the experimental results. Consideration of this kind of punitive behavior is likely to induce people to steal who otherwise would not.

When the evidence left behind is completely ambiguous (draw has a 50% chance of being black or white), player A steals 78% of the time. A rational agent who is concerned only with their payout would choose to steal, leaving an ex ante expectation that this number would approach 100%. Perhaps an economist would find this experimental figure low, but given other-regarding preferences that would provide disutility for harming others, this 78% result is not surprising. When there is a 100% chance that the evidence they leave behind will be incriminating (a black ball will be left), the subjects still steal 25% of the time. This is very surprising and suggests several possibilities. Perhaps the participants are still somehow unclear about the experimental design, despite the practice rounds in which they participated. More likely, it is that potential thieves believe either that punishers will still decide not to punish them or that punishers will punish them regardless of their decision, so they decide to steal. In both scenarios, we are likely inducing expectations that are not relatable to standard prosecution behavior in the real world.

In addition, the experimental results suggest that changing the sanction level while holding harm, and evidentiary uncertainty, constant does not affect stealing behavior. Evidence also suggests that punishers are only weakly deterred by the harm they inflict on others under certain circumstances. It does not seem reasonable that the level of punishment does not deter potential criminals and that the harm they inflict on their victim only weakly deters them. This raises some concerns about what we can interpret from their behavior in this experiment. Ultimately, we are not very concerned with the behavior of the players in group A. Rather, we are more concerned about an analysis of the punishment decisions of players in group C.

This concern arises because of the main research question: Do punishers interpret reasonable doubt with legal understanding, or with economic concerns regarding the costs of legal error minimization? Evidence from this experiment suggests that experimental subjects concern themselves with evidentiary uncertainty and not minimization of legal error costs. Empirical findings, and the enormous rate of type I and II errors, in the article reflect this.

It is fair to ask if this analysis is really an interpretation of reasonable doubt or simply evidence that punishers do not allow relative costs associated with variables such as harm or sanction level to cloud their interpretation? Likely, this will be addressed in subsequent research.

Regardless of the interpretation, the evidence in this article is very insightful. It suggests that a whole stream of research and theory, regarding how potential punishers consider harm and the level of punishment when making sentencing decisions, may be faulty. It does this in a sound experimental framework, with a great experimental design, and is a great addition to the legal error literature.

These results will likely be questioned, given the foundational underpinnings regarding harm, and sanction, levels in the existing theory. Earlier in this article, external validity concerns were raised, given how some of the behavior and actions may not necessarily reflect actual human behavior in the legal system. Other concerns may arise from the research subjects' age, education level, profession, and location because the subjects are primarily young, undergraduate-educated law students at a university in Germany. A skeptic may question whether the experimental results would apply to people of other ages, education levels, professions, and locations. Given that the main result of this article is a conclusion about how people pass judgment and interpret burden of proof, we should be concerned about this validity. Perhaps future studies will explore these results with subjects in different locations or with a field study using older individuals in other professions.

5. CONCLUSION

This comment raises no objections to the methodology or practices in this article. The underlying theory is explained in detail, great care is taken with the experimental design, and the results are reported in understandable ways. The results provide evidence that punishers interpret reasonable doubt with legal understanding and do not necessarily consider economic concerns regarding the costs of legal error minimization. This directly addresses a concern raised by Miceli (2009) in the legal error literature, which explains that there is a lack of evidence regarding how legal decision makers interpret reasonable doubt. Although there may be objections regarding external validity, this is likely to be the case with any laboratory experiment, and the authors take great care to address potential concerns. I look forward to future research in this area to see if, in fact, sanction and harm levels play smaller roles in these decisions than the current theory suggests.

REFERENCES

Andreoni, James. 1991. "Reasonable Doubt and the Optimal Magnitude of Fines: Should the Penalty Fit the Crime?" *RAND Journal of Economics* 22:385–95.

Baumann, Florian, and Tim Friehe. 2017. "Crime and Punishment under Evidentiary Uncertainty: Laboratory Evidence." *Supreme Court Economic Review* 25:65–104.

Feess, Eberhard, Hannah Schildberg-Hörisch, Marcus Schramm, and Ansgar Wohlschlegel. 2015. "The Impact of Fine Size and Uncertainty on Punishment and Deterrence: Theory and Evidence from the Laboratory." IZA Discussion Paper no. 9388. Institute of Labor Economics, Bonn.

Miceli, Thomas. 2009. "The Economics of Criminal Procedure." In *Encyclopedia of Law and Economics*, 2nd ed., vol. 3, *Criminal Law and Economics*, edited by Nuno Garoupa. Cheltenham: Elgar.

Zeiler, Kathryn, and Erica Puccetti. 2018. "Crime, Punishment, and Legal Error: A Review of the Experimental Literature." Unpublished manuscript. Boston University School of Law, September. https://ssrn.com/abstract=3250393.

Explaining the Standard of Proof in Criminal Law: A New Insight

Nuno Garoupa*

Legal economists have explained the standard of proof in criminal law by exploring the asymmetry between social costs of false negatives (acquitting guilty defendants) and false positives (convicting innocent defendants). In a recent article, a model of punitive preferences (individuals with stronger-than-average punishment preferences) was introduced to explain police behavior, law enforcement, and rules of criminal procedure. We extend that model to provide for a new explanation for a more demanding standard of proof in criminal law without relying on exogenous assumptions about the social cost of false negatives and false positives.

1. INTRODUCTION

Legal economists have developed formal models to discuss criminal law and procedure from the perspective of optimal deterrence (Becker 1968; Becker and Stigler 1974; Polinsky and Shavell 2009). The possibility of false negatives (acquittal of criminals) and false positives

* Texas A&M University Law School, Católica Global School of Law; nunogaroupa@law.tamu.edu. I am grateful to Dhammika Dharmapala and Richard McAdams for exciting discussions about the idea of extending our work on punitive preferences to explain standards of proof in criminal litigation. One anonymous referee, Henrik Lando, Murat Mungan, Matteo Rizzolli, and AEDE 2017 participants have helped me with stimulating observations. Abe Wickelgren and participants at the 2018 Supreme Court Economic Review Research Roundtable on the Economics of Legal Error offered excellent suggestions. Any remaining errors or omissions are, of course, my own.

Electronically published: December 4, 2018

(conviction of innocents) has been one of the main concerns of this literature. Its effect on deterrence has been a matter of controversy (Png 1986; Kaplow and Shavell 1994; Ognedal 2005; Lando 2006; Garoupa and Rizzolli 2012; Rizzolli and Saraceno 2013; Lando and Mungan 2018). There seems to be no consensus on whether legal errors enhance or dilute deterrence. Adequate enforcement of sanctions deters harmful acts, whereas wrongful acquittals have the opposite effect. However, the overall impact of a mistaken conviction is ambiguous due to the nature of its incentives. Another aspect related to the possibility of false negatives and false positives is the impact on legal defense spending (Gravelle and Garoupa 2002). The nature of enforcement, public or private, including compensation for enforcement mistakes, is also likely to affect the social cost of wrongful acquittals and mistaken convictions (Garoupa 1997; Fon and Schaefer 2007; Doménech and Puchades 2015; Mungan and Klick 2016).

Because evidence rules inevitably shape the likelihood of false negatives and false positives, there is related literature on how evidence should be evaluated and appropriate rules designed (Rubinfeld and Sappington 1987; Posner 1999; Demougin and Fluet 2006; Mungan 2011; Kaplow 2011a, 2011b, 2012). Behavioral arguments and experimental evidence have been used to support current legal policy in terms of assessing and determining standards of proof in criminal litigation (Rizzolli and Stanca 2012; Sonnemans and van Dijk 2012; Nicita and Rizzolli 2014).[1]

A standard approach in the formal models is to consider the varying social costs of false positives and false negatives (Rizzolli, forthcoming). In particular, it is frequently assumed that false positives are more socially costly than false negatives. This conventional wisdom is derived from Blackstonian reasoning by which one wrongful conviction is worse than 10 wrongful acquittals (DeKay 1996; Volokh 1997). This cost asymmetry has been used to justify important rules of criminal procedure and explain a "beyond reasonable doubt" standard in criminal law.

In a recent seminal article, Kaplow (2011a) shows that the optimal threshold varies according to the complexities of the situation. For example, when individuals engage in benign behavior potentially sub-

---

[1] As Kaplow (2011a) recognizes, the treatment of burden of proof in the economic literature is confusing. The distinction between burden and standard of proof is not always clear. We understand the economic analysis of the burden of standard of proof as a theory explaining which side in criminal litigation should satisfy a given standard. A theory justifying a certain "strength of evidence required for the imposition of sanctions" would fall within the economic theory of the standard of proof. These two questions are obviously related, but for pedagogical reasons it is important to distinguish between burden and standard.

ject to sanctions, the choice of standard of proof varies with the distribution of signals about the harmful nature of a particular act.[2] However, Kaplow recognizes that in the simple version of the model where individuals decide whether or not to commit a harmful act, the question is to determine the standard of proof that maximizes deterrence, given enforcement and social costs. The problem is, thus, reduced to the standard trade-off between false negatives and false positives (see Kaplow 2011a, subsec. III.E).

In this article, we provide for an alternative explanation for a high standard of proof in criminal law. Rather than relying on the asymmetry of social costs, we introduce the possibility that punitive preferences exhibited by law enforcement agents explain a beyond reasonable doubt standard in criminal law. Based on previous work by Dharmapala, Garoupa, and McAdams (2016), we propose that a high standard of proof might be needed because law enforcers have stronger than average taste for punishment. Because enforcers with punitive preferences might be overzealous, an effective way to mitigate such effect is to raise the standard of proof accordingly. In this context, we provide an argument for a beyond reasonable doubt standard even if the social costs of wrongful enforcement decisions are exactly the same.

The article goes as follows. Section 2 presents the formal model. Section 3 addresses policy implications and possible caveats. Section 4 concludes the article.

2. THE MODEL

Following Dharmapala et al. (2016), let p be the probability that a given suspect is guilty, L the cost of wrongful law enforcement, and β the parameter that represents the relative cost of punishment errors against acquittal errors.[3] The cost of accurate punishment (true positives) and accurate acquittal (true negatives) is normalized to zero.[4] Given a suspect with probability p of guilt, the expected cost from punishment is $(1 - p)\beta L$, whereas the expected cost from acquittal is pL. The latter will exceed the former when p is sufficiently large. Specifically, according to social welfare, a suspect should be punished if:

---

[2] In fact, Kaplow (2011b) introduces an explicit critique concerning the way legal economists have interpreted a preponderance of the evidence standard in the face of ex ante and ex post probabilities of harmful behavior. See also Lando (2002).

[3] As emphasized by Dharmapala et al. (2016), the parameter β might conform to Blackstone's famous dictum that "it is better that ten guilty persons escape, than that one innocent suffer"—so β should substantially exceed 1.

[4] We are making use of a reduced form. Generality and caveats of this formulation are extensively discussed by Dharmapala et al. (2016).

$$p > \frac{\beta}{\beta + 1} \equiv p^*, \tag{1}$$

where the relative magnitude of the parameter β determines the threshold p^*.

A couple of results are interesting to note. If punishing the innocent is very costly compared with not punishing the guilty (β is substantially larger than 1), p^* will be close to 1. As β approaches infinity, p^* approaches 1. If $\beta = 1$ (so that wrongful punishment and wrongful acquittals are equally costly), then $p^* = .5$. If β approaches 0, p^* approaches 0.

Consider now punitive preferences as introduced by Dharmapala et al. (2016). They define mL, where $m > 0$ is a parameter that represents the intensity of the taste for punishment of the guilty (relative to the loss L from erroneous law enforcement). Given a suspect with probability p of guilt, the expected costs to the enforcer from punishment and acquittal are $(1 - p)\beta L - pmL$ and pL, respectively.

A punitive enforcer (either police or prosecutor) wishes to punish suspects if:

$$p > \frac{\beta}{m + \beta + 1} \equiv p^m. \tag{2}$$

It easily follows from equations (1) and (2) that

$$p^m < p^*.$$

Dharmapala et al. (2016) develop a model to explain hiring of enforcers and the role of punitive preferences in determining rules of criminal procedure (they distinguish between strong and weak criminal procedure protections). They conclude there is a trade-off between law enforcement costs (enforcers with punitive preferences are cheaper) and law enforcement accuracy (enforcers with punitive preferences want to sanction suspects with lower p than otherwise).

In this extension, we abstract from the hiring decision to focus on the impact of punitive preferences on the standard of proof. Also, without loss of generality, we assume all enforcers have punitive preferences. Otherwise, we just need to average the relevant parameters of the model according to the proportion of enforcers with and without punitive preferences.

The sequence of the game developed by Dharmapala et al. (2016) under these assumptions is the following:

i. Court announces a critical threshold for securing a conviction given by p';
ii. Enforcers observe p, whereas court cannot observe p;

iii. Enforcers report p'', which might be different from p;
iv. Court convicts if $p'' > p'$.

As a pedagogical exercise, let us start by considering the case without punitive preferences.

Trivially, $p^* = p^m$ from equations (1) and (2). Because all enforcers have the same nonpunitive preferences, we know that $p'' = p$ (they report the accurate probability) and $p' = p^*$, that is, enforcers do not lie and courts define the efficient threshold.

A higher standard of proof for criminal convictions, in this context, is simply a function of β. Criminal cases have higher standard of proof because β is perceived to be relevant (under the conventional thesis that criminally convicting innocents is costlier than acquitting guilty individuals). We obtain the standard result in the literature.

A second exercise is to consider punitive preferences but with symmetric information between enforcers and court. We need some further notation before we discuss the implications. Let us assume that lying has some cost for the enforcer due to the need to manipulate or fabricate evidence, and so forth. For simplicity, the cost is defined as $cL(p'-p)$, that is, it varies linearly with L to make the analytics easier.[5] It increases with the difference between the actual p and the threshold that guarantees conviction p'. A bigger lie is costlier to the (punitive) enforcer.[6]

With symmetric information, there is no point in lying because the court can observe p accurately (and lying is costly). Therefore, $p'' = p$ (enforcers do not lie because there is a cost with no benefit) and $p' = p^*$ (court sets the efficient threshold).

The situation we want to explore is the case of punitive preferences with asymmetric information. The punitive enforcer knows that any $p > p'$ is convicted and, therefore, these cases are truly reported. At the same time, because lying is costly, there is a new threshold p''' such that (i) if p is below p''', it is truly reported as p and the defendant gets acquitted, whereas (ii) if p is above p''' and below p', it is reported as p' and the defendant is ("mistakenly") convicted.

Using the same approach of Dharmapala et al. (2016), the objective function to be maximized by enforcers is the following:

---

[5] For simplicity, we use a reduced form with linear costs. A more complex game could include a perjury stage also subject to severity and probability of punishment.

[6] There are, of course, more extreme possibilities. Enforcers could take justice into their own hands because, according to them, criminals are acquitted on technicalities. Although this possibility is not modeled explicitly, the reasoning we derive is applicable to such situations. The standard of proof might have to be adjusted to take into account the costs of vigilante justice.

$$-\int_0^{p'''} pL dp_+ \int_p^{p'''p'} [pm - (1-p)\beta - c(p'-p)]L dp + \int_p^{'1} [pm - (1-p)\beta]L dp. \ (3)$$

Enforcers maximize equation (3) by setting p''' as conditional on the threshold p' previously announced by the court. Easy calculations show the following result:

$$p''' = \frac{\beta + cp'}{m + \beta + 1 + c}$$

A few quick notes about the new threshold p''' are of particular interest and relevance:

i. If $m = 0$ (no punitive preferences) and $p' = p^*$ (court announces efficient punishment), then $p''' = p^*$ (enforcers comply with efficient punishment);

ii. If $p' = p^m$ (court is equally punitive), then $p''' = p^m$ (court and enforcers agree on being punitive and, therefore, enforcers do not lie about probability of guilt);

iii. If c goes to zero (enforcement lying is costless), then $p''' = p^m$ (enforcers engage in widespread lying and punishment is imposed according to their punitive preferences);

iv. If c goes to infinite (enforcement lying is extremely costly), then $p''' = p'$ (enforcers do not engage in lying and comply with the threshold announced by the court).

We turn now our attention to the court. Following Dharmapala et al. (2016), under the assumption of a benevolent social-welfare maximizing court, we have the following objective function:

$$-\int_0^{p'''} pL dp - \int_p^{'''1} (1-p)\beta L dp. \tag{4}$$

Broadly speaking, the court seeks to define p' so as to manipulate p''' because the principal anticipates the decision by the agents.

We know, by construction of the model in equation (1), that $p''' = p^*$, that is, the court should force the enforcers to report those and only those who are above p^*. To do that, the court will solve the following equation:

$$\frac{\beta + cp'}{m + \beta + 1 + c} = p^*.$$

Quite easily we can see that:

$$p' = \frac{p^*(m + \beta + 1 + c) - \beta}{c} = \frac{\beta(m + c)}{(1 + \beta)c} = \frac{\beta}{(1 + \beta)\left(1 + \frac{m}{c}\right)}. \tag{5}$$

Notice, for example, that when $\beta = 1$, we have:

$$p' - \frac{1 + \frac{m}{c}}{2}.$$

The ratio m/c determines the additional standard of proof. It provides for a new rationale for a beyond reasonable doubt standard that is independent of β. Even if $\beta = 1$ (costs of not acquitting the innocent are equal to costs of not convicting the guilty), we predict a higher standard for criminal litigation as long as m/c is positive. A beyond reasonable doubt standard is more likely when there are strong punitive preferences and when the cost of enforcement lying goes down. So we find that there are three related policy dimensions: standard of proof, preferences of enforcer, and cost of lying (additional evidence). Specifically, preferences of enforcer and evidence technology (cost of lying) determine the additional standard of proof in the absence of exogenous β—social preferences.

In particular, notice that:

i. If $m/c = 0$ (no punitive preferences or enforcement lying is extremely costly), then $p' = p^*$ (court sets efficient punishment and enforcers comply with efficient punishment);

ii. If m/c goes to a very large number (significant punitive preferences or enforcement lying is costless), then $p' > p^*$ (court sets a very high standard of proof so that enforcers pick only individuals above efficient punishment because lying will be prevalent).

3. DISCUSSION

3.1. Posterior and Prior Probability of Guilt

In Dharmapala et al. (2016), the probability of guilt p is the posterior probability because the production of evidence is not modeled as an endogenous process. Let us denote guilt by G and evidence by E. It is the case that $p = p(G|E)$.

Criminal convictions require not only a higher standard of proof (beyond a reasonable doubt) but also a presumption of innocence. Rules concerning the presumption of innocence are fundamental to determine evidence gathering based on a prior probability of guilt. The use of posterior probability suppresses consideration of the presumption of innocence in the formal model, as the standard of proof based on the posterior includes the effect of both the strength of evidence and the presumption of innocence.

We can suggest that the possibility of punitive preferences has an implication to the presumption of innocence (or other criminal procedure protections) similar to the one it has on the standard of proof. Punitive enforcers are expected to gather evidence or disrespect the presumption of innocence in more active ways than otherwise. Therefore, it could be efficient to develop more demanding evidence rules, enhance the presumption of innocence, or reinforce criminal procedure protections to balance out possible biases introduced by punitive preferences.

3.2. Other Reasons for Nonbenevolent Objective Functions

Punitive preferences introduce a gap between social welfare maximization (principal's objective function) and private utility (agent's objective function). In this light, punitive preferences seem to be one specific example of a broader case for heightened standards of proof. For example, when enforcers prefer to convict because of private benefits (consider the effects of higher conviction rates on reputation and postemployment gains), there is a situation similar to punitive preferences because the incentives induce overreporting. Another possible context is in civil forfeiture cases, where authorities keep the proceeds from seizures, which could be a direct incentive to be overzealous.

A few previous articles have considered the need to adjust law enforcement parameters in the presence of these private benefits (Garoupa 1997; Garoupa and Klerman 2002; Hylton and Khanna 2007), but they have not discussed the interaction between its direct implication for the standard of proof and the varying social costs from false positives and false negatives.

It seems that in the absence of varying social costs from false positives and false negatives, a beyond reasonable doubt standard (or a more demanding "clear and convincing evidence" standard in the particular case of civil forfeiture) can be justified by an existing fundamental divergence between social and private interests in law enforcement.

3.3. Alternative Legal Policies

Punitive preferences introduce a gap between the principal's objective function and the gains for the agent. The formal model shows that overenforcement arises when there is asymmetric information (with symmetric information, the principal is able to address agency costs and delegate socially optimal enforcement). Imposing a stronger standard of proof is a solution to reduce the costs imposed by this gap.

This reasoning opens the possibility that less costly alternative legal policies might be developed to address the identified problem. In particular, in the context of the formal model, enforcement rules that reduce asymmetric information would eliminate the need for a higher standard of proof. Rules that limit the private nature of the information obtained by enforcers could be equally efficient. These rules could include mandatory disclosure, open file duties, and ex post auditing of enforcement agents. However, as shown in the literature (Garoupa and Rizzolli 2011), these alternative legal policies have intrinsic costs that could be as significant as the ones considered in the formal model.

3.4. Applications Outside of Criminal Law

One possible critique to an explanation based on punitive preferences rather than social costs is why it plays a role in criminal law but not in other areas of the law where some form of punishment is relevant (i.e., regulation and administrative law, immigration law, tax law). There are a few justifications of why m/c is likely to be much more relevant in criminal law. For example, the form or the nature of punishment is more severe or the cost of manipulating evidence to secure conviction is likely to be costlier in criminal law than in other areas of public law. Punishment in regulation or tax law usually takes a monetary form, whereas punishment in criminal law is a nonmonetary sanction in many contexts. Punitive preferences are likely to be more acute for nonmonetary sanctions that involve imprisonment or some form of incapacitation.

Notice that we can argue that these same additional explanations are very much needed in the context of justifying why social costs of false positives and false negatives are different across areas of public law. Thus we do not think a standard proof theory based on variations of β has fewer caveats than an explanation based on variations of m/c.

4. CONCLUSION

By making use of the model introduced by Dharmapala et al. (2016) on punitive preferences in law enforcement, we have derived a higher standard of proof in criminal law without relying on exogenous assumptions about the social costs of false positives (convicting innocents) and false negatives (acquitting criminals).

Our analytics were applied under the assumption that only punitive enforcers are hired. If we reframe the problem in the more general context of Dharmapala et al. (2016), our results suggest that a beyond reasonable doubt standard makes sense in the particular case of strong criminal procedure protections. That is precisely the outcome in which only punitive enforcers are recruited because they are cheaper (government saves on enforcement costs), whereas more effective rules of criminal procedure are needed to prevent excessive punishment.

There are three important implications for a new explanation for a beyond reasonable doubt standard. The first is clearly empirical. Which of the two explanations, asymmetric social costs or punitive preferences, is more likely to matter? It is easy to accept that neither explanation is mutually exclusive. However, the legal policy consequences are different. Unfortunately, the experimental literature, fundamentally influenced by the "social costs of false negatives and false positives" approach, is not yet helpful to answer the empirical question.

The second important implication is, indeed, related to policy considerations. An explanation based on asymmetric or varying social costs simply points out that a particular standard of proof is shaped by largely exogenous social preferences (subject to crucial ad hoc assumptions about these given social preferences). Our alternative explanation integrates the choice of a standard of proof in a more general mind-set, particularly, the design of the law of police (McAdams, Dharmapala, and Garoupa 2015). From that viewpoint, new policy questions emerge such as the use of strong criminal procedure protections in relation to the selection of enforcement agents (selection) and their performance (shirking, moral hazard more generally).

A third possible implication is comparative in nature. If this new explanation is correct, we should expect jurisdictions where the gap between social preferences and law enforcement preferences is narrow (either because everyone is punitive or because everyone dislikes punishment) to be less exposed to the problem we have analyzed in this article. Therefore, we should observe weaker criminal procedure protections in place. On the contrary, jurisdictions with very heterogeneous preferences that result in a consistent gap between social preferences and law enforcement preferences should exhibit stronger criminal procedure protections.

REFERENCES

Becker, Gary S. 1968. "Crime and Punishment: An Economic Approach." *Journal of Political Economy* 76:169–217.

Becker, Gary S., and George J. Stigler. 1974. "Law Enforcement, Malfeasance, and Compensation in Enforcers." *Journal of Legal Studies* 3:1–18.

DeKay, Michael L. 1996. "The Difference between Blackstone-Like Error Ratios and Probabilistic Standards of Proof." *Law and Social Inquiry* 21:95–132.

Demougin, Dominique, and Claude Fluet. 2006. "Preponderance of Evidence." *European Economic Review* 50:963–76.

Dharmapala, Dhammika, Nuno Garoupa, and Richard McAdams. 2016. "Punitive Police? Agency Costs, Law Enforcement, and Criminal Procedure." *Journal of Legal Studies* 45:105–41.

Doménech, Gabriel, and Miguel Puchades. 2015. "Compensating Acquitted Pre-trial Detainees." *International Review of Law and Economics* 43:167–77.

Fon, Vincy, and Hans-Bernd Schaefer. 2007. "State Liability for Wrongful Conviction: Incentive Effects on Crime Levels." *Journal of Institutional and Theoretical Economics* 163:269–84.

Garoupa, Nuno. 1997. "A Note on Private Enforcement and Type I Error." *International Review of Law and Economics* 17:423–29.

Garoupa, Nuno, and Daniel Klerman. 2002. "Optimal Law Enforcement with a Rent-Seeking Government." *American Law and Economics Review* 4:116–40.

Garoupa, Nuno, and Matteo Rizzolli. 2011. "The Brady Rule May Hurt the Innocent." *American Law and Economics Review* 13:168–200.

Garoupa, Nuno, and Matteo Rizzolli. 2012. "Wrongful Convictions Do Lower Deterrence." *Journal of Institutional and Theoretical Economics* 168:224–31.

Gravelle, Hugh, and Nuno Garoupa. 2002. "Optimal Deterrence with Legal Defense Expenditure." *Economic Inquiry* 40:366–79.

Hylton, Keith N., and Vikramaditya Khanna. 2007. "A Public Choice Theory of Criminal Procedure." *Supreme Court Economic Review* 15:61–118.

Kaplow, Louis. 2011a. "On the Optimal Burden of Proof." *Journal of Political Economy* 119:1104–40.

Kaplow, Louis. 2011b. "Optimal Proof Burdens, Deterrence, and the Chilling of Desirable Behavior." *American Economic Review* 101:277–80.

Kaplow, Louis. 2012. "Burden of Proof." *Yale Law Journal* 121:738–859.

Kaplow, Louis, and Steven Shavell. 1994. "Accuracy in the Determination of Liability." *Journal of Law and Economics* 37:1–16.

Lando, Henrik. 2002. "When Is the Preponderance of the Evidence Standard Optimal?" *Geneva Papers on Risk and Insurance—Issues and Practice* 27:602–8.

Lando, Henrik. 2006. "Does Wrongful Conviction Lower Deterrence?" *Journal of Legal Studies* 35:327–38.

Lando, Henrik, and Murat C. Mungan. 2018. "The Effect of Type-1 Error on Deterrence." *International Review of Law and Economics* 53:1–8.

McAdams, Richard H., Dhammika Dharmapala, and Nuno Garoupa. 2015. "The Law of Police." *University of Chicago Law Review* 82: 135–58.

Mungan, Murat C. 2011. "A Utilitarian Justification for Heightened Standards of Proof in Criminal Trials." *Journal of Institutional and Theoretical Economics* 167:352–70.

Mungan, Murat C., and Jonathan Klick. 2016. "Reducing False Guilty Pleas and Wrongful Convictions through Exoneree Compensation." *Journal of Law and Economics* 59:173–89.

Nicita, Antonio, and Matteo Rizzolli. 2014. "In Dubio Pro Reo: Behavioral Explanations of Pro-defendant Bias in Procedures." *CESifo Economic Studies* 60:554–80.

Ognedal, Tone. 2005. "Should the Standard of Proof Be Lowered to Reduce Crime?" *International Review of Law and Economics* 25: 45–61.

Png, Ivan P. L. 1986. "Optimal Subsidies and Damages in the Presence of Judicial Error." *International Review of Law and Economics* 6:101–5.

Polinsky, A. Mitchell, and Steven Shavell. 2009. "Public Enforcement of Law." In *Criminal Law and Economics*, edited by Nuno Garoupa, 1–59. Northampton, MA: Elgar.

Posner, Richard. 1999. "An Economic Approach to the Law of Evidence." *Stanford Law Review* 51:1477–546.

Rizzolli, Matteo. Forthcoming. "Adjudication: Type I and Type II Errors." In *Encyclopedia of Law and Economics*, edited by Alain Marciano and Giovanni Ramello. New York: Springer.

Rizzolli, Matteo, and Margherita Saraceno. 2013. "Better That Ten Guilty Persons Escape: Punishment Costs Explain the Standard of Evidence." *Public Choice* 155:395–411.

Rizzolli, Matteo, and Luca Stanca. 2012. "Judicial Errors and Crime Deterrence: Theory and Experimental Evidence." *Journal of Law and Economics* 55:311–38.

Rubinfeld, Daniel L., and David E. M. Sappington. 1987. "Efficient Awards and Standards of Proof in Judicial Proceedings." *RAND Journal of Economics* 18:308–15.

Sonnemans, Joep, and Frans van Dijk. 2012. "Errors in Judicial Decisions: Experimental Results." *Journal of Law, Economics and Organization* 28:687–716.

Volokh, Alexander. 1997. "*n* Guilty Men." *University of Pennsylvania Law Review* 146:173–216.

Comment on "Explaining the Standard of Proof in Criminal Law: A New Insight"

*Abraham L. Wickelgren**

"Explaining the Standard of Proof in Criminal Law: A New Insight" by Nuno Garoupa (2017) is one of the first articles to apply the insights from the principal-agent literature in economics to standard of proof issues.[1] Given that our justice system relies on the actions of many different agents, all of whom almost certainly have objective functions different from that of the social planner, Garoupa's approach is clearly a valuable one. As a first step in applying an agency model, the article naturally has some limitations. Because a comment is more interesting and useful when it focuses on the limitations of an article, most of my remarks will be about why there might be advantages in applying the principal-agent approach to model burden of proof in a somewhat different way. First, I will discuss the advantages of taking a more comprehensive, from first principles, approach to finding the socially optimal burden of proof and how that might affect the results. Then, I will discuss how a more explicit integration of the agency issues in law enforcement might affect the results. But, at the outset, I want to make clear that Garoupa's approach represents a clear step forward for this literature. As such, I hope it will inspire future authors to build on and improve upon the path that this article has begun.

1. DERIVING THE WELFARE FUNCTION FROM FIRST PRINCIPLES

The central agency problem in the article is that enforcers have stronger relative preferences for not acquitting the guilty than for not con-

* University of Texas at Austin.
[1] Articles such as Wickelgren (2003) have discussed related issues with respect to punishment.

Electronically published: December 6, 2018

victing the innocent (punitive preferences) than does the court. The enforcer, however, has the information that the court uses to decide whether to convict a suspect or not. That is, the enforcer knows p, the probability that the suspect is guilty. In the model, the court moves first, setting a threshold level for p, which the article calls p'. If the enforcer reports that $p > p'$, the court convicts, otherwise it acquits. Because lying is costly for the enforcer (and more costly, the larger the lie), the court can induce the enforcer to only recommend conviction (reporting a p that exceeds the threshold) when the true value of p is above the court's ideal threshold simply by setting the nominal threshold far enough above the ideal threshold.

This strategy works, and it achieves the court's first best outcome given the specified objective function. That said, it does not achieve the first best outcome in terms of social welfare because the enforcers have to incur lying costs (which are not included in the court's objective function in the model). If one includes lying costs in the social welfare function, then the optimal standard of proof is probably lower (so as to induce less lying) than the standard that re-creates the same set of convictions and acquittals that a perfectly informed court would prefer.

Because the revelation principle (Myerson 1979) does not always hold with reporting costs, the optimal solution might still involve some deception on the part of the enforcer. The general solution to this problem would involve the enforcer announcing some p' and having the court commit to a function that maps this announcement to a probability of conviction. If the court is maximizing social welfare, including reporting costs, my guess is that the solution to this second best optimal mapping is probably not a step function like the outcome in the article. That said, the small literature on mechanism design with reporting costs (see, e.g., Crocker and Morgan 1998; Lacker and Weinberg 1989; Maggi and Rodriguez-Clare 1995) does suggest that it will likely involve some misreporting and some biasing of the mapping away from the first best in the direction of higher standards of proof.

However, even if the court/social planner brings lying costs into its objective function, the planner's objective function and the article's analysis seem too ex post focused. That is, the planner is taking the crime rate, the number of suspects brought before it, and the social costs of mistakes as given despite the fact that the legal rules surrounding standard of proof likely affect all of these. Why not model the decision to commit a crime as a function of the standard of proof and other parameters (e.g., the probability of detection and the punishment if detected and convicted)? This generates a crime rate that can be put into a social welfare function—thus, generating costs for mistaken acquittals endogenously and possibly wrongful convictions as well, depending on whether you think of criminal opportunities as exclusive or not—that might also include social costs from imprisonment and maybe other costs from wrongful convictions.[2]

Based on this social welfare function, one could then incorporate the agency problem in the article. This would involve allowing the enforcer to learn p and lie about it and then also incorporating lying costs into the social welfare functions as well. One way to view the Garoupa (2017) article is that it takes a reduced-form approach to all of this. It is imagining that all of this optimization from first principles is going on in the background to generate an optimal standard of proof, and then its problem is how to implement that given that enforcers have an incentive to lie about p. If we ignore lying costs as part of the social planner's objective function, this works well because the article finds that we can implement the first best real threshold for p by creating a formal threshold that exceeds p. If we view the lying costs as social costs, however, then we not only need to know the socially optimal p, we also need the social loss function for when the actual threshold differs from the socially optimal one.

Again, one could take a reduced-form approach and just specify an arbitrary loss function, $L(p)$, that is minimized at zero, the socially optimal threshold. This article, however, is implicitly assuming a particular functional form for this function when it assumes a constant social cost for each wrongful conviction and mistaken acquittal. This is not the loss function that a first-principles analysis of social welfare would generate. The advantage of deriving a social welfare function that depends on p from first principles is that it would enable us to get much more insight into how the agency function affects the optimal formal p than simply specifying an arbitrary loss function.

2. EXPLICITLY INCORPORATING AGENCY PROBLEMS

Because I really like the incorporation of the agency problem into a model of optimal legal rules, I would have also liked to see a fuller integration of that problem. The motivation for the assumption that law enforcers have stronger punishment preferences is from Dharmapala, Garoupa, and McAdams (2016). In that model, it is optimal to hire punitive enforcers because they are willing to work for lower wages as a

---

[2] If criminal opportunities are not exclusive, then if I don't commit a particular crime, someone else might. The probability that I might be convicted for that crime if I don't do it would give me an incentive to commit it. If criminal opportunities are exclusive, then if I don't commit a given crime, it won't happen. The fact that I might be wrongfully convicted for a different crime will not affect my incentive to commit this crime if the punishments are additive (see Schrag and Scotchmer 1994).

result of the utility they get from the act of punishing. I find this plausible, but it means that our social welfare function should take into account the cost of hiring the enforcer. If we do not, then we might as well hire nonpunitive enforcers. If we do, then this may interact with our optimal evidence threshold. For example, if the cost of hiring an enforcer depends on the utility that enforcer receives from doing the job, then establishing a legal rule that either (a) requires the enforcer to bear lying costs to obtain the convictions that increase its utility and/or (b) leads to fewer convictions that reduce the utility from the job and will increase the wages required to hire enforcers and will tend to lead us to choosing a nominal standard of proof that is less than the unconstrained optimum. It would be nice to have explicit conditions for the interaction of the cost of hiring effect and the need to control the different preferences of the agent. It is also possible that in such a world, it would be less costly to simply try to screen out punitive enforcers.

The downside of doing so, however, is its effect on another important agency problem, the canonical problem of inducing effort. An enforcer's job is to exert costly effort to gather evidence that can both help identify the perpetrator of a crime and lead to that individual's conviction. It is certainly easier to induce the enforcer to exert any given level of effort if the enforcer gets utility from the outcome of the effort. This is a reason to prefer punitive enforcers despite the costs associated with controlling their divergent preferences. But, if we raise the standard of proof and impose lying costs on the enforcer, then the net utility from gathering evidence that leads to a conviction is lower because it requires incurring lying costs. This suggests another reason why we might want punitive enforcers but not want to bias our standard of proof very much to compensate for their divergent preferences.

Garoupa's (2017) article represents a clear step forward in its integration of agency considerations into models of optimal standards of proof. I hope that this comment provides some suggestions for ways that Garoupa and others could build on this first step in future work in this area.

REFERENCES

Crocker, Keith J., and John Morgan. 1998. "Is Honesty the Best Policy? Curtailing Insurance Fraud through Optimal Incentive Contracts." *Journal of Political Economy* 106:355–75.
Dharmapala, Dhammika, Nuno Garoupa, and Richard McAdams. 2016. "Punitive Police? Agency Costs, Law Enforcement, and Criminal Procedure." *Journal of Legal Studies* 45:105–41.

Garoupa, Nuno. 2017. "Explaining the Standard of Proof in Criminal Law: A New Insight." *Supreme Court Economic Review* 25:111–122.

Lacker, Jeffrey M., and John A. Weinberg. 1989. "Optimal Contracts under Costly State Verification." *Journal of Political Economy* 97: 1345–63.

Maggi, Giovanni, and Andres Rodriguez-Clare. 1995. "Costly Distortion of Information in Agency Problems." *Rand Journal of Economics* 26:675–89.

Myerson, Roger. 1979. "Incentive Compatibility and the Bargaining Problem." *Econometrica* 47:61–73.

Schrag, Joel, and Suzanne Scotchmer. 1994. "Crime and Prejudice: The Use of Character Evidence in Criminal Trials." *Journal of Law, Economics, and Organization* 10:319–42.

Wickelgren, Abraham L. 2003. "Justifying Imprisonment: On the Optimality of Excessively Costly Punishment." *American Law and Economics Review* 5:377–411.

Judicial Compensation and Performance

Gregory DeAngelo [*]
Bryan C. McCannon

*Judges have considerable influence over legal proceedings
and outcomes. Intrinsic motivations are an important component of the explanation of why individuals seek out the
bench. It has been argued, though, that judges maximize the
same things that everybody else does, including income. In
this research we utilize a unique data set from New York
State on appealed felony convictions to identify the impact
of judicial salary on performance. We exploit a large increase
in judicial salaries, which followed a 12-year period of un-
changed salaries, to identify the impact. We differentiate
two alternative explanations for salary's effect on outcomes.
Increased salaries can act as efficiency wages to induce currently sitting judges to work harder to continue their employment. Also, higher salaries can affect occupational
choice, encouraging high-quality attorneys to instead seek
the bench. In both instances, we anticipate an increase in
the number of cases that are upheld upon appeal. By examining judges who served both before the wage increase and
after, we can test for the presence of selection and effort separately. First, we document that the rate at which appealed*

[*] Gregory DeAngelo and Bryan C. McCannon are affiliated with the Department of
Economics, College of Business and Economics, West Virginia University. We appreciate the help from Paul Lewis, who provided us with information on the case handling at
the local level in New York State. We also thank Scott Baker, Scott Cunningham, and
Todd Zywicki for useful discussions. Finally, we thank the Koch Foundation for financial support.

Electronically published: December 4, 2018

convictions were reversed or modified decreased by 4.2% af-
ter the salary change went into affect. Second, although we
do record a slight selection effect, we find that this change
comes primarily from the higher salary encouraging higher
quality decision making. Specifically, judges on the bench
before the wage increase were significantly more likely to
have their appealed cases upheld after the salary increase
went into effect than before. Thus, efficiency wages are an
important driver of the legal system's quality.

1. INTRODUCTION

Judges are the linchpins of the legal system. They exercise a substantial amount of discretion with little external oversight. Appreciating
what motivates them is needed to evaluate the legal system's efficacy. In a seminal contribution to our understanding of judicial decision making, Posner (1993) asks a straightforward question: "What do
judges maximize?" His parenthetical response provides his answer:
"The same thing everybody else does." Judges prefer to do their job
well, want to avoid mistakes (exposed in part by appealed cases), enjoy
leisure, and derive utility from consumption (and thus desire to receive satisfactory salaries), among other things. Contributing to the
dilemma of judicial motivation, as advanced in one of Tullock's (1971)
seminal contributions, judging itself is a public good. As he points out,
there is little chance a judge will directly benefit from his own ruling;
therefore, the time and effort invested in reaching a good decision suffers
from free-riding concerns. This has led legal scholars to point out that
the free-riding, principal-agent concerns combined with the substantial
discretion and minimal checks on the exercise of that discretion mean
that a judge's intrinsic motivation is of primary importance (Ash and
MacLeod 2015).

A potentially important dimension of the job of being a judge is the
salary provided. Although nonmonetary, intrinsic benefits may be
important, readily available alternative occupations exist for individuals who possess the formal human capital and experience generally
demanded to be an effective judge. Consequently, a concern has been
raised that this important public service is unable to attract the best
individuals. Although an issue across the country, a prominent example is New York State. Trial court justices did not receive any increase
in their nominal wage for 12 consecutive years. Concerns arose that
the state was losing viable individuals to the private sector as the opportunity cost of being a justice rose. Beginning in April 2012, a series
of aggressive pay increases was initiated with the goal of bringing
lower court judge salaries up to those of federal judges. This event

provides a unique opportunity to evaluate how judicial compensation affects the legal system's quality.

We explore a unique data set of every appealed felony conviction in New York State since 2007. More than 20,000 appeals were ruled upon. Although errors are, by their very nature, difficult to assess directly, we argue that the appellate court's evaluation of the lower court's decisions is a reasonable metric of mistakes.[1] This is especially relevant given the argument by Judge Posner (1993, 2008) that appeal avoidance is an important component to the judicial utility function. Using case-level data, we examine the determinants of upheld appeals of lower court convictions.

Our empirical strategy is to differentiate judges who serve only before the pay increase, those who serve only after the pay increase, and those whose careers straddle the salary change. With the first group as the reference, those who joined the bench after the pay adjustments went into effect can be affected both by selection effects (they ran for office in part because of the high wage) and efficiency wages (their effort is enhanced because of the risk of losing the high wage). If the quality of their rulings were higher, we would not be able to differentiate the source of that improvement. Those who straddle the pay increase, though, allow us to differentiate the two effects. Relative to the preperiod, if ruling quality improves within this cohort, then efficiency wages matter. If their decision making does not improve, then a measurable bump in affirmation rates after the pay increase would be driven by selection effects.

We find that after the pay increase, the proportion of appealed trial court convictions that were not upheld decreased by 4.2%. Differentiating justices, we find that those who joined the bench after the wage improvement experienced an increase in the probability that an appealed conviction would be upheld, by approximately 16 percentage points. For cases overseen by a justice who straddled the pay change, in the period before the wage increase, the probability that the conviction would be upheld increased by 1.4 percentage points, but after the wage increase, the affirmation likelihood increased by 14.0 percentage points. These results strongly suggest that efficiency wages are a driving factor in judicial effort provision, and selection effects, although they exist, are a more minor contributor to legal system quality. Given our results, we find some empirical support for New York State's stated policy goal of bringing higher quality justices to the bench. Moreover, the unstated outcome—that higher wages incentivize judicial effort—is shown not only to exist but to have a meaningful impact on case outcomes.

[1] A similar strategy is employed by McCannon (2013) and DeAngelo and McCannon (2017).

Our work contributes to the robust literature on judges' behavioral responses to retention concerns. This research focuses primarily on judicial election's impact on sentencing decisions (Berdejo and Yuchtman 2013; Lim 2013; Cohen, Klement, and Neeman 2015). Alternatively, the comparison between election and appointment mechanisms has received attention (Shepherd 2009; Choi, Gulati, and Posner 2010; Iaryczower, Lewis, and Shrum 2013). Choi, Gulati, and Posner (2009) address the issue of whether judges are underpaid. They conduct a cross-sectional analysis of state supreme court opinion writing and do not find a relationship between wages and output. However, their analysis is unable to differentiate salary's causal impact on effort from selection effects.[2] In addition, the existing literature does not examine lower court judges, for whom job retention, promotion possibilities, and compensation are all relevant. To the best of our knowledge, we are the first to evaluate the direct impact of judicial pay on the quality of legal system outcomes.

Our work complements research on prosecutor salaries as well. Boylan (2004) shows that assistant US attorneys experience higher turnover when their salaries are lower, which, consequently, lowers output. Furthermore, Boylan and Long (2005) provide evidence that they take more cases to trial when private labor-market opportunities are better. Relatedly, both the intensive and extensive margins of prosecution improve when the funding of the prosecutor's office improves (Rasmusen, Raghav, and Ramseyer 2009). Economies of scale can have important effects on prosecutorial production (Detotto and McCannon 2017a, 2017b).

The article proceeds as follows. In section 2, we briefly outline the history of judicial wages in New York State and develop our working hypotheses. Section 3 presents the data and data collection techniques. The empirical analysis is presented in section 4, and in section 5, we conclude.

2. JUDGES' SALARY IN NEW YORK AND TESTABLE HYPOTHESES

Felony criminal cases in New York State are initially heard in county court or supreme court, which is the state's (rather than the county's) trial court. Each of the 62 counties in New York State has one county court. Also, the state is divided into 13 supreme court districts. Each

---

[2] Legal scholars have debated the issue, but the discussion has focused on selection effects, relatively ignored efficiency wage arguments, and focused on higher courts (Frank, 2003; Baker, 2008; Anderson and Helland, 2012).

county in New York is served by one county court and one supreme court, but with potentially many justices within each system.

The supreme court has unlimited jurisdiction in civil and felony criminal cases. Each county court handles felony cases, misdemeanors, and lawsuits less than $25,000. Supreme court justice pay is set by the state legislature. By law, the county court justices are paid 95% of the salary of supreme court justices. Judges in New York State are selected in popular, partisan elections serving 10-year (county) and 14-year (supreme) terms. In addition, the governor is able to make appointments to fill vacancies.

On January 1, 1999, judges' salaries were increased. The lower court judges in New York State then went 12 years without an increase in their nominal salary. In 2011, amid growing concerns that judicial quality was being hampered as skilled individuals chose higher paying, private-sector jobs, judicial pay was increased (Commission on Legislative, Judicial, and Executive Compensation 2015). The first salary increase took effect April 1, 2012, and increased annually thereafter. Again, in 2015 a state bill was passed to continue the wage improvements with the objective of having the pay of state supreme court justices equal federal judge salaries by 2018.[3] Quoting the commission's findings, "to sustain and enhance that stature, New York must maintain and strengthen its ability to attract the best and brightest legal minds to its Judiciary and retain them" (Commission on Legislative, Judicial, and Executive Compensation 2015, 1). The adjustment represents a 41% increase in pay between April 2012 and April 2016, with additional increases in 2017 and 2018.

New York State does not conform to either the federal judiciary or other states. To illustrate this, we collected data from the National Center for State Courts, which provides annual surveys of judicial compensation across the country. Figure 1 tracks trial court justice's salaries in New York State and compares them with federal judges and judges in neighboring states New Jersey, Pennsylvania, and Connecticut. Salaries are normalized to their 1999 levels within each state.

New York State sits well below the comparison states across the entire time period. Interestingly, growth in salary in New Jersey, Pennsylvania, and Connecticut outpaces the federal judge salary, which is New York's benchmark. Prior to 1999, justice salaries in New York were updated regularly. For the decade of the 1990s, for example, New York justices received nominal wage increases in 7 of the 10 years. Overall, justices' nominal salaries increased by more than 28% in the

---

[3] Part E, chap. 60, of the Laws of New York State (2015) was enacted to create a quadrennial commission to "examine, evaluate and make recommendations with respect to adequate levels of compensation and non-salary benefits" for judges.

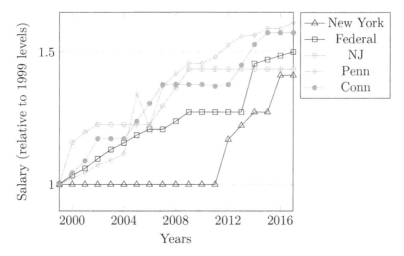

Figure 1.   Judge salaries across time

1990s, compared with 0% in the 2000s. Thus, the wage disparity was different not only from other states but from New York's own history.[4]

How might judges' salaries affect the legal system's outcomes? One clear channel is through selection. The commission's report provides information on the salaries of private attorneys in the major cities across the state. If an individual is making a career decision, higher private market wages can shift the occupational choice decision for many individuals. Under a reasonable assumption that the wage an individual can receive in the private sector is correlated with the individual's professional quality, then the wage disparity creates a lower average quality for those who choose to serve as a judge. Therefore, an occupational selection framework would hypothesize that judicial quality should improve with salary.

In addition, the theory of efficiency wages (Shapiro and Stiglitz 1984) suggests that the threat of losing one's job, and the high wage it provides, has the benefit of discouraging shirking by employees. Applied to judges, there is the threat that they will either not be reelected by the voters or not be reappointed by the governor. If wages are high, then this becomes a threat that incentivizes the effort required to do a good job.[5] Therefore, the efficiency wage theory would hypothesize that

[4] Appellate justices in New York State earn a slight premium over the trial court justices. This is because they are selected by the governor from the set of elected lower court justices.

[5] Alternatively, high wages can trigger a preference for reciprocity, expressed as more effort being expended as a reciprocal exchange for the greater salary (Akerlof, 1982). Our analysis is unable to differentiate the two sources of effort provision.

there is a change in the judges' incentives that should improve the quality of their decisions when compensation improves. Our identification strategy is to use this dramatic pay increase in New York State to differentiate the effect of the salary's selection effect from its efficiency wage effect.

3. DATA DESCRIPTION

Our primary data source comes from New York State's appellate court. To adequately describe the data used in the project, we provide a brief description of New York State's appellate court and the published opinions we use in our analysis. Second, we detail the information on judge biographies and backgrounds.

3.1. Appellate Court

Whether a case originates in the county court or supreme court, appeals of those convictions are handled by the Appellate Division. New York State is partitioned into four appellate departments. Within each department there are 12–15 appellate justices who serve in, typically, five-person panels. Throughout the year, the panels rotate in composition. The appellate justices are selected by the governor from the pool of elected supreme court justices to serve 5-year terms. The appellate court hears appeals of all criminal and civil cases across the department.[6]

For each appeal decided, a slip opinion is published. The length and content of each slip opinion varies. Each, though, provides basic information on the dispute: decision, lower court involved, dates, appellate justices, lower court judge and defensive representation, and so forth. A short narrative is included providing a justification for the decision reached. Frequently, a brief summary of the appellant's claims and the court's response is provided. Relevant case law is cited.

Each slip opinion is maintained in portable document format on each of the four appellate department's websites, which we scraped, then cleaned for further analysis. Our data contain slip opinions that start in 2007 and extend through April 2017. A total of 117,398 slip opinions were collected. Of these, 20,644 involve appeals of criminal

---

[6] Although not included in the data studied here, appeals of misdemeanor convictions are handled by the County Court in the Third and Fourth Departments (upstate New York), whereas the Appellate Term reviews such convictions in the First and Second Departments. We restrict attention to felony crimes. In addition, although the selection and effort of appellate justices are likely to be important issues, it is unclear how and whether they would affect conviction affirmations.

convictions. The remainder are appealed civil cases. These slip opinions correspond to original court cases that extend back as early as 1981.

The corpus of slip opinions was converted into a flat file database. Classifiers were then developed to conduct a series of regular-expression and "bag of word" extractions of specific information from the slip opinions. The date of the original case and the appeal, the outcome of the appeal, and the court in which the case was heard were collected. The outcome can affirm, dismiss, modify, or reverse the trial court's conviction. In addition, indicator variables were created to indicate whether the original case was decided in a bench trial or a jury trial or whether a guilty plea was entered. The document length (in words) was also gathered. Finally, we recorded the name of the original justice who presided over the case, the county where the case was heard, and the identity of the appellate justices on the panel that ruled on the appeal.[7]

Two additional, important pieces of information were also collected from the slip opinions. First, the crime being appealed was recorded. Overall, 31 separate crime categories were identified with a unique indicator variable created for each. Second, the grounds of the appeal were identified from the text.[8] A total of 12 separate grounds for appeal were recorded. Table A7 contains a full list of the crimes and grounds for appeal that were extracted from the slip opinions. These extractions were completed utilizing both standard regular expression and bag of words extractions. The extractions were manually checked to confirm their accuracy.

Regarding the decision reached on a slip opinion, we considered a distinct measure of the appellate court's ruling on the trial court's conviction. Specifically, our dependent variable is binary, taking a value of 1 if the lower court's decision stands on appeal. It is common for a particular individual's conviction to involve multiple crimes. Each conviction can be appealed; therefore, multiple decisions are made by the appellate court and published on one slip opinion. As such, we consider only cases in which the appellate justices believed no errors were made in the original judgment (i.e., no conviction was reversed or

---

[7] Regarding the original justice who presided over the case, in some cases, multiple justices were involved. For example, one justice might have handled the preliminary hearing while another justice handled the trial. In these instances, we coded only the justice who handled the trial portion of the court proceedings.

[8] Crimes were identified by conducting a regular expression extraction from the plea or conviction statement in the slip opinion. So, the crimes were extracted from either the statement "upon his/her plea of guilty of [CRIME HERE]" or "convicting him/her of [CRIME HERE], upon." Grounds for appeal were extracted using a regular expression extraction of the grounds for appeal from McCannon (2013).

modified). We denote this as the indicator variable "upheld," which is the same dependent variable used in McCannon (2013) and DeAngelo and McCannon (2017).

3.2. Data on Judges

To supplement the case-level data, a biography was created for each justice in New York State. Of the 20,644 slip opinions in our data set, a total of 518 justices appear in the data. Biographical information is primarily identified from the New York State Unified Court System (2018).[9]

From these sources, we recorded basic information, such as the justice's gender, law school attended, and the year graduated from law school. Graduation year allows us to calculate an experience measurement.[10] We differentiate justices who attended a law school within the state from out-of-state justices, recognizing that selection is driven in part by local political connections. Information on the justice's career prior to becoming a judge was also collected. Specifically, we identified whether the individual worked as a prosecutor or a public defender. In addition, we recorded which courts the justice served in over his or her career.[11]

Finally, information on the election cycles was used. For each justice we identified the year in which he or she became a judge and

[9] The New York State Unified Court System (2018) provides biographies for all active justices. Missing information was gathered from Ballotpedia (https://www.ballotpedia .org), which provides biographical information on elected politicians across the country. In a small number of situations, online web searches are used to fill in missing information. For example, local media coverage of a justice's retirement provides missing career information. Additional information from media sources was collected for only 44 justices (6.7% of all justices in the sample), which represents 7.8% of the cases in our data set. Our data collection efforts resulted in the coverage of 88.5% of the justices and 98.82% of all slip opinions; therefore, the justices with unrecoverable biographical information are those involved in very few cases. Indicator variables were created for the missing information.

[10] One justice in New York State did not attend law school. Thus, the year used is 1 year less than the year he was admitted to the bar. This justice presided over 126 appealed felony convictions in our data set.

[11] Supreme court justices are distinguished by whether they hold an elected position or are appointed by the governor. Justices in the supreme court are separated into three categories: those who only have an appointed position (SCAJ), those who only have an elected position (SC), and those who were first appointed but then elected to the position (SCAJ-SC). It is not uncommon for an elected county court justice to also receive an associate justice appointment in the supreme court. Also, it is not rare for an individual to first be elected to serve as a county court justice (labeled as the indicator variable CC) and, later in his or her career, run for a supreme court position. Such an individual would be recorded as having served in both.

which years he or she ran for reelection. This information allows us to identify the pay regime under which a justice served.

Table A1 is divided into two sections (tables A1–A8 are available online). The first panel provides judge-level summary statistics, whereas the second panel provides the case-level summary statistics used in the empirical analysis. In panel (a), we examine the average total number of appeals per justice and the outcome of appealed cases, as well as the justice's experience at the time of the ruling and the court on which the justice served. On average, justices have approximately 36 judgments appealed. There is a substantial amount of variation in judicial experience. Cases are distributed rather equally across the two court systems. On average, a justice runs for just more than one reelection.

A conviction is upheld approximately 80% of the time and affirmed 90% of the time. Dismissals, modifications, and reversals of cases each occur approximately 10% of the time. As stated previously, because one slip opinion can provide the appellate ruling for an individual with more than one conviction, these rulings sum to a number greater than 1. Similar outcome breakdowns arise in panel (b). It is noteworthy that the standard deviations are greater. This suggests more consistency across justices than within one justice over time. It is also consistent with the hypothesis that variation in incentives over time is important.

In panel (b) we examine case-level data from the 20,644 criminal appeals in our data set. On average, we find that each appealed case takes almost 2.5 years to reach the appellate court. There is wide variation in opinion length. Jury trials are almost as prevalent as guilty pleas. Plea bargaining typically occurs in 95% of felony cases, and this suggests an important selection effect in which convictions are appealed.[12]

We divide our justices into three groups based on the April 2012 wage increase. First, we identify justices that exist in our data only before the wage change (*Prewage*). Second, we identify those who were in office both before and after the wage change (*Both*). Finally, we identify justices who were in office only after the wage change (*Postwage*). In table A2 we provide summary statistics for these three groups of justices. The most notable difference is that justices in the Prewage group have more experience and more appealed cases compared with either the Postwage or Both group. If the ratio of appeals per year is calculated, the pre- and postwage cohorts are similar. Otherwise, we do not observe obvious differences in appeal outcomes in our summariza-

---

[12] The omitted category is opinions that do not reveal the mode of conviction. Even if all of these were in fact plea-bargained cases, jury trials would still represent almost a quarter of all cases.

tion of the data. To further examine the relationship between the likelihood that a case is upheld and wage increases for judges, we turn to a more robust empirical analysis.

4. EMPIRICAL ANALYSIS

To engage in the empirical analysis, we first present the main results highlighting the change in upheld, appealed convictions. Second, we decompose the intertemporal effects, both the gradual change over time after adoption and the possible anticipation beforehand. Finally, we evaluate the robustness of the main results.

4.1. Main Results

To examine the effect of a justice's wage on performance, equation (1) employs a standard difference-in-differences approach to determine the effect of the wage increase.

$$\text{Upheld}_{ijmy} = \beta_1 \text{Postwage}_{ijmy} + \beta_2 \text{Both}_{ijmy} + \beta_3 (\text{Both}_{ijmy} \times \text{Postperiod})$$
$$+ X_j + X_{jmy} + m \times y + \delta_i + \varepsilon_{ijmy} \tag{1}$$

As noted, we divide our sample into three groups of judges: (1) justices who are only in our data before the wage increase, (2) justices who are only in our data after the wage increase, and (3) justices who are in our data both before and after the wage increase. Our omitted group is the justices who were active only before the wage increase.[13] The group of justices who appear only after the wage increase are captured in the Postwage$_{ijmy}$ variable. These denote justice j in county i of month m and year y, who only experience the high wage after April 2012. We separate the remaining justices into the variables Both$_{ijmy}$ and Both$_{ijmy}$ × Postperiod. The Both$_{ijmy}$ variable captures the justice's behavior in the period before the wage increase, whereas the Both$_{ijmy}$ × Postperiod variable measures the April 2012 wage improvement's effect on justices who were in their position before the salary change.

Additional controls are included in the analysis. With regard to each justice, we include controls for gender, previous experience (pre-

[13] Another way of thinking about these groups is that there are four types of opinions in our data. Opinions that are generated (1) preincrease by a justice who was only on the bench before the wage increase, (2) preincrease by a justice who was on the bench before and after the wage increase, (3) postincrease by a justice who was only on the bench after the wage increase, and (4) postincrease by a justice who was on the bench both before and after the wage increase.

viously an assistant district attorney or assistant public defender), and whether the justice attended a New York State law school. Our case-level controls include whether the case was handled in the supreme court or county court, whether the case was a jury or nonjury trial, and the number of days between the original judgment and initial appeal date. Last, 31 controls for the crime committed in the original case and 12 controls for grounds for appeal are also included in our analysis.

Utilizing this specification allows us to separately identify two effects of the wage increase. First, β_1 identifies whether trial court outcomes are improving. It cannot, though, tell us the source of improvement. In other words, if $\beta_1 > 0$, then either higher wages are inducing the selection of more capable individuals or encouraging higher effort from those holding the judicial seat. Second, β_3 measures the effect of the wage increase on the performance of those currently holding the judicial office. If $\beta_3 > 0$, then this implies that justices are responding to higher wages by performing their job with fewer errors in the period following the wage increase. The coefficient β_2, in contrast, considers this cohort's decisions before the wage increase; therefore, it can only be affected by selection. If only β_3 is nonzero, then the efficiency wage argument dominates. Alternatively, if only β_2 is nonzero, then selection alone is driving the improvements. If the interaction term is dropped from equation (1), then β_2 would capture both the selection and effort effects. By including the interaction term, the two effects are disentangled. Comparing the two coefficients allows us to gauge the relative importance of the two factors that we hypothesize affects outcomes.

Table A3 examines the likelihood that an appealed case is upheld. In the first column we run an ordinary least squares (OLS) model that includes county, month, and year fixed effects while controlling for the convicted crimes in the original case, grounds for appeal, and a trend for the number of appealed cases in a given month.[14] The specification in the second column is identical to the first column, except that we estimate a probit model. Columns 3 and 4 are similar to the first two columns, except that we now include month-by-year fixed effects rather than separate month and year fixed effects.

We find that justices who joined the bench after April 2012 are approximately 6 to 16 percentage points more likely to have their cases upheld on appeal, relative to justices who are on the bench only in the period before the wage change. From table A1, this represents as much

---

[14] Less saturated models with very similar results generate the same qualitative results.

as a 19.5% increase in the affirmation rate. Thus, the effect is non-negligible. Of those justices who were on the bench both before and after the April 2012 wage change, we observe a 1.4-percentage point higher likelihood that their appealed case is upheld relative to justices on the bench only in the preperiod. In addition, for those judges in both the pre- and postperiod, we observe a 3- to 14-percentage point higher likelihood that their case is upheld in the postperiod. The probit analysis finds similar results. Moreover, our Akaike information criterion is much smaller when we include month-by-year fixed effects, so we will focus on this model as we proceed in our analysis.

These findings strongly suggest that the salary increase achieved its goal of improving the quality of the legal institutions in New York State. Our novel finding is that the selection effect, which is the dominant argument for proponents of the wage increase, is minimal. The efficiency wage effect is substantial.

We conduct an F-test to determine whether the Postwage, Both, and Both × Postperiod coefficients are statistically different from each other using the specification in the first column. The β_2 / β_3 and β_1 / β_2 pairs are significantly different from one another. As such, we find support for both an entry and efficiency wage effect. Because β_1 and β_3 are not statistically different from one another, this implies that entering judges are no better than those currently sitting on the bench. However, because β_2 is statistically different from β_3 (and β_1), this implies that the efficiency wage argument induces "better" decision making for justices on the bench. Moreover, this means that those entering and those staying on the bench are both higher quality justices than those who have historically sat on the bench.

4.2. Event Study Analysis

To more directly examine the effect of the wage change on the quality of the judgments, we conduct an event study analysis by dividing our appeals data into 6-month intervals before and after the wage change. We then rerun the above specification but include separate indicators for each 6-month period, as seen in Greenstone and Hanna (2014), with separate month and year fixed effects. The control group is comprises those individuals who either have not received the wage increase yet or who will not receive the wage increase because they leave the data set prior to the wage increase. The treatment group is comprises the justices who have received a wage increase in the postperiod. This approach allows us to identify whether heterogeneous effects of the wage change exist over time.

Figure 2 plots the difference-in-difference estimates in the 6-month intervals leading up to and after the wage change, including all previ-

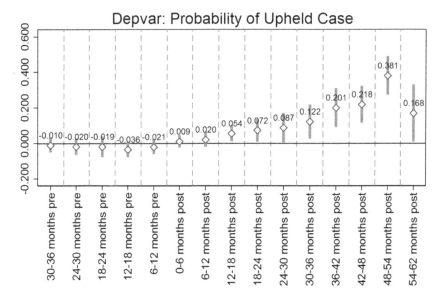

Figure 2.   Likelihood of a case being upheld

ous controls. Importantly, the estimates satisfy the parallel trends assumption, as the differences in the likelihood that a case is upheld in the preperiod between the treatment and control groups are not statistically different from one another. This can be seen by all difference-in-difference estimates and confidence intervals hovering around zero. However, in the postperiod, we see our estimates pulling apart. In all but the first two 6-month intervals in the postperiod, we find significant differences in the likelihood that a case is upheld. In fact, by 3 to 6 years after the wage change, the likelihood that a case is upheld is 20%–40% higher than the control group. Thus, when we break our difference-in-difference estimates apart, we find even stronger evidence that the wage change dramatically affected the quality of the judicial performance.

4.3. Testing for Anticipation Effects

Although table A3 identifies significant positive effects of justices who were in the position of a justice before and after the wage change on the likelihood a case is upheld, this could be an anticipation effect (Ashenfelter, Eisenberg, and Schwab 1995). In other words, individuals could be anticipating the wage increase and running for the elected judicial positions prior to the higher wages being put in place. Thus, we have argued that the positive value of β_2 is coming from a selection effect. Alternatively, justices in the Both group could have been in the position before any knowledge that a wage increase was announced. They choose to run for the seat when the real wages are low. Therefore, we further divide the Both group into those judges who were in the position prior to 2009 (*Entry pre-2009*) and those entering the position after 2009 but before April 2012 (*Entry post-2009*). This enables us to examine whether the wage increase improved legal outcomes by inducing more effort from those already in a judicial position or better quality candidates to seek the position.

In table A4 we separately identify whether entry or effort appears to be driving the increase in judicial quality that occurs when wages increase. As noted, we have divided the justices in the Both group so the Entry pre-2009 subgroup will be justices who are increasing their effort in response to the wage increase, whereas the Entry post-2009 subgroup will be justices who entered the judge position and were likely knowledgeable about the forthcoming wage increase. We examine the separate effects of these groups on the likelihood that a case was upheld in both the pre- and postperiods.

Examining the same specifications from table A3, we find evidence that supports both the effort and entry stories. Again, the effort story appears to be much more pronounced and rather uniform across the two groups. Examining the first column, in which we run an OLS regression, we note that the Both × Entry pre-2009 and Both × Entry post-2009 variables capture any differences in the likelihood that a case would be upheld in the preperiod relative to those justices who are in our data only for the preperiod. Interestingly, we find weak evidence that the group of justices who are likely unaware of the forthcoming wage change (Both × Entry pre-2009) are the ones with an effect statistically distinguishable from zero; however, the estimated effects are nearly identical for the two. Therefore, the argument for selection effects is weak.

When we examine the postperiod, we observe significant differences in behavior. First, the Entry pre-2009 group is approximately 14 percentage points more likely than the Prewage justices (omitted group) to have their case upheld in the postperiod, whereas the Entry post-2009 group is only 11 percentage points more likely. Although distinct, the two cannot be statistically differentiated from each other. Moreover, neither of these coefficients is significantly different from the Postwage coefficient in the postperiod. By breaking up the justices who remain on the bench after the wage change into those who could have anticipated the effect and justices who likely could not have anticipated the wage change, we find that these justices, in addition to the justices who join the bench after the wage increase, converge toward higher quality performance, as measured by a higher likelihood of having their cases upheld on appeal.

4.4. Robustness Checks

To examine the effect of the wage change on judge behavior, we conducted a permutation test in which we randomly assigned a wage change date and examined the effect of this random assignment on the behavior of justices who were in the position both before and after the actual wage change. This creates a "placebo" salary adjustment. The regression coefficients were calculated (using the specification in table A1, first column) and recorded. This process was repeated 1,000 times, creating 1,000 estimates from the placebo wage changes. If our results arise from a spurious correlation, then the randomly created placebo wage changes will frequently have a statistically significant correlation with appeal outcomes. Alternatively, if the wage change has a direct effect, then the placebo policy changes will rarely correlate with upheld conviction likelihoods.

Table A5 presents the results of this permutation test. The coefficients on the Both and Both × Postperiod variables are presented. In the preperiod, our results are not statistically different from the results that we would have obtained by randomly assigning a wage change date. However, when we examine the interaction between the Both group and the postperiod, we find that our estimates are significantly different. Examining the estimated coefficient of the 1st and 99th percentiles, our estimate falls outside this interval. It is very unlikely that the upheld rate increase observed is due to random chance. Therefore, we conclude that the increase in effort exerted by the group of justices who straddle the change in the postperiod is not due to spurious correlation but rather is a unique effect that is driven by the introduction of the wage increase in April 2012.

In addition, we ran a falsification test of the wage change by dropping all observations after 2009 from our sample and then imposing a false wage change in April 2005. We chose this date because it is in the middle of a time period when justices received no change in their compensation. We then reestimated the specification in table A3, which we present in table A6.

Importantly, we do not find any effect of the false wage change on the behavior of justices who joined the bench after 2005 or for those who were on the bench before 2005 and remained on the bench after 2005.[15] These falsification results further reinforce the impact of the true wage changes because they appear to be unique to the environment in which an actual wage change occurred and not due to spurious correlation.

---

[15] Our results are not sensitive to the use of 2005 as a false wage change date. In fact, we ran 48 falsification tests for each month of the years 2004–7 and obtained nearly identical estimates for all of these results.

5. CONCLUSION

In 2012 New York State began a series of aggressive pay increases for its lower court justices, raising their wage more than 40%. This increase rectified a 12-year freeze in their nominal wage. Under concerns that low relative pay was driving highly qualified individuals to pursue alternative legal careers, New York acted with the intention to improve the quality of its legal system. Using this event, we evaluate the impact of judicial salary. To measure a trial court's quality, we utilize a data set of more than 20,000 felony conviction appeals. First, we document that the probability that an appealed conviction is upheld increases after the pay increase. Second, we explore the driver of this change. Although the policy makers' stated objective was to select highly skilled individuals, we provide evidence that higher pay acts as an efficiency wage that can induce more effort, which leads to better outcomes. We disentangle the two effects and find that although selection effects are prevalent, most of the increase in the quality of the lower court's rulings in criminal cases comes from greater effort.

We provide direct empirical evidence not only that improved judicial pay leads to better outcomes of the legal system but also that it is an unstated determinant that leads to the improvement. As famously argued by Posner (1993), judges maximize the same things as everyone else. Thus, incentivizing judicial effort is an important and relatively unexplored area of empirical legal research.

Our analysis focuses on the criminal justice system. Presumably, judicial compensation improves the decision making in civil cases as well. Documenting this effect is left for future research. In addition, within criminal law, we use appeals as our metric of mistakes. Successful appeals will primarily be driven by procedural problems. Consequently, it is a test of the judge's officiating function. Sentencing is a different, important action that justices perform. We also leave for future research an evaluation of whether sentencing differences occur with pay changes.

Our analysis evaluates the effect that wages have on incentivizing judges to perform their job well. Numerous other external motivations also matter. For example, a lower court justice may be interested in advancing politically to higher positions. Although for most judges, the position is the pinnacle of previous advancements, for a few, promotions to a higher court, for example, may be possible. One would expect that motivations such as this are orthogonal to wages and, therefore, unrelated to the dramatic wage shift that occurred.

Some important empirical limitations should be considered. For example, the decision to file an appeal is endogenous. Although the factors that influence the decision to appeal are likely unrelated to the judge's salary directly, it is an open question whether our results are causal. Relatedly, the legislative decision to raise salary opens up potential endogeneity concerns. Falsification tests and permutation tests strongly suggest a direct effect. In addition, we use as our data set a comprehensive collection of appealed convictions. We do not have information on the universe of all criminal cases ruled on during the period. Thus, our results are best interpreted as conditional on the case being appealed.

REFERENCES

Akerlof, George A. 1982. "Labor Contracts as Partial Gift Exchange." *Quarterly Journal of Economics* 97:543–69.

Anderson, James M., and Eric Helland. 2012. "How Much Should Judges Be Paid? An Empirical Study on the Effect of Judicial Pay on the State Bench." *Stanford Law Review* 64:1277–342.

Ash, Elliott, and W. Bentley MacLeod. 2015. "Intrinsic Motivation in Public Service: Theory and Evidence from State Supreme Courts." *Journal of Law and Economics* 58 (4): 863–914.

Ashenfelter, Orley, Theodore Eisenberg, and Stewart J. Schwab. 1995. "Politics and the Judiciary: The Influence of Judicial Background on Case Outcomes." *Journal of Legal Studies* 24 (2): 257–81.

Baker, Scott. 2008. "Should We Pay Federal Judges More?" *Boston University Law Review* 88:63–112.

Berdejo, Carlos, and Noam Yuchtman. 2013. "Crime, Punishment, and Politics: An Analysis of Political Cycles in Criminal Sentencing." *Review of Economics and Statistics* 95 (3): 741–56.

Boylan, Richard T. 2004. "Salaries, Turnover, and Performance in the Federal Criminal Justice System." *Journal of Law and Economics* 47 (1): 75–92.

Boylan, Richard T., and Cheryl X. Long. 2005. "Salaries, Plea Rates, and the Career Objectives of Federal Prosecutors." *Journal of Law and Economics* 48 (2): 627–51.

Choi, Stephen J., G. Mitu Gulati, and Eric A. Posner. 2009. "Are Judges Overpaid? A Skeptical Response to the Judicial Salary Debate." *Journal of Legal Analysis* 1 (1): 47–117.

Choi, Stephen J., G. Mitu Gulati, and Eric A. Posner. 2010. "Professionals or Politicians: The Uncertain Empirical Case for an Elected Rather Than Appointed Judiciary." *Journal of Law, Economics, and Organization* 26:290–336.

Cohen, Alma, Alon Klement, and Zvika Neeman. 2015. "Judicial Decision Making: A Dynamic Reputation Approach." *Journal of Legal Studies* 44 (S1): S133–S159.

Commission on Legislative, Judicial, and Executive Compensation. 2015. *Final Report on Judicial Compensation.* New York: Commis-

sion on Legislative, Judicial, and Executive Compensation. http://
www.nyscommissiononcompensation.org/pdf/compensation
-report-dec24.pdf.

DeAngelo, Gregory, and Bryan C. McCannon. 2017. *Using Appellate Decision to Evaluate the Effect of Judicial Elections*. SSRN Working Paper No. 2988272. https://ssrn.com/abstract=2988272.

Detotto, Claudio, and Bryan C. McCannon. 2017a. "Economic Freedom and Public, Non-market Institutions: Evidence from Criminal Prosecution." *Economics of Governance* 18 (2): 107–28.

Detotto, Claudio, and Bryan C. McCannon. 2017b. *Consolidation of Prosecutor Offices*. SSRN Working Paper No. 2735760. https://ssrn.com/abstract=2735760.

Frank, Michael J. 2003. "Judge Not, Lest Ye Be Judged Unworthy of a Pay Raise: An Examination of the Federal Judicial Salary 'Crisis.'" *Marquette Law Review* 87:55–122.

Greenstone, Michael, and Rema Hanna. 2014. "Environmental Regulations, Air and Water Pollution, and Infant Mortality in India." *American Economic Review* 104 (10): 3038–72.

Iaryczower, Matias, Garrett Lewis, and Matthew Shrum. 2013. "To Elect or to Appoint? Bias, Information, and Responsiveness of Bureaucrats and Politicians." *Journal of Public Economics* 97:203–44.

Lim, Claire S. H. 2013. "Preferences and Incentives of Appointed versus Elected Public Officials: Evidence from State Trial Court Judges." *American Economic Review* 103 (4): 1360–97.

McCannon, Bryan C. 2013. "Prosecutor Elections, Mistakes, and Appeals." *Journal of Empirical Legal Studies* 10 (4): 697–715.

New York State Unified Court System. 2018. "Judicial Directories." https://www.nycourts.gov/judges/directory.shtml.

Posner, Richard A. 1993. "What Do Judges and Justices Maximize? (The Same Thing Everybody Else Does)." *Supreme Court Economic Review* 3 (1): 1–41.

Posner, Richard A. 2008. *How Judges Think*. Cambridge, MA: Harvard University Press.

Rasmusen, Eric, Manu Raghav, and Mark Ramseyer. 2009. "Convictions versus Conviction Rates: The Prosecutor's Choice." *American Law and Economics Review* 11 (1): 47–78.

Shapiro, Carl, and Joseph E. Stiglitz. 1984. "Equilibrium Unemployment as a Worker Discipline Device." *American Economic Review* 74 (3): 433–44.

Shepherd, Joanna M. 2009. "The Influence of Retention Politics on Judges' Voting." *Journal of Legal Studies* 38 (1): 169–206.

Tullock, Gordon. 1971. "Public Decisions as Public Goods." *Journal of Political Economy* 79 (4): 913–15.

Comment on "Judicial Compensation and Performance"

J.J. Prescott *

The most significant challenges to better understanding judicial behavior are lack of data and the absence of plausible exogenous variation in judicial environments. The random assignment of judges to
cases has admittedly been helpful in gaining traction on the effects
of judicial decisions (e.g., Dobbie, Goldin, and Yang 2018). Yet devel-
oping a full empirical account of "what judges maximize" (Posner
1993) would require a setting in which judges are randomly subjected
to a wide variety of (real-world) environments with different costs,
constraints, and rewards. This prospect remains pie in the sky, but
that does not mean that we have not made some headway on the
ground. For instance, researchers have deployed the random assignment of cases to judges to back out how judges respond to differences
in case attributes when the characteristics of cases (e.g., severity) can be
assessed ex ante (Leibovitch 2016) and to attempt to gauge how judicial
decision making evolves over the course of the day or in response to an
empty stomach (Danziger, Levav, and Avnaim-Pesso 2011; Weinshall-
Margel and Shapard 2011). These lines of research, however, have more
to say about when judges depart from the merits of cases than about which
traditional institutional features (e.g., compensation, selection) enhance judicial effort and improve accuracy.

In "Judicial Compensation and Performance," DeAngelo and Mc-
Cannon (2017) seek to make progress on the question of what judges
maximize by, first, collecting detailed appellate data from New York
slip opinions and, second, exploiting plausibly exogenous variation in

* University of Michigan Law School.

Electronically published: December 5, 2018

judicial compensation between 2007 and 2017 to better understand judicial behavior. The data assembled for the article are valuable in and of themselves, but the idea of using a sharp discontinuity in state-level pay to explore the role that financial compensation plays in judicial effort and performance is also a meaningful methodological contribution. By comparing patterns in outcomes—specifically, accuracy, in the form of decisions being "upheld"—of three sets of judges, with a focus on those judges serving before and after the shift in compensation, the authors aim to distinguish between two theories for why the accuracy of judicial decisions might improve after a pay increase: (1) better jurists choose to serve as judges when compensation is more generous and/or (2) jurists simply work harder when they are better compensated. With respect to the latter possibility, the authors briefly postulate an efficiency-wage hypothesis in which better compensated judges choose to work harder for fear of losing their position during the next election, but the article is largely agnostic about precisely why higher wages might lead to better outcomes.[1]

DeAngelo and McCannon's (2017) decision to approach their work atheoretically has costs, however. Although little of their article appears to turn on the precise relationship between compensation and effort, there are at least two ways in which their not being more explicit about the possible characteristics and fundamental nature of this relationship has resulted in missed opportunities.

First, more theoretical precision would have allowed the authors to distinguish between different competing theories of judicial effort (i.e., efficiency wages versus reciprocity). The "shirking model" version of the efficiency-wage hypothesis they cite (Shapiro and Stiglitz 1984) depends on employees fearing the consequences of shirking. In this context, low effort equates to a higher probability of being made to leave the bench and find employment elsewhere. The authors' data are from New York, a state that is geographically diverse, and therefore one that presumably presents very different employment opportunities for former judges in New York City than may be available in Ithaca or Phoenicia. If judicial salaries are constant statewide, then the potential loss from shirking (exogenously) varies from jurisdiction to jurisdiction with this variation in outside options. If the authors were to detect differences in outcomes that align with these different environments, they would have a much stronger case for an efficiency-wage hypothesis relative to other hypotheses (e.g., some versions of reciprocity theory). One can also imagine similar empirical strategies

---

[1] In a footnote, the authors also allow for a reciprocity theory in which judges exert more effort following a salary increase simply to reciprocate the state's decision to compensate them more generously.

taking advantage of political polarization and geographic concentration. It must be the case that many trial judges realistically face no
possibility of electoral challenge, despite needing the endorsement
of a partisan nominating convention.[2]

Second, more theoretical precision would have nudged the authors
to scrutinize their otherwise intuitive measure of performance—the
likelihood that a judge's decision is upheld on appeal. An efficiency-
wage hypothesis implicitly incorporates a theory of termination and
thus an understanding of the terms and conditions of judicial positions generally. The authors recognize this, and we learn that judges
have rather long terms in New York—10 or 14 years, depending on
the court—and are generally subject to partisan elections. Assuming that
most judges expect to seek reelection, the critical question becomes,
What sort of performance is likely to generate electoral victory?[3]

It is not obvious—and may even run against expectations—that
avoiding reversals in criminal cases is how a judge best pursues reelection.[4] For one, if avoiding reversals is truly the goal, studying criminal
appeals may be inappropriate, given the asymmetry in criminal appeal
rights. A judge can avoid reversal entirely by granting motions of acquittal for insufficient evidence (which prosecutors generally cannot
appeal), and so might do this in cases with well-represented defendants to avoid reversal. This would produce a correlation between
electoral motivation and the rate at which decisions are upheld, but
that correlation would be the result of judges manipulating the composition of the appellate docket and would actually be a sign that
greater incentives lead to additional distortions rather than additional
effort. The politics of criminal justice, however, seem more likely to

[2] One response to this point is that it also implies that the article's empirical results would be even stronger if the authors categorized only judges facing heightened
incentives as receiving the treatment. The authors' case would benefit from exploring
this idea explicitly. One concern with this possibility is that the estimated effect sizes
are already quite large, which points to either extreme shirking in the preperiod or a
spurious relationship in the data.

[3] Exogenous variation in the number of years until reelection and the demographic
characteristics that are themselves exogenously correlated with a judge's likelihood of being
interested in reelection (e.g., age) are also available to probe the robustness of the efficiency-
wage hypothesis. Note that judicial terms in New York are long. The authors report
that judges are reelected on average approximately only once, hinting that a large percentage of New York judges are indifferent to their reelection chances because they are in their
second term, close to retirement, etc. Presenting data on the frequency with which judges
seek reelection and/or retire in the middle of a term would have been very useful for better
understanding judicial employment dynamics in New York.

[4] DeAngelo and McCannon (2017) ought to be able to empirically assess, for instance, whether judges in New York, all else equal, are more likely to lose a bid for
reelection if they are reversed relatively more often.

be consistent with a different dynamic. Judges are purportedly rewarded in many places for being "tough" on criminal defendants. If true, a judge seeking reelection might favor the prosecution more aggressively to the point of becoming *more* likely to be reversed, on average. Moreover, judges might be just fine with being reversed in particular cases. An appeals court refusing to uphold a trial court's punitive treatment of a criminal defendant might be political gold when the district court judge below wants to signal to the public that he or she is concerned first and foremost with public safety or that, unlike many "out-of-touch" judges, he or she is more interested in "the truth" than procedural niceties.[5]

If one accepts that there is an empirical relationship between the sharp increase in judicial wages in New York beginning in 2012 and judicial "effort" as measured by an increase in the likelihood a conviction is upheld, one can still profitably ask how we ought to interpret such a finding. Although a sharp discontinuity in judicial wages is more salient to all concerned, and any association with behavioral outcomes is both easier to detect and more likely to be causal, its use also raises a few difficult questions.

First, a sharp, politics-driven, media-reported increase in judicial wages may be endogenous to judicial behavior, perhaps a response to declining judicial performance or quality, followed by subsequent regression to the mean.[6] Although a sharp discontinuity initially presents as an ideal situation in which to study the effects of compensation on judicial performance, judicial salary changes that occur according to a predetermined formula or a standardized procedure established without reference to recent judicial behavior may allow for findings that are more amenable to a causal interpretation.

Second, exploiting a significant, salient, and apparently long-overdue increase in compensation raises important questions about precisely what the authors are measuring—and, ultimately, whether the article provides valuable lessons on how to reduce judicial error. Put another way, does DeAngelo and McCannon's (2017) analysis teach us about the effect of wages on judicial behavior or, instead, the effect of a *change* in wages on judicial behavior? An increase in compensation, especially a large one, is infused with many other meanings (e.g., a showing of respect to the employee or a recognition of the employee's inequality aversion) that would not accompany stable wages at a higher

---

[5] The authors could explore this idea empirically in their data by looking to see whether appeal rates (without trial-level data, the authors would need to assume a constant flow of a cases) and reversal rates vary for trial judges over the tenure cycle.

[6] DeAngelo and McCannon's (2017) theory also suggests that we should observe an increasing trend in reversals prior to the 2012 raise because judges' real wages were declining steadily (at least in relative terms) during that period.

level many years later. A simple efficiency-wage hypothesis imagines a constant effect of the higher salary over time, whereas the effect of a change in wages would presumably diminish over time (although one can imagine alternative theories). DeAngelo and McCannon's figure 2 seems at odds with both theories, assuming the figure shows the timing of the trial judge's behavior along the x-axis. The figure reveals a slow increase over time with, at best, relatively small effects at the outset—notwithstanding the large and salient increase in compensation at that time. One explanation might be that it takes judges time to respond or that higher effort levels only make a difference in cases initiated after the rise in compensation. On this latter score, it is worth observing that judicial wages continued to increase after 2012. DeAngelo and McCannon do not use this variation in their work, but a model of effort in which judicial compensation had to cross some threshold, one not crossed in New York until years after 2012, might explain the patterns in their data.[7]

The New York slip opinions that DeAngelo and McCannon (2017) have collected and coded for their analysis will be of considerable value for future research. Nevertheless, the data do have important limitations. First and foremost, the authors' data include solely appellate-level decisions, meaning that we cannot know how the underlying population of cases evolved over time—perhaps in reaction to policy changes, although it seems unlikely that an increase in judicial salaries would alter criminal behavior or prosecutorial charging decisions (unless prosecutors also experienced a contemporaneous change in compensation).[8] More generally, the composition of appellate cases may have evolved over the sample period in unobservable (or at least unobserved) ways. Future researchers using these data would likely benefit by examining crime, arrest, charging, and trial court data in New York for compositional change. DeAngelo and McCannon do attempt to control for such selection in their work but do so by including likely endogenous re-

---

[7] DeAngelo and McCannon do not use the size or timing of the salary increases (other than the timing of the first increase) in their analysis. This makes how best to interpret their results less obvious and seems to leave a significant amount of useful information on the table. Thinking about how to assess a 12-year lull in salary increases and then a subsequent catch-up requires context, including an understanding of how unusual this pattern is for state employees and whether New York judges suffered alone or with other fellow civil servants.

[8] DeAngelo and McCannon also ought to have clarified whether and how New York's appellate judges were affected by the salary increases evaluated in the article. The outcome of interest is necessarily a function of both the trial judge's performance and the appellate judge's performance. Even if appellate judges are assigned randomly to lower-court decisions, significant effort and selection effects at the appellate level would alter the interpretation of the authors' findings.

gressors—for example, whether the case involved a trial or a guilty plea, the number of days between judgment and appeal, and the grounds for appeal. Given the power of trial court judges to influence these case dimensions, they are best categorized as outcomes themselves. By controlling for them, the authors introduce potential bias into their primary estimates of interest.

REFERENCES

Danziger, Shai, Jonathan Levav, and Lieora Avnaim-Pesso. 2011. "Extraneous Factors in Judicial Decisions." *Proceedings of the National Academy of Sciences* 108 (17): 6889–92.

DeAngelo, Gregory, and Bryan C. McCannon. 2017. "Judicial Compensation and Performance." *Supreme Court Economic Review* 25:129–48.

Dobbie, Will, Jacob Goldin, and Crystal S. Yang. 2018. "The Effects of Pretrial Detention on Conviction, Future Crime, and Employment: Evidence from Randomly Assigned Judges." *American Economic Review* 108 (2): 201–40.

Leibovitch, Adi. 2016. "Relative Judgments." *Journal of Legal Studies* 45 (2): 281–330.

Posner, Richard A. 1993. "What Do Judges Maximize? (The Same Thing Everybody Else Does)." *Supreme Court Economic Review* 3 (1): 1–41.

Shapiro, Carl, and Joseph E. Stiglitz. 1984. "Equilibrium Unemployment as a Worker Discipline Device." *American Economic Review* 74 (3): 433–44.

Weinshall-Margel, Keren, and John Shapard. 2011. "Overlooked Factors in the Analysis of Parole Decisions." *Proceedings of the National Academy of Sciences* 108 (42): E833.

Error and Regulatory Risk in Financial Institution Regulation

*Jonathan Macey**

This article provides a rationale for why past and present efforts to regulate systemic risk have failed to create incentives for bankers to limit their own excessive risk taking. Specifically, the bureaucratic proclivity to systemize and generalize regulation leads large, systemically important financial institutions to conduct business and to analyze risk in a single, uniform way. This proclivity generates error and has the unintended consequence of increasing systemic risk in the economy by causing a herding effect. In other words, by reducing the heterogeneity of firm behavior in an economy, regulation—even regulation aimed at reducing systemic risk—often increases such risk. The second insight is that rational regulators will be averse to type I risk, which is defined as the perceived risk that a systemically important financial institution will be mischaracterized as nonsystemically important and left underregulated. The professional consequences of such an error in categorization would be significant for the regulator or bureaucracy making such an error, and therefore regulators will attempt to avoid this type of error at all costs. Type II error occurs when regulators characterize institutions that are not systemically important as being systemically important. There are few bureaucratic consequences for regulators

* Yale Law School. I am grateful for helpful comments from Ian Ayres, Roberta Romano, and participants in the Yale Law School Faculty Workshop and anonymous referees.

Electronically published: December 4, 2018

who commit this type of error. As such, type I risk leads to the overcategorization of financial firms as systemically risky, which leads to homogeneous regulation and herding. These problems exacerbate the ongoing dialectic between government, which seeks to control excessive risk taking, and the banking sector, which seeks to engage in such risk taking because the owners of the firms in this sector can diversify their holdings and thereby obtain the rewards of such risk taking without experiencing the consequences.

It is the duty of the United States to provide a means by which the periodic panics which shake the American Republic and do it enormous injury shall be stopped.

—Robert L. Owen[1]

1. INTRODUCTION

What is now known as the "Financial Crisis" (see, e.g., Havemann 2009) has been analyzed from virtually every conceivable perspective, from the committed free market to the Marxian view.[2] The single point of agreement is that the crisis represents what was "at root a massive failure of regulatory practice" (Froud et al. 2012, 35). As usual, the government's response was to reaffirm its role as the chief strategist in the government's new jihad against financial crisis (see, e.g., Rivlin 2009; US Department of the Treasury 2009), calling regulators before congressional committees and asking them to explain what

---

[1] Robert L. Owen was chairman of the Committee on Banking and Currency, US Senate, 1913–19 (Carlson and Wheelock 2012, 1).

[2] This financial crisis has many names, including "The Great Recession," "The Financial Crisis of 2007–8," "The 2008 Financial Crisis," and "The Global Financial Crisis." In this article, I will refer to the financial crisis that reached its crescendo in 2008 as the "Financial Crisis." On the free market, e.g., Peter Wallison (2009) has argued persistently that government intervention in free markets is to blame for the Financial Crisis. Wallison (2009) posits that "government policies and especially the Community Reinvestment Act (CRA) and the affordable housing mission that Fannie Mae and Freddie Mac were charged with fulfilling, are to blame for the financial crisis. Regulators also deserve blame for lowering lending standards that then contributed to riskier homeownership and the housing bubble" (1); see also Wallison (2011); Calomiris and Wallison (2008), who blamed the crisis on government interference with markets. On the Marxian, e.g., Peter Burnham (2010) argues that the Financial Crisis is "an aspect of the constitution of capital and of the process of the accumulation of capital itself," and that the "growing and chronic separation between financial (fictitious) accumulation and productive accumulation is the key to understanding the latest crisis of capital expressed as a global credit crunch." Burnham concludes that "Marx opens the door to the development of an overtly 'political' theory of crisis stressing the 'capitalist use of crisis' as a means for the violent reassertion of the fundamental class relation" (27).

they are doing to reduce systemic risk in the capital markets.[3] A major casualty of the Financial Crisis was the decades-long commitment to treat financial markets regulation as relatively apolitical and to leave the details of regulation in the hands of technocrats (Froud et al. 2012). Starting with Congress's rejection of the first version of the Troubled Assets Recovery Program (TARP), the Financial Crisis allowed politicians to replace bureaucrats at the center of financial markets regulation (see, e.g., Paulson 2010; Swagel 2009). After the crisis, "Debates about regulation shifted arenas: They were no longer confined to the domain of low politics, populated by technocrats, but were the subject of investigation by elected politicians, and the stuff of front pages rather than financial pages" (Froud et al. 2012, 37).

Statutes that address systemic risk aimed at avoiding financial crisis have a long history.[4] Such regulation emerges during times of crisis like flooding after a storm. For a time, bureaucratic action takes a back seat to political action. And sweeping new laws and regulations in the financial sector can be premised, justified, and even enacted on the ground that they mitigate systemic risk of the kind that manifests during a financial crisis.[5]

---

[3] See, e.g., *Mitigating Systemic Risk in the Financial Markets through Wall Street Reforms: Before the United States Senate Comm. on Banking, Housing, and Urban Affairs*, 113th Cong. (2013) (testimony of Mary Jo White, Chair, Securities and Exchange Commission).

[4] These statutes have developed over more than half a century; see, e.g., Federal Deposit Insurance Act of 1950, 12 U.S.C. § 1811 (deposit insurance); Federal Deposit Insurance Act, Pub. L. No. 81-797, 64 Stat. 873 (part of the Banking Act of 1933, amending the Federal Reserve Act of 1913 [1950]) (deposit insurance); 12 C.F.R. 5 (rules, policies, and procedures for corporate activities); 12 C.F.R. 100 (rules applicable to savings associations); Office of the Comptroller of the Currency (2018; entry requirements including licensing); Office of the Comptroller of the Currency (2017; restrictions on services and product lines); Board of Governors of the Federal Reserve System, Federal Deposit Insurance Corporation, and Office of the Comptroller of the Currency (2014b; liquidity requirements); Elliott (2014; liquidity requirements); 12 U.S.C. § 461(b) (reserve requirements); Board of Governors of the Federal Reserve System (2017; reserve requirements); Feinman (1993; reserve requirements); 12 U.S.C. § 371(a) (interest rate ceilings on deposit accounts); 12 C.F.R. 217 (interest rate ceilings on deposit accounts preventing banks from paying interest on certain accounts from 1933 until 2011); 12 U.S.C. § 371(c) (restrictions on intracorporate transactions); 12 U.S.C. § 343(3)(A)-(B) (restrictions on intracorporate transactions); Dodd-Frank Wall Street Reform and Consumer Protection Act, Pub. L. No. 111-203, 124 Stat. 1376 (2010) (special liquidation and distress resolution rules).

[5] Restrictions on intracorporate transactions, special liquidation and distress resolution rules, and other aspects of financial system architecture are all justified in whole or in part on the grounds that they reduce systemic risk, as are many of the operations of central banks, particularly on the grounds that they make liquidity available to financial institutions in times of crisis in their capacity as lenders of last resort.

For political scientists, the Financial Crisis is an important phenomenon because it was "a multinational and international . . . failure of many different regulatory regimes, configured in many different institutional ways, in many different political environments, and exhibiting many different regulatory cultures" (Froud et al. 2012, 44). This article seeks to advance our understanding of the interaction between systemic risk and the law by showing how the laws and regulations that emerged in the wake of the crisis are being shaped and twisted by entrenched bureaucratic culture and private bureaucratic interests. Until these pathologies are better understood, legislative initiatives to control systemic risk are not likely to be successful. This article consists of two parts.

With respect to bureaucratic culture, in section 2 of this article, I argue that the bureaucratic proclivity toward regularity, which manifests itself in the commitment to standardized procedures that treat like cases alike, actually increases systemic risk by causing herding among regulated financial institutions that greatly magnifies the effects of regulator error. In this part of the article, I also show that the Dodd-Frank Wall Street Reform and Consumer Protection Act (Dodd-Frank), the major legislative response to the crisis, errs because it has made the herding problem worse, not better.[6] In Dodd-Frank, as in previous regulatory efforts to control systemic risk, the penchant for treating like cases alike exacerbates systemic risk in two ways: by stifling innovation of risk reduction technologies and by reducing and sometimes eliminating the critical heterogeneity in business practices that reduces systemic risk.

With respect to the bureaucratic proclivity for blame avoidance, I argue in section 3 of this article that this characteristic manifests itself in regulators' inevitable and strong incentives to avoid, at almost all costs, *type I error*, defined as rejecting a true null hypothesis (e.g., "The failure of Bank A will cause the collapse of the economic system"). In contrast, an example of type II error would be to falsely hypothesize that the failure of a bank will cause the failure of the financial system. Bureaucrats strongly prefer the side of committing type II error and avoiding type I error (a phenomenon I call "type I error avoidance"). The antipathy of regulators to committing type I error results in overinclusive regulation and excessive caution on the part of judges and regulators.

The point is not that regulators are inept. Quite the opposite is true. The analysis in this article indicates that honest, objective, well-

---

[6] Dodd-Frank Wall Street Reform and Consumer Protection Act, Pub. L. No. 111-203, 124 Stat. 1376 (2010).

meaning regulators attempting to regulate systemic risk are likely to fail (or even more likely to fail) if they do not recognize these short-comings. These shortcomings should be taken into account when regulating and lead to different approaches to regulation. In particular, I argue that failing to understand the inherent challenges of systemic risk regulation makes the government itself an inadvertent source of systemic risk.

Nor is the point that regulation is pointless. In fact, the production of systemic risk by individual firms in the economy is a paradigmatic example of the sort of negative externality that justifies regulatory intervention—Acharya et al. (2013) argued that "by its very nature, systemic risk is a negative externality" (178). But as with global warming and perhaps other systemic problems, the fact that financial institutions present broad risks with dire consequences that are not internalized by those who make fortunes by generating such risk does not mean, unfortunately, that there is a known way to ameliorate these consequences.

2. TREATING LIKE CASES ALIKE

In this section, the core of the argument is that the entrenched legal norm of treating like cases alike, and similarly situated firms and similarly situated people similarly, clashes with the principle of diversification as a means of risk reduction and increases systemic risk. The point is that if firms are required by regulation to behave similarly, particularly where there is great uncertainty about the consequences of their behavior, systemic risk will increase because firms' private heterogeneous responses to market conditions will be replaced by lockstep, industry-wide responses. Such industry-wide responsive actions actually create systemic risk because the failure of particular strategies becomes industry-wide rather than firm specific.

2.1. Risk-Based Capital

In the intensely regulated banking sector, the regulation of bank capital is considered to be the most important form of regulation there is.[7] In light of the critical need to have meaningful regulation of bank

---

[7] "Capital is the foundation on which a bank's balance sheet is built" (Hoenig 2012). As used here, the term "capital" refers to the total value of a bank's assets minus the amount of debt and other commitments that the bank has a contractual commitment to repay. Capital is important because it represents the funds available as a cushion or buffer against insolvency in case the value of the bank's assets declines or its liabilities rise. The following example represents the role of bank capital in avoiding bank fail-

capital, there also is strong consensus that bank capital levels must be harmonized internationally to avoid harmful "races to the bottom" and the concomitant unfair competitive advantage that banks in regulatory regimes with low required levels of capital are perceived to enjoy (Simmons 2001). Another entrenched norm in banking regulation is that capital requirements should be risk-based such that capital levels for various classes of assets should reflect the riskiness of those assets, with higher capital levels required for riskier assets than for less risky assets—Grenadier and Hall (1995) wrote that "bank risk-based capital (RBC) standards require banks to hold differing amounts of capital for different classes of assets, based almost entirely on a credit risk criterion" (1). Adoption of risk-based capital standards is universal among the G-10 countries and in the European Union, and these standards have been adopted in hundreds of other countries as well (Tarbert 2000).[8]

The need for harmonization reflects the fact that capital in the form of equity is expensive relative to other forms of funding. Because of the expense of adding equity to a bank's balance sheet, left unregulated, banks will fund themselves disproportionately with debt (that is often subsidized by government deposit insurance) and abjure the accumulation and maintenance of capital. Although Franco Modigliani and Merton Miller (1958) have shown that, under certain conditions, altering the mix of debt and equity on a firm's balance sheet does not affect the firm's overall cost of capital and therefore debt-equity ratios are irrelevant, a variety of institutional features of the banking industry combine to create a financial environment in which equity is very costly relative to debt. For example, Karlo Kauko (2011) of the Bank of Finland argues that the Modigliani-Miller irrelevance theorem is not valid for

---

ure. Suppose that a bank has $100 of loans outstanding, funded by $92 of deposits and $8 of common stock invested by the bank's owners, resulting in $8 or an 8% capital level on a non-risk-adjusted basis. This $8 is available to protect creditors (including depositors) against losses. If $7 worth of the loans were not repaid, there would be $1 with which to repay the bank's depositors without having to draw on the government's deposit insurance fund, although the shareholders would suffer a loss in the value of their equity of 87.5% (from $8 to $1) (Elliott 2010). Tarullo (2008, 15) wrote that "over the past 25 years . . . capital adequacy requirements have become the most important type of regulation designed to protect safety and soundness." In addition, Elliott (2010) noted that "there is a strong consensus among policymakers that there need to be higher minimum capital requirements for banks in order to foster a more stable financial system and to help avoid the recurrence of a financial crisis of the magnitude of the recent one."

[8] The G-10 consists of the "ten industrial nations that agreed in 1962 to lend money to the International Monetary Fund. They are Belgium, Canada, France, Italy, Japan, Netherlands, Sweden, Germany, the United Kingdom, and the United States" (Scott and Wellons 1999, 1239). Tarbert (2000) discussed the countries that have adopted the Basel Capital Accords.

banks because banks' balance sheets are opaque and, as such, banks face a "need to pay high dividends in order to signal good asset quality even in a bad state." Banks keep capital levels low to reduce the burden of paying the high dividends required by a heavy reliance on equity funding: "Unlike in other industries, not paying the expected dividend may trigger a deposit run" (Kauko 2011).

More straightforwardly, Franklin Allen, Elena Carletti, and Robert Marquez (2014) have shown that where bank deposits are insured, funding projects with insured debt becomes so inexpensive that banks "no longer have any incentive to hold capital, instead choosing to finance themselves entirely with deposits" (3; see also DeAngelo and Stulz 2013; Berger, Herring, and Szego 1995).

There is reason to believe that banks will try to reduce capital levels where possible, and secular declines in bank capital are considered a major causal and exacerbating factor in the Financial Crisis. Specifically, between 1999 and 2007, the banking industry's tangible equity to tangible asset ratio declined from 5.2% to 3.8%, and for the 10 largest banking firms it was only 2.8% in 2007 (Hoenig 2012). Of immediate relevance to the point in this part of the article about the destructive herding effects of treating like cases alike, the total risk-based capital ratio of the 10 largest firms remained relatively high at around 11%, an apparently anomalous state of affairs that was achieved by shrinking assets using ever more favorable risk weights to adjust the regulatory balance sheet (Hoenig 2012).

Strong empirical support for the point made by Allen et al. (2014) lies in the historical evidence. Prior to the founding of the Federal Reserve System in 1913 and the Federal Deposit Insurance Corporation (FDIC) in 1933, when bank equity levels were primarily market driven rather than a by-product of regulatory incentives, the US banking industry's ratio of tangible equity to assets ranged between 13% and 16%, regardless of bank size (Hoenig 2012).

Thus, although risk-based capital rules seem desirable in theory, in a world characterized by uncertainty and error, actually applying these principles is fraught with danger. The problem arises when the risk of a particular asset class is underestimated so that capital levels are set too low. This may occur because regulators erroneously interpret historical information about default rates, or because they overestimate the efficacy of hedging or other risk-reduction techniques, or because they succumb to political pressure to favor certain asset classes, such as home mortgages or securitized assets.

To illustrate the risk-exacerbating role of risk-based capital requirements, consider the following example. Imagine a bank with four classes of assets: (1) cash and US government-issued Treasury notes, (2) mortgage-backed securities issued by the government-sponsored entity the Federal National Mortgage Association (FNMA; Fannie Mae), (3) single-family mortgages that are held on the bank's balance sheet, and (4) commercial loans.[9] Using the risk-based capital rules in place at the time of the Financial Crisis, the risk-weighted capital guidelines would mandate that the bank maintain the levels of capital shown in table 1.

The risk weightings are used to adjust asset size on the basis of risk. On a non-risk-adjusted basis, the firm's total assets are $4,000. A bank would have to maintain minimum capital of $320 to comply with an 8% minimum capital requirement.[10] In contrast, on a risk-adjusted basis, $320 in capital reflects a capital level not of 8% but of an impressive 19%.[11] If the hypothetical bank in this example were required to comply only with a risk-weighted capital requirement of 8%, the bank would be able to reduce its total level of capital by 58%, from $320 to $136.

A profit-maximizing bank subject to risk-based capital regulation would reduce its capital level by $184 (from $320 to $136), replacing the lost equity with debt in the form of government-insured deposits. As can be seen in this example, the risk-based capital guidelines that were in place leading up to the Financial Crisis created industrywide incentives for banks to favor the purchase of residential mortgage-backed securities (RMBSs) issued by FNMA over commercial loans and other loan categories with identical risk-return characteristics. By purchasing assets with low risk weights (20%), banks increased profitability by decreasing their cost of capital.

Thus, risk-based capital requirements increased banks' demand for assets that were subject to low risk weights and high returns. Modern portfolio theory teaches that rational investors should assemble an *efficient portfolio*, one with expected returns to investors that generate the highest return for any given level of risk. In capital markets, obtaining higher returns requires accepting higher levels of risk.

Because returns are correlated with risk, in that higher returns are required to attract investors to higher risk investments, risk-based capital requirements incentivized banks to move into risky asset-backed securities in the form of RMBSs. In the absence of risk-based capital insurance, banks would have more fully internalized the costs of holding

---

[9] FNMA is a private, publicly traded company created in 1938 by Congress to improve opportunities to obtain housing finance and thus homeownership. FNMA supplements housing finance by purchasing housing loans from lenders who can then make additional loans with the proceeds of the purchase. FNMA finances its purchases by issuing debt and by selling in securitized form the loans it has purchased (see FNMA 2014, 1).

[10] $4,000 \times 0.08 = \$320$.

[11] $\$320 / \$1,700 = 0.1882$

Table 1.   Mandated Levels of Capital To Be Maintained by the Bank

		ASSET VALUE ($)	
ASSET CLASS	RISK WEIGHT (%)	Total	Risk Adjusted
Cash and US government-issued Treasury notes	0	1,000	0
Mortgage-backed securities issued by FNMA	20	1,000	200
Single-family mortgages held on the bank's balance sheet	50	1,000	500
Commercial loans	100	1,000	1,000
Total		4,000	1,700
Simple capital ratio/risk-adjusted capital ratio (assuming capital of $320)		8%	18.82%

risky assets, and banks would have been indifferent to the particular identity of the assets on their balance sheet. Risk-adjusted capital rules had the effect of herding banks into mortgage-backed securities and therefore exacerbated the consequences of the collapse of the housing market and likely caused, or at least contributed to, the asset bubble in real estate by artificially increasing the demand for home mortgages due to the subsidized borrowing costs caused by risk-based deposit insurance premiums.

In 2004, the Office of Federal Housing Enterprise Oversight imposed greater capital requirements on FNMA's securitized mortgage products. This might have led to a decline in demand for RMBSs, but in the same year, the Basel II international capital accords were passed. The 2004 Basel II rules reduced risk-based capital levels for home mortgages for banks from the 50% level required by Basel I, to levels ranging from 15% to 35%, which incentivized banks to create special-purpose vehicles that could issue mortgage-backed securities on their own. These entities securitized mortgages made to low-income people and to borrowers who chose not to document their income and net worth on their loan applications.

To avoid systemic events, regulators should eschew regulations that lead to the natural diversification in the economy that is generated by the uncoordinated profit-seeking activities of innovative competitors. Risk-based capital guidelines had the opposite effect. These rules exacerbated systemic risk by creating incentives for profit-maximizing firms to all pursue the same strategy—investing in the mortgage-backed securities that lay at the heart of the Financial Crisis.

As a consulting firm with a substantial financial-sector practice has observed, "The most recent financial crisis has brought into question previous views that capital in the financial sector had been both adequate and adequately regulated" (Buehler, Samandari, and Mazingo 2009, 2). The primary regulatory response to the dissatisfaction with the pre-Financial Crisis focus on risk-based capital was for regulators to reemphasize simple leverage ratios. Leading up to the Financial Crisis, regulation focused on risk-based capital, and particularly on the ratio of tier 1 capital to risk-weighted assets.[12] After the Financial Crisis, there was a renewed regulatory emphasis on non-risk-adjusted capital levels (generally known as "leverage ratios"), or the simple ratio of tier 1 capital to total assets. The goal of leverage ratios is to put a ceiling on the buildup of overall leverage in the banking sector (Sun and Tong 2015). Globally, the Basel III framework sets the minimum leverage ratio at 3%, but in July 2013, the US authorities announced that the minimum leverage ratio would be raised to 6% for systemically important US banks (Sun and Tong 2015).[13]

Leverage ratios are not a complete answer to the problem of asset herding identified in this article. The regulatory error reflected in leverage ratios is that they require the same amount of capital for assets regardless of their risk, which, in essence, penalizes banks for holding safe assets and rewards them for holding risky assets. This is because leverage ratios require banks to hold risky assets to improve profitability and returns on assets because of the trade-off between risk and return. If two banks have identical balance sheets, and they cannot increase leverage (reduce capital) because of the leverage ratio, they will be required to shift their investments into riskier classes of assets to increase profitability. And because the postcrash capital rules do not eliminate or reduce the risk-based capital requirements, the herding ef-

---

[12] The main component of Tier 1 capital is common shareholders' equity, including retained earnings (see FDIC 2018).

[13] Regulatory Capital Rules: Regulatory Capital, Implementation of Basel III, Capital Adequacy, Transition Provisions, Prompt Corrective Action, Standardized Approach for Risk-Weighted Assets, Market Discipline and Disclosure Requirements, Advanced Approaches Risk-Based Capital Rule, and Market Risk Capital Rule, 78 Fed. Reg. 55340 (Sep. 10, 2013). All banks with $50 billion or more in assets are deemed systemically important under Dodd-Frank; see § 165(d), 124 Stat. at 1377; see also, *Systemically Important Financial Institutions and the Dodd-Frank Act: Before the Subcomm. on Financial Institutions and Consumer Credit, Comm. on Financial Services, US House of Representatives*, 112th Cong. (2012) (testimony of Michael S. Gibson, Director, Division of Banking Supervision and Regulation, FDIC).

fect that occurs when funds are shifted to higher risk asset classes will be exacerbated.

Previous accounts of the role of risk-based capital requirements have focused on errors that were made in assigning risk categories (see, e.g., Calem and LaCour-Little 2004). It appears highly unlikely that simple mistake accounts for the low-risk rating assigned to mortgage loans and mortgage derivatives. Rather, political pressure appears to explain this problem (Macey 2000a, 2000b). Attributing the cause of the errors in assigning risk categories is relevant for this article because it indicates that the problem is not susceptible to being solved by better data or stronger analytics. To address systemic risk, changes must occur in the industrial structure of the banking industry that not only degrade the ability of banks to influence, capture, and control their regulators but also increase the number of competitors in the capital markets and shadow banking sector of the economy so that business practices become more heterogeneous.[14]

2.2. "Skin in the Game": Dodd-Frank's Retention Rules

In traditional retail banking, banks would lend money to people to purchase houses, cars, and other items and then retain those loans on their balance sheets.[15] Banks' profits largely were determined by the spread between the relatively low cost of consumer deposits (especially those that were FDIC insured) and the higher returns received on the loan payments from borrowers—Hoenig and Morris (2012) described the "traditional banking model of making loans and holding them to maturity [to] earn profits from loan-deposit rate spreads."

As technology improved and markets developed, this business model, which focused on interest spreads, was replaced by a new model, known as the "originate-to-distribute" model, in which banks earned fees rather than spreads. These fees were generated by making loans, bundling them together into asset-backed securities, and then selling those securities.[16]

Because securitization inevitably results in moving assets off of a bank's balance sheet, banks that sold loans in securitizations rather

[14] Macey and Holdcroft (2011) argued in favor of breaking up the banks to curb their political power.

[15] For an observation of the history of deposits by banks to fund loans, see Bord and Santos (2012). In addition, Rosen (2010) described the "traditional model that combines originating a loan with holding it to maturity."

[16] See Bord and Santos (2012), describing the move from the traditional originate-to-hold business model to the originate-to-distribute model; see also Rosen (2010), describing that "with the [originate-to-distribute] model, banks originate mortgages and then sell them off to be part of a securitization."

than retaining them on their balance sheets did not internalize the full costs associated with making bad loan decisions. By the time a borrower defaults, the bank has received the fees and profits from selling the loan, and the losses are borne by those who have invested in the securities rather than by the banks or loan originators who made the loan decision. The direct exposure by banks to the consequences of making bad loan decisions is called "having skin in the game." When loans were packaged as asset-backed securities, banks were said to no longer have sufficient skin in the game to make them appropriately concerned about the risks associated with those loans.

The securitization of assets and the associated diminution in skin in the game was considered to be "a glaring flaw of the asset-backed securities (ABS) market revealed by the financial crisis" (Aguilar 2014). Congress directly addressed this "glaring flaw" in Dodd-Frank by directing the federal banking agencies and the Securities and Exchange Commission jointly to prescribe regulations that require any bank or other firm engaged in securitizations to retain a material portion of the credit risk of any asset that the firm transfers, sells, or conveys to a third party through the issuance of an asset-backed security. As Chris Dodd, a principal architect of the bill, opined, "When securitizers [sic] retain a material amount of risk, they have 'skin in the game,' aligning their economic interests with those of investors in asset-backed securities."[17] Securitizers who retain risk have a strong incentive to monitor the quality of the assets they purchase from originators, package into securities, and sell.[18] Dodd-Frank went even further, prohibiting securitizers from hedging or otherwise transferring the credit risk they are required to retain.[19] The goal of the statute was to require "securitizers to retain an economic interest in a material portion of the credit risk for any asset that securitizers transfer, sell, or convey to a third party. This 'skin in the game' requirement will create incentives that encourage sound lending practices, restore investor confidence, and permit securitization markets to resume their important role as sources of credit for households and businesses."[20]

Prior to the Financial Crisis, the received wisdom about securitization was that it was an efficient means for allocating risk. For ex-

[17] 156 Cong. Rec. 3131 (daily ed. May 5, 2010); see Arnholz and Gainor (2014), 1–5.
[18] Restoring American Financial Stability Act of 2010, S. Rep. No. 111-176, §§ 37, 129 (2010).
[19] Dodd-Frank § 941, 124 Stat. at 1890–96. These "skin in the game" rules require that the rules be jointly adopted by the Office of the Comptroller of the Currency, the Board of Governors of the Federal Reserve System, the Federal Deposit Insurance Corporation, the Federal Housing Finance Agency, the Department of Housing and Urban Development, and the Securities and Exchange Commission.
[20] Restoring American Financial Stability Act, S. Rep. No. 111-176, § 37 (2010).

ample, Alan Greenspan (2004) lauded the fact that securitization moved risky assets off of the balance sheets of highly leveraged banks and onto the balance sheets of less-regulatcd, more-capitalized investors. From Greenspan's perspective, securitization was a "new [instrument] of risk dispersion" that "enabled the largest and most sophisticated banks in their credit-granting role to divest themselves of much credit risk by passing it to institutions with far less leverage." The general consensus was that, in modern capital markets characterized by the widespread securitization of assets, certain market participants could specialize in making loans, and others could specialize in investing in securitized assets. These investors could assemble diversified portfolios of assets, mixing types of securitized assets and other investments in the portfolio to reduce or eliminate firm-specific risk and shift risk to the parties best able to bear it.[21]

In other words, after 2008, policy makers' views shifted from holding securitization out as an important source of risk reduction for banks to holding securitization out as a major contributor to the excessive risk that led to the Financial Crisis. This new wisdom demanded regulatory change. Before the Financial Crisis, regulators encouraged securitization as a means for moving risky assets off of banks' balance sheets, whereas after the Financial Crisis, Congress instructed regulators to require that these same assets be kept on banks' balance sheets so that banks would have skin in the game.

As Ryan Bubb and Prasad Krishnamurthy (2015) trenchantly observed: "A requirement that securitizers retain a minimum amount of the credit risk of the assets they securitize concentrates risk. Twelve underwriters accounted for about 80% of the total volume of private-label MBS [mortgage-backed securities] issuance during the recent boom. The leading sponsors of MBS in the run-up to the crisis included many of the largest banks and broker-dealers—Lehman Brothers, Bear Stearns, Merrill Lynch, Bank of America, and Citigroup. By concentrating housing market risk on the balance sheets of such large, systemically important financial institutions, risk retention increases systemic risk" (1579).

The key insight of Bubb and Krishnamurthy (2015) is that asset bubbles are a major cause of systemic failure and that the new risk-

---

[21] Firm-specific risk, also known as "unsystematic risk," is the risk that a particular event will occur, such as bankruptcy, or the loss of a patent, or a new, narrowly targeted regulation. In contrast, systemic risk or market risk is the risk associated with an event such as a recession, or a war, or inflation, or a general change in interest rate levels. The capital asset pricing model (CAPM) shows that systemic risk cannot be eliminated, but that firm-specific risk can be eliminated through portfolio diversification (Sharpe 1964; see also Linter 1965; Tobin 1958).

retention rules embedded in Dodd-Frank and reflected in subsequent regulation "radically [undermine] the case for mandatory risk retention" (1579). The problem with the risk-retention rules is that they lead to the very behavior—herding behavior in the form of industry-wide accumulations of toxic assets—that caused the Financial Crisis in the first place.

This problem of regulation causing herding behavior can be expanded even beyond the important confines of Dodd-Frank's risk-retention rules. As we saw in the context of risk-based capital requirements, other regulations have the proclivity either to cause or to exacerbate the problem of herding. This phenomenon is ironic because, in a variety of contexts, government regulation designed to reduce systemic risk is, in fact, exacerbating such risk.

Regulation such as the risk-retention rules and the risk-based capital rules, which induce herding behavior, increase systemic risk because they lead to a lack of diversification in the portfolios of the financial institutions that are subject to these regulations. As such, these policies are inconsistent with the core analytical and empirical insight of modern portfolio theory that diversification reduces risk.

As initially developed by Harry Markowitz (1970), portfolio theory teaches that investors can reduce portfolio risk at any given level of returns through diversification. This insight is relevant in analyzing governmental action regarding risk because, as scholars long have recognized, the government, in its capacity as the recipient of corporate income taxes, is in the same economic position as an investor in a portfolio that includes all of the firms in the economy (see, e.g., Macey 2006).[22] In this capacity, the government, were it acting as a rational actor with an interest in maximizing the risk-controlled returns on its portfolio, would seek regulatory outcomes that encourage diversification.

It appears, however, that a lack of understanding of the herding effects of regulation, or a lack of comprehension of the dangers of herding itself, or both, are leading to defective regulation that increases rather than decreases systemic risk (see generally, Shojai and Feiger 2013). In the following section, I identify and explore the ways in which other widespread regulatory pathologies increase systemic risk.

2.3. The Federal Reserve's Emergency Lending Authority

The third feature of Dodd-Frank on which I focus is the reform of the Federal Reserve's primary monetary weapon in the battle against

---

[22] Berle (1991) stated that corporate income taxes make the government "virtually . . . an equal partner . . . as far as profits are concerned" (xxviii).

systemic risk: its authority to act as lender of last resort, which is contained in section 13(3) of the Federal Reserve Act.[23] It was this provision that empowered the Federal Reserve to support nonbanks as well as banks during the Financial Crisis, such as by extending a $29 billion loan to a limited liability company called Maiden Lane LLC, which was established to acquire certain assets of Bear Stearns Institutions to incentivize JPMorgan Chase & Co. to acquire Bear Stearns and to loan billions to the American Insurance Group (AIG), which was bailed out despite the fact that it was not chartered, insured, or even regulated by the federal government.[24]

Concerned that working capital loans were required to save small industrial firms during the Great Depression (Federal Reserve Board 1934), Congress added section 13(3) to the Federal Reserve Act when it enacted the Emergency Relief and Construction Act of July 1932 (Hackley 1973). Until amended by Dodd-Frank in 2010, section 13(3) empowered the Federal Reserve, "in unusual and exigent circumstances . . . to discount for any individual, partnership, or corporation, notes, drafts, and bills of exchange of the kinds and maturities made eligible for discount for member banks" (Hackley 1973, 128). The provision stipulated that before extending credit, "the Federal Reserve Bank shall obtain evidence that such individual, partnership, or corporation is unable to secure adequate credit accommodations from other banking institutions" (Hackley 1973, 128).

Prior to the Financial Crisis, section 13(3) was not used extensively (Carlson and Wheelock 2012). Until the passage of the Federal Deposit Insurance Corporation Improvement Act of 1991 (FDICIA), loans extended under section 13(3) had to be secured by collateral "of the kinds and maturities made eligible for discount for member banks under other provisions of the Act" (Hackley 1973, 222). The FDICIA removed this limitation on the Fed's lending power to nonbanks, replacing it with the same requirement that governed the Fed's cash advances to depository institutions, which was that such lending need only be secured "to the satisfaction of the Reserve" (Todd 1993, 20).

As is well known, the Financial Crisis of 2008 unleashed a massive wave of lending by the Federal Reserve under authority provided by the Federal Reserve Act's section 13(3) and other statutory provisions. By the end of the crisis, the government had provided $700 bil-

---

[23] 12 U.S.C.§ 343: "any reference in any provision of Federal law to the third undesignated paragraph of section 13 of the Federal Reserve Act [FRA] shall be deemed to be a reference to Section 13(3) of the FRA."

[24] *American International Group: Before the Committee on Financial Services, US House of Representatives*, 111th Cong. (2009) (testimony of Ben S. Bernanke, Chairman, Federal Reserve).

lion under TARP, which was used to bail out banks and two major automotive manufacturers: Chrysler and General Motors car companies. Total commitments to support the financial system amounted to $14.7 trillion, according to the *New York Times* (2011). Among these, the $53 billion bailout of AIG and the $29 billion bailout of Bear Stearns under section 13(3) were perhaps the most unpopular (*New York Times* 2011). In its bailout of AIG, the Federal Reserve provided venture capital funds to create new investment vehicles to buy and hold bad securities held or insured by AIG (*New York Times* 2011). In its bailout of Bear Stearns, the Fed bought distressed assets from Bear Stearns to facilitate its sale to JPMorgan Chase (*New York Times* 2011). By themselves, both the AIG bailout and the Bear Stearns bailout ranked alongside the bank rescue of 2008, the Great Depression, the savings and loan bailout of 1989, and the bailout of Fannie Mae and Freddie Mac as among the six largest bailouts in US history (Davis 2008).[25]

There was widespread public dissatisfaction with the bailouts, which enabled particular failed financial institutions not only to stay alive but also to pay out hundreds of millions of dollars in bonuses to top executives and traders. The bailouts seemed particularly lawless because they were not the result of general legislation but of bespoke regulatory action that funneled billions to particular financial institutions such as Bear Stearns and AIG, which were known for their excessively aggressive trading practices and lavish salary and bonus payments to top executives.

AIG was bailed out on September 17, 2008, when the government extended an $85 billion line of credit to the firm (Shinkle 2008). Under the plan, AIG was to pay $165 million in bonuses, including bonuses to be paid to traders in its Financial Products division, which was the part of the firm that sold credit insurance on derivatives in the form of the credit default swaps that "every other financial institution relied upon to 'insure' its collateralized debt obligation (CDO)" (Martin and Scotto, 2010, 4).[26] According to a *Washington Post* article, AIG offered its Financial Products division employees more than $400 million in reten-

---

[25] This was the bailout effectuated by the Emergency Economic Stabilization Act of 2008, which created TARP. The act authorized (1) the US Treasury to buy risky and nonperforming debt, such as mortgages, auto loans, and college loans, from banks; and (2) a cash infusion of $250 billion into the banking system to facilitate and encourage bank lending.

[26] A *credit default swap*, or CDS, is an ersatz insurance contract whose value rises or fall with the value of an underlying credit, such as securities backed by subprime mortgages. The CDO contract calls for the obligor (seller) of the CDO protection to pay the buyer of such protection an agreed-upon amount (often the principal and interest due on the underlying security) in the event that a stipulated "credit event" such as default or downgrade is deemed to have occurred.

tion pay, with lump sums due in March 2009 and March 2010 (Dennis 2010).

Six months later, in March 2009, bonus season rolled around and AIG's "retention bonus plan" became public. As a measure of the unpopularity and political salience of bonuses paid to Wall Street executives whose firms received bailouts: (a) President Obama pledged that he would "pursue every single legal avenue to block" (*Wall Street Journal* 2009) these bonus payments; (b) legislators introduced a bill that would have taxed the payments to Financial Products employees at 90%; and (c) the New York attorney general threatened to publicize the recipients' names, prompting executives at AIG Financial Products to hastily agree to return about $45 million in bonuses by the end of 2009, as the *Washington Post* reported (Dennis 2009).

In 2007, just before the bailout of Bear Stearns, a transaction that was said to have "rocked Wall Street and possibly permanently altered Wall Street's relationship with the government" (Robb 2008), CEO Jimmy Cayne received compensation of $34 million and became the first Wall Street CEO to own a company stake worth more than $1 billion (Kelly 2007). Thus, even though Bear Stearns did not pay bonuses in 2007, previous pay packages to Bear Stearns executives were described as "prime examples of why some critics decry corporate pay for performance" schemes that provide jacked-up pay based on unsustainable performance (Levisohn 2008). As Lucian Bebchuk, Alma Cohen, and Holger Spamann (2010) have observed, the top five executives at Bear Stearns accumulated bonus payments exceeding $300 million in the period from 2000 to the closing of the firm.

In light of the political fallout from the bailouts made pursuant to section 13(3), it is not surprising that this provision was the subject of scrutiny and, ultimately, revision in Dodd-Frank. The new version of section 13(3) was designed to prohibit one-off bailouts of individual firms and to require that regulators only effectuate bailouts on an industry-wide basis as a response to a systemic problem (Skeel 2011, 136). The new version of section 13(3) implemented by Dodd-Frank has several "rule of law" provisions intended to ensure that regulators will stop the pre-Financial Crisis practice of singling out particular firms for bespoke bailouts.

First, the Fed is now required to obtain prior written approval from the Treasury before doling out cash to troubled financial institutions.[27] As David Skeel (2011) has observed, however, this provision is likely to change little if anything about the way that bailouts are done. With regard to this particular provision, Skeel notes, "It is hard to imagine a situation in which the Treasury—the most political of agencies, whose

[27] 12 U.S.C. § 343; see 12 C.F.R. 201 (Regulation A).

head answers directly to the President—would balk at a bailout or other intervention the Fed wished to make" (136).

Second, Dodd-Frank attempts to amend section 13(3) so as to remove the Fed's "general authority to lend to an individual, partnership, or corporation and to replace that general authority with the limited authority to extend emergency credit only to participants in a program or facility with broad-based eligibility designed for the purpose of providing liquidity to the financial system."[28]

The new statutory provisions also forbid any government program or facility that is designed to remove assets from the balance sheet of a single and specific company or established for the purpose of assisting a single and specific company to avoid bankruptcy or resolution under a Federal or State insolvency proceeding, because such a program or facility "would not be considered a program or facility with broad-based eligibility."[29]

Skeel (2011) makes a reasonably convincing case that these restrictions on extraordinary loans to individual companies can be circumvented with ease:

> Dodd-Frank authorizes the Fed to guarantee the debt of banking institutions, which would give it considerable power to buttress a bank's stability. While the Fed is now prohibited from making single-company loans, it may be able to circumvent this restriction by establishing a broad-based program that just so happens to benefit a systemically important firm that is stumbling. The program could include restrictions that exclude nearly every firm other than the troubled institution, for instance, or the Fed could simply bail out the industry more broadly. As the Panic of 2008 revealed, regulatory creativity is at its height when regulators are cobbling together a bailout. Alternatively, using the leverage the Dodd-Frank Act gives them, regulators can force the peer institutions of a troubled bank to pitch in for a bailout. Several of the bailouts of recent decades were privately funded, including the bailout of Long-Term Capital Management in 1998 and a rescue package put together for Korea during roughly the same period. In the past, regulators have been forced to rely on moral suasion, and they couldn't be certain everyone would go along. (139)

Thus it is likely that the revisions to section 13(3) create the illusion that like cases will be treated alike while retaining the traditional system of permitting the Fed to engage in idiosyncratic bailouts to individual firms such as AIG and Bear Stearns. Conversely,

---

[28] Dodd-Frank § 1101(a)(2), 124 Stat. at 2113.
[29] Dodd-Frank § 1101(a)(2), 124 Stat. at 2113.

it is conceivable that section 13(3) will require system-wide bailouts and that such bailouts could replace the individualized bailouts like the Bear Stearns and AIG bailouts. Although the "rule of law" reforms to section 13(3) may have had a cathartic effect on voters disgusted with the bailout of fat-cat investment bankers and derivatives traders, it is unlikely that requiring industry-wide bailouts in place of bailouts of individual firms will reduce the future costs of bailouts.

3. FOCUSING ON THE MEASURABLE: DODD-FRANK, THE FINANCIAL STABILITY OVERSIGHT COUNCIL, AND TYPE I ERROR AVOIDANCE

Financial regulators cannot regulate institutions that pose systemic risk without first identifying which institutions pose systemic risk. This portion of the article focuses on the way that the legal system identifies which institutions pose systemic risk. Dodd-Frank created a new bureaucracy, the Financial Stability Oversight Council (FSOC), which is supposed to act as the centralized regulator of systemic risk. Dodd-Frank gave the FSOC the authority to designate certain financial companies as "systemically important financial institutions" (SIFIs), a designation that would subject such institutions to heightened regulatory scrutiny. In addition, Dodd-Frank requires that any bank holding companies with $50 billion or more in assets be categorized as systemically important and regulated by the FSOC.

On the basis of clear and accepted theories of bureaucratic behavior, one would predict that politicians' and bureaucrats' incentives would lead to the overinclusion of financial institutions on any list of institutions designated as systemically risky. This is because rational regulators who understand that they are not perfect (or that even though they are perfect themselves, they are hampered because they are not operating in an environment of perfect information) will vastly prefer committing what is known in the world of statistical hypothesis testing as type II error rather than type I error. As noted in the introduction, *type I error* is defined as rejecting an accurate null hypothesis such as, "The failure of Bank A will cause the collapse of the economic system" (Neyman and Pearson 1933a, 1933b; see, Mitchell and Jolley 2013; Lockhart 1998). In other words, type I error by the FSOC of Congress would consist of declining to designate a financial institution as systemically important even though the institution actually is systemically important. This type of error is highly visible and salient. It will be front-page news and lead to denunciations and congressional investigations. As one pundit observed, when type I error is committed, "the media pounces, the public denounces and Congress pronounces" (Miller 2010).

In contrast, regulators suffer virtually no consequences for committing errors of the type II variety. In this context, *type II error* consists of concluding that the collapse of a particular financial institution would harm the financial system when in fact it would not. This sort of error is neither visible nor salient. And because nobody notices this type of error, there are no negative consequences for a bureaucrat or an administrative agency committing this type of error.

As such, we would expect to see the FSOC and Congress designate too many and not too few financial institutions as systemically important. And this appears to be the case. As discussed in the next subsection, aversion to type I error clearly seems to explain the otherwise inexplicable automatic trigger in Dodd-Frank that causes any bank with $50 billion or more in assets to be subject to extensive new regulation.[30]

3.1. The $50 Billion Threshold for Designation of Banks as Systemically Important

In addition to the nonbanks that have been designated as SIFIs, which are discussed below, there are at present 37 bank holding companies with assets greater than $50 billion that are subject to enhanced supervision and heightened regulatory requirements (Ryan 2014). The purpose of these enhanced prudential supervision requirements is to ensure that "banks and non-banks that could generate substantial risk to the financial system by their failure . . . have a different and enhanced level of regulation applied to them" (Neiman and Olson 2014).

Financial institutions subject to the $50 billion threshold are quite heterogeneous: "They vary widely in both size and the scope of their operations, from multinational financial conglomerates to banks with narrower business lines and regional geographic scope" (Ryan 2014). In fact, there is reason to be concerned that regulatory resources have been misallocated, with too much time spent on supervision of institutions that do not pose a systemic risk and insufficient time spent on those that do (Neiman and Olson 2014). Indeed, the Federal Reserve Board implicitly acknowledged in 2014 that the $50 billion threshold was too low by setting the new supplementary leverage ratio for banks at $700 billion in assets rather than at $50 billion in assets (Board of

---

[30] Dodd-Frank § 165(a), 124 Stat. at 1423–24. Dodd-Frank requires that such institutions comply with heightened risk-based capital requirements and leverage limits, heightened liquidity requirements, heightened risk management requirements, heightened concentration limits, and be subject to annual stress tests. Such banks must also develop so called "living will" resolution plans and comply with heightened credit exposure reporting requirements.

Governors of the Federal Reserve System, Federal Deposit Insurance Corporation, and Office of the Comptroller of the Currency 2014a).

Regulators, lawmakers, and bankers have all recently taken issue with the $50 billion threshold—above which banks are considered systemically important—arguing that it subjects several less risky institutions to burdensome and unnecessary regulations (Finkle 2014). Providing evidence of the general consensus that the $50 billion threshold is too low, former representative Barney Frank, one of the architects of Dodd-Frank and among history's most enthusiastic regulators, testified before the House Banking Committee in 2015 that the $50 billion threshold should be revisited (Klein and Hall 2014). Federal Reserve Governor Dan Tarullo and Comptroller of the Currency Thomas Curry concurred in this assessment (Finkle 2014). Although identifying the appropriate threshold is difficult, raising the threshold indicative of systemic importance makes sense for two principal reasons.

First, in the context of the financial sector and the economy as a whole, banks with assets of $50 billion are relatively small. This is due to the fact that the industrial structure of the US banking industry is disproportionate, and the six largest bank holding companies dwarf the next several cohorts of banks (National Information Center 2018). As the Bipartisan Policy Center (Ryan 2014) correctly observes:

> One would have to combine the assets of all 22 bank holding companies that fall between the current and proposed thresholds in order to arrive at an asset size equivalent to that held by the country's largest bank. The six largest bank holding companies average $1.2 trillion in assets, while the average size of the 22 banks in the $50–$250 billion range is just one-tenth of that amount (for reference, the comparable medians are similar: $1.5 trillion and $108 billion respectively). Based on size alone, it is difficult to imagine that the collapse of any single institution below the $250 billion threshold would result in system-wide negative externalities.

In addition, the smaller banks in the cohort automatically designated by Dodd-Frank as systemically important do not present systemic risk because they are not interconnected. They are regional and have negligible exposure to foreign investments, holding 90% of their assets in the United States (National Information Center 2018). These banks "are significantly less integrated into the global financial markets than the largest institutions . . . [and] generate the vast bulk of their revenue from traditional 'boring banking' activities such as deposit taking and lending, not complex trading and investment activities. As such, it is extremely unlikely that the failure of any one of these banks would produce domino effects with systemic consequences for either the U.S. or international banking sectors" (Ryan 2014).[31]

Ironically, the overdesignation of banks as SIFIs likely increases rather than decreases risk. First, as the economist James Barth has noted, "The static and arbitrary [$50 billion] threshold provides an incentive to those institutions just below the threshold to curtail their growth to remain below $50 billion, while those just above the threshold have an incentive to take actions to increase their size to spread the additional costs incurred due to being subjected to enhanced potential supervision over a bigger asset base" (quoted in Carter 2015).

Second, the massive resources deployed by the Fed and other regulators in providing increased monitoring of risk management programs at such banks, and in performing the required annual stress testing, could instead be deployed to the largest financial institutions in the economy that actually pose systemic risk. In addition, many of the costs of complying with the added regulations imposed by Dodd-Frank are fixed rather than variable, which means that they do not vary much depending on the size of the institutions that must comply with them. As such, these costs fall disproportionately on smaller banks, making them more likely to fail.

Using MetLife Inc. as an example, the next subsection focuses on the provisions in Dodd-Frank that empower the FSOC to designate nonbanks, regardless of size, as systemically important. Decisions by the FSOC are deeply flawed in a way that seeks to make it possible to designate firms as systemically important despite evidence they are not. FSOC decisions to date do not distinguish plausible risks from implausible ones, do not understand the balance sheets of the firms—and, indeed, the industries—of the companies that it is analyzing, and do not recognize the well-established principle that collateral is a valid hedge against risk. In its recent decision to designate the insurance company MetLife as a SIFI, for example, the FSOC failed to consider even basic principles of risk regulation, such as the principle that risk assessment should "consider the relationship between the likelihood of an adverse event and the potential impact on an institution" (Federal Reserve System 1997, 25).

3.2. The FSOC Has Refused to Distinguish Plausible Risks from Implausible Ones

The FSOC's analysis thus far has been inconsistent with this basic principle of risk regulation that plausible risks should be distinguished

---

[31] Neiman and Olson (2014, 40) wrote that "the task force believes that banks of about $50 billion are not systemically important—or at least the threshold is arbitrary and does not take other important factors into account."

from implausible risks. For example, in its assessment of whether Met-
Life is a SIFI, the FSOC overtly refused to give any consideration to
whether its scenarios were even remotely likely to occur—whether
to MetLife specifically, to an insurance company more generally, or
to anyone at all (FSOC 2014a). The FSOC asserted that because the statute does not expressly incorporate a standard of likelihood, the FSOC
may assess harm to the financial stability of the United States based
on risks that lack even basic plausibility in the relevant context. This
rejection of any consideration of the probability of a negative event ever
occurring is a clear expression of a strong aversion to accepting even a
modicum of type I risk.

The FSOC's approach ignores the fact that distinguishing between
plausible and implausible risks is an essential part of any coherent system of risk regulation.[32] The agency disregards the fact that Dodd-
Frank asks the FSOC to examine not simply possible financial distress
but *"material* financial distress at the U.S. nonbank financial company."[33] Examining material financial distress as required by the statutory text, the FSOC must address financial distress as it could plausibly occur at such a company—just as one would expect in light of
fundamental principles of risk regulation.

The FSOC's aversion to type I risk also led it to consider highly unlikely scenarios to conclude that MetLife's material financial distress
could pose a threat to US financial stability. For instance, the FSOC's
analysis placed a strong emphasis on the "run-on-the-bank" scenario.
The FSOC (2014a) suggested that "beyond the direct effect of MetLife's
asset liquidation on the financial markets, a run on MetLife necessitat-
ing significant asset liquidations could spark a loss of confidence in the
broader insurance industry, potentially leading to runs at other major
insurers" (153).

The FSOC expressed the same concerns in its determinations that
two other nonbank financial institutions, American International
Group and Prudential Financial, were SIFIs (see, e.g., FSOC 2013). This
run-on-the-bank scenario is wholly improbable in the context of an insurance company and other nonbank financial institutions such as
MetLife because of several important aspects of the insurance industry
(discussed in the next section). The FSOC's baseless assumption that a
run-on-the-bank scenario will occur renders its analysis fundamentally
incoherent because runs on banks are a manifestation of particular fi-

---

[32] See Memorandum of Points and Authorities in Support of Plaintiff MetLife,
Inc.'s Cross-Motion for Summary Judgment and in Opposition to Defendant's Motion
to Dismiss, or, in the Alternative, for Summary Judgment at 27 (No. 40), on file with
author.

[33] 12 U.S.C. § 5323(a)(1); emphasis added.

nancial characteristics of banks and shadow banks that do not appear in insurance companies. Specifically, unlike insurance companies, banks face an acute mismatch in the term structure (maturity) of their assets and liabilities that insurance companies do not. Banks' assets are long term, opaque, and illiquid, whereas their liabilities are short term, transparent, and liquid. It is this balance sheet "imbalance" that makes bank runs a real risk, but this imbalance simply is not reflected in insurance company balance sheets the way that it is in bank balance sheets.

Even assuming that runs on life insurance companies present a systemic risk problem, the FSOC's analysis reflects hyperaversion to type I risk because it does not account for the significant difference between runs on life insurers and runs on banks. In the United States, state regulators deal with a run on an insurer by seizing control of the insurer and freezing outflows. But unlike depositors in banks, policyholders in insurance companies are not relying on money due to them under their policies to fulfill short-term liquidity needs. Insurance policyholders do not have the same immediate liquidity rights as do counterparties to repurchase agreements in the shadow banking system and depositors in banks. As such, runs on insurance companies can be and are managed by state regulators in a more orderly way than runs on banks.

The FSOC's (2014a) aversion to type I error, as reflected in its rejection of standard risk assessment analysis, also caused the council to ignore or minimize certain important protections in its assessment of MetLife, such as the use of collateral to mitigate risk. Risk regulators universally treat obligations secured by collateral as less risky than unsecured obligations; indeed, the quality of collateral itself may be a factor in risk assessment, as is the extent to which the collateral secures the obligation. Those well-accepted principles would evaporate in a regime where the regulator simply assumes that everything that can go wrong will go wrong—for example, that good collateral will provide no more protection than bad collateral, or none.

3.3. The FSOC Declined to Consider the Structure of MetLife's Balance Sheet

The presence or absence of transparency, liquidity risk, and maturity mismatch on a bank's balance sheet are elemental determinants of the safety and soundness of a financial institution. *Balance sheet transparency* refers to the ease of ascertaining the actual market value of the assets and liabilities on a bank's balance sheet (Macey and O'Hara, forthcoming).

Liquidity risk in this context refers to the fact that banks' assets are illiquid instruments such as loans, whereas their liabilities are highly liquid instruments such as certificates of deposit (CDs), savings accounts, and demand deposits. This mismatch is managed by banks, which use historical patterns and probability estimates to forecast their clients' expected demand for liquidity and hold reserves sufficient to meet that expected demand. When the financial system encounters liquidity problems, however, companies are forced to sell their assets at an illiquidity discount (a price cheaper than would be available under conditions of liquidity), often referred to as a *fire sale*. In turn, lower asset prices lead to losses that deplete capital and further compromise liquidity. The result is a feedback mechanism (Allen and Gale 2004).

Maturity mismatch refers to the fact that banks' liabilities are very short term, again in the form of CDs, savings accounts, and demand deposits, whereas their assets are long term in duration. This maturity mismatch "affects a company's ability to survive a period of stress that may limit its access to funding and to withstand shocks in the yield curve."[34] Maturity mismatch can cause or exacerbate liquidity risk.

Economists have found that maturity mismatch causes self-fulfilling panics among bank depositors. This happens in the banking context because of the very nature of banks, which engage in maturity transformation, turning short-term liabilities into longer term assets (Diamond and Dybvig 1983). Put another way, a bank gives its demand depositors almost instant access to their funds, but it receives repayment of loans from consumers and businesses over a longer period of time. In this sense, the risk of maturity mismatch is a natural and integral feature of the business model of banks (Diamond and Dybvig 1983).

This results in two equilibriums. First, "If confidence is maintained, there can be efficient risk-sharing, because in that equilibrium a withdrawal will indicate that a depositor should withdraw under optimal risk-sharing." Second, "If agents panic, there is a bank run and incentives are distorted. In that equilibrium, everyone rushes in to withdraw their deposits before the bank gives out all of its assets. The bank must liquidate all its assets, even if not all depositors withdraw, because liquidated assets are sold at a loss" (Diamond and Dybvig 1983, 403).

In the financial sector, maturity mismatch is often measured by asset-liability duration and gap analysis. Duration analysis involves the calculation of the "time-weighted" maturity for each asset and liability of a company. In turn, gap analysis involves the estimation of differences between the duration of those assets and liabilities. Thus,

[34] Authority to Require Supervision and Regulation of Certain Nonbank Financial Companies, 77 Fed. Reg. 21637, 21659 (Apr. 11, 2012).

to measure maturity mismatch, one needs to examine a company's balance sheet closely. With life insurers, by contrast, it is not primarily their ability to do gap analysis and asset-liability management that makes them less susceptible to liquidity risk. Rather, the primary factors are the fundamental structure of such companies' liabilities, particularly the stability of such liabilities; the long-term nature of those liabilities; and the reluctance of policyholders to liquidate due to surrender penalties, taxes, and other restrictions.

In contrast to the business model of banks, however, maturity mismatch is not a natural and integral feature of the business model of insurance companies, which are better positioned to pursue asset-liability management. Insurance companies operate by pooling and managing risk. Although the structure of their balance sheet varies significantly by the type of insurance product, insurance companies tend to have long-term liabilities. In turn, insurance companies are well positioned to estimate the duration of their liabilities and assign probability to payouts.

Mirroring the above discussion, MetLife describes itself as a "liability-driven business with long-term, predictable cash flows" (FSOC 2014a, 284). This structural feature distinguishes banks from insurance companies such as MetLife and allows the latter to avoid the maturity mismatch problem by buying assets with maturities that correspond to the term structure of their liabilities and to avail themselves of the option to hold such assets to maturity.

Moreover, unlike bank depositors, insurance policyholders have greater disincentives to early withdrawal, such as contractual penalties and loss of tax benefits, and thus are less likely to run on a moment's notice.

The differences in the business models of banks and insurance companies have three primary consequences. First, insurance companies can manage maturity mismatch significantly better than banks, and it is in the insurance companies' interest to do so. Unlike banks, maturity mismatch is not an inherent feature of insurance companies' business model. In fact, all insurance companies, including large firms such as MetLife, pursue asset-liability management by matching the terms of their asset profile with those of their liability profile FSOC 2014a, 284).

Second, the insurance industry has far greater resilience against liquidity risk than other financial firms because their liabilities tend to be illiquid. These illiquid liabilities give them the opportunity to invest in longer term assets. This characteristic of insurance not only reduces risk; it has a huge societal benefit in light of the great social value created by investors with longer term time horizons. That benefit may be lost by treating insurance companies as if they were no different from banks.

Third, insurance companies are less susceptible to liquidity problems through their management of what maturity mismatch they do experience. To begin with, insurance policyholders have greater disincentives to early withdrawal than bank depositors, including "federal income tax liability, federal income tax penalties, surrender penalties, and the loss of guarantees" (Huff 2013). Moreover, insurance companies, especially life insurance companies, "are generally buy-and-hold investors, with the goal of generating predictable and stable income in the long run, and having sufficient funds available to pay claims when due" (NAIC 2014).

In other words, insurance companies, because of the inherent structure of their business, are less likely to face an immediate need for liquidity. MetLife, for instance, manages $458 billion in its general account investment portfolio, but more than 20% of the portfolio's securities are held in "cash, short-term investments, U.S. Treasury securities, agencies, and agency RMBS" (FSOC 2014a, 284). Thus, "liquidity risk is negligible in the insurance sector" (Plantin and Rochet 2007, 92).

The FSOC's analysis of MetLife is a classic example of type I risk aversion.[35] Consistent with this theory, as S. Roy Woodall, the sole member of the FSOC with insurance expertise, observed in his dissenting statement to MetLife's SIFI designation, the FSOC's analysis "relies on implausible, contrived scenarios as well as failures to appreciate fundamental aspects of insurance and annuity" (FSOC 2014b, 2). And Adam Hamm, the state insurance commissioner representative on the FSOC, noted that "the Basis implicitly assumes material financial distress at all

---

[35] In its Final Rule and Interpretive Guidance, the FSOC proposed a number of sample metrics to assess liquidity and maturity mismatch (see "Authority to Require Supervision and Regulation of Certain Nonbank Financial Companies," 77 Fed. Reg. at 21,637, 21,660 [April 11, 2012]). These metrics help determine a nonbank financial company's vulnerability to financial distress. For instance, "short-term debt as a percentage of total debt and as a percentage of total assets . . . indicates a nonbank financial company's reliance on short-term debt markets" (Authority to Require Supervision and Regulation of Certain Nonbank Financial Companies," 77 Fed. Reg. at 21,637, 21,660 [April 11, 2012]). In addition, the FSOC acknowledged that "asset-liability duration and gap analysis . . . indicate[s] how well a nonbank financial company is matching the re-pricing and maturity of the nonbank financial company's assets and liabilities" (Authority to Require Supervision and Regulation of Certain Nonbank Financial Companies," 77 Fed. Reg. at 21,637, 21,660 [April 11, 2012]). The FSOC, however, failed to apply its own metrics in assessing MetLife. It virtually ignored the fact that MetLife's short-term debt is only 0.27% of its assets (see FSOC 2014a, 286). FSOC also glossed over the fact that "MetLife has a substantial portfolio of highly liquid assets" (see FSOC 2014a, 17). Not only did the FSOC fail to measure the degree of MetLife's maturity mismatch, but it also failed to measure the actual risk that MetLife's maturity mismatch poses to the financial system, and it failed to apply its own sample metrics to MetLife.

insurance entities at the same time, yet the Basis cites no historical examples of that having ever occurred" (Hamm 2014, 10).

Furthermore, with respect to type II risk aversion, the FSOC (2014a) acknowledged in its analysis that "approximately 88 percent of the securities lent by MetLife are U.S. government and agency securities, whose liquidity helps to protect counterparties" (156). In addition, the FSOC (2014a) recognized that "MetLife invested $6.6 billion of the cash collateral in U.S. Treasury and agency securities, which would be sold to satisfy any cash requirements due to the termination of securities lending agreements" (157). These facts, however, did not prevent the FSOC (2014a) from speculating that MetLife "could transmit material financial distress to other market participants as a result of a rapid liquidation of invested collateral to produce the necessary liquidity to return cash collateral to its securities lending counterparties" (157). Thus, in its final determination, the FSOC failed to consider MetLife's access to significant liquid assets.

3.4. The FSOC Failed to Recognize That Insurance Companies Are Less Interconnected with One Another and with the Financial System

Banks are institutionally interconnected. They extend loans to one another through the interbank lending market and transact in over-the-counter derivatives. Therefore, the financial system is susceptible to systemic risk arising from banks. Financial distress at a large bank can have impact on the financial system at large and pose a threat to US financial stability. In particular, banks routinely encounter counterparty risk that stems from their trading partners, including other banks. Counterparty risk comes in various forms, such as default risk, replacement risk, and settlement risk. Moreover, the magnitude of counterparty risk increases with the degree of interconnectedness of the trading partners. During the 2008 Financial Crisis, "increased counterparty risk contributed to" (Taylor and Williams 2009, 58) the unfolding of the financial market turmoil.

In contrast, insurance companies lack the banking system's interconnectedness in two distinct ways. First, insurance companies are less interconnected with one another than banks are. There exists no "insurance system" comparable to the banking system. Insurance companies are not directly linked to one another through their balance sheets. Although insurance companies cede some of their risks through reinsurance agreements, reinsurers only take up portions of the primary risks of insurers, acting as a backstop.

Second, insurance companies are not as interconnected with the rest of the financial system as banks are. On the one hand, insurance companies act as financial intermediaries and invest in financial markets. On the other hand, "the degree to which insurance companies are interconnected with other financial institutions is generally less significant than the interconnection among banks and brokerage firms" (NAIC 2013).[36]

Because insurance companies are less interconnected with one another and with the financial system than banks, their exposure to the financial system is more limited. Moreover, insurance companies do not impose the same level of counterparty risk on the financial system as banks do. Indeed, empirical studies point toward a lack of "any evidence in favor of contagion of failures in insurance" (Plantin and Rochet 2007, 92).

In sum, insurance companies are less interconnected, and thus less likely to pose a threat to US financial stability than banks. The FSOC's antipathy to type I risk appears to best explain why these important institutional features of the insurance industry seem to be ignored by the council in its SIFI designation process.

At first blush, it would appear that type I risk aversion does little harm. After all, if a regulator is going to make a mistake, it seems obvious, at least initially, that it would be better for the regulator to commit type II error, which results only in the award of a SIFI designation to a nonsystemically risky company, than to commit type I error, which results in no SIFI designation for a company that is in fact systemically risky. The problem with this sanguine analysis is that it ignores the effects of herding. If my hypothesis that the FSOC will continue to overdesignate nonrisky institutions as SIFIs is correct, then we will observe increasing homogeneity in the regulations of firms. In particular, large insurance companies like MetLife, which are currently regulated at the state level, will come under the federal regulatory umbrella. Thus, the overdesignation of firms as SIFIs likely will magnify the consequences of regulatory error by increasing the number of firms subjected to such error.

Put simply, the SIFI designation threatens to undermine the current patchwork of regulation in which different sorts of firms, banks, insurance companies, hedge funds, investment banks, and private equity firms are subjected to a diverse array of regulators and regulations. Although this system may be inefficient, it has the virtue of mitigating the effects of regulatory error by insuring that regulatory mistakes are limited to the cohort of firms actually subject to that regulation. As more and more firms become designated as SIFIs, the patchwork will be replaced by the relatively more consistent set of regulations imposed on SIFIs.

---

[36] For example, insurance companies participate in low-risk activities such as securities lending, but they do not participate in interbank lending (see NAIC 2011).

To date, FSOC has designated four nonbanks as SIFIs: the insurers AIG, MetLife, and Prudential and one other firm, GE Capital. The FSOC is considering whether to designate firms in other sectors of the financial system and held a conference in 2014 on the potential systemic importance of asset managers such as pension funds, hedge funds, and private equity firms (Labonte 2015).

In addition, the designation of a firm as a SIFI increases expectations that the government will prevent that firm from failing. This in turn leads to moral hazard, as creditors and counterparties of a too-big-to-fail firm believe that the government will bail out that too-big-to-fail firm if need be, causing their incentives to monitor and control the firm's risky behavior to decline. In other words, the overbroad application of the SIFI designation increases moral hazard and increases public and market expectations that firms with the designation will be bailed out in the future.[37]

4. CONCLUSION

Building on simple economic insights, this article provides a rationale for why past and present efforts to regulate systemic risk have failed to create incentives for bankers to limit their own excessive risk taking. Specifically, the bureaucratic proclivity to systemize and generalize regulation causes error by leading financial institutions to conduct business and to analyze risk in a single, uniform way. This well-meaning tendency actually has the unintended consequence of increasing systemic risk in the economy by causing herding. In other words, by reducing the heterogeneity of firm behavior in an economy, regulation—even regulation aimed at reducing systemic risk—can increase such risk.

The second insight is that rational regulators will be averse to type I risk, which in this context is defined as the perceived risk that a SIFI will be mischaracterized as nonsystemically important and left unregulated. The professional consequences of such an error in categorization would be significant for the regulator or bureaucracy making such an error. As such, we should expect to observe institutions that are not systemically important to be categorized that way. This type of error increases systemic risk by moving more firms under the umbrella of a single regulator than there would be in the absence of the provisions in Dodd-Frank that created the FSOC and arrogates to that new agency regulatory control over a diverse group of institutions (including insurance companies, hedge funds, and private equity firms) that

[37] *Examining the Dangers of the FSOC's Designation Process and Its Impact on the US Financial System: Hearing Before the Comm. on Financial Services*, 113th Cong. (2014).

otherwise would be regulated by a diverse set of regulators. In this way, type I risk leads to the overcategorization of financial firms as systemically risky, which leads to homogeneous regulation and herding. These problems exacerbate the ongoing dialectic between government, which seeks to control excessive risk taking, and the banking sector, which seeks to engage in such risk taking because the owners of the firms in this sector can diversify their holdings and thereby obtain the rewards of such risk taking without experiencing the consequences.

REFERENCES

Acharya, Viral V., Lasse H. Pedersen, Thomas Philippon, and Matthew Richardson. 2013. "How to Calculate Systemic Risk Surcharges." In *Quantifying Systemic Risk*, edited by Joseph G. Haubrich and Andrew W. Lo, 175–222. Chicago: University of Chicago Press.

Aguilar, Luis A. 2014. "Skin in the Game: Aligning the Interests of Sponsors and Investors." Public statement. US Securities and Exchange Commission. http://www.sec.gov/News/PublicStmt/Detail/PublicStmt/1370543250034.

Allen, Franklin, Elena Carletti, and Robert Marquez. 2014. "Deposits and Bank Capital Structure." Working paper. University of Pennsylvania Wharton School.

Allen, Franklin, and Douglas Gale. 2004. "Financial Intermediaries and Markets." *Econometrica* 72:1023–61.

Arnholz, John, and Edward E. Gainor. 2014. *Offerings of Asset-Backed Securities* (Supplement), 2nd ed. New York: Wolters Kluwer.

Bebchuk, Lucian, Alma Cohen, and Holger Spamann. 2010. "The Wages of Failure: Executive Compensation at Bear Stearns and Lehman 2000–2008." *Yale Journal on Regulation* 27:257–82.

Berger, Alan, Richard Herring, and Giorgio Szego. 1995. "The Role of Capital in Financial Institutions." *Journal of Banking and Finance* 19:393–430.

Berle, Adolph A. 1991. "Property, Production and Revolution: A Preface to the Revised Edition." In *The Modern Corporation and Private Property*, 2nd ed., edited by Adolph A. Berle and Gardiner C. Means, xix–xl. Piscataway, NJ: Transaction.

Board of Governors of the Federal Reserve System. 2017. *Reserve Maintenance Manual*. Washington, DC: Board of Governors of the Federal Reserve System.

Board of Governors of the Federal Reserve System, Federal Deposit Insurance Corporation, and Office of the Comptroller of the Currency. 2014a. "Agencies Adopt Enhanced Supplementary Leverage Ratio Final Rule and Issue Supplementary Leverage Ratio Notice of Pro-

posed Rulemaking." Press release, April 8, 2014. https://www
.federalreserve.gov/newsevents/pressreleases/bcreg20140408a.htm.
Board of Governors of the Federal Reserve System, Federal Deposit Insurance Corporation, and Office of the Comptroller of the Currency.
2014b. "Federal Banking Regulators Finalize Liquidity Coverage Ratio." Press release, September 3, 2014. https://www.federalreserve
.gov/newsevents/pressreleases/bcreg20140903a.htm.
Bord, Vitaly M., and João A. C. Santos. 2012. "The Rise of the Originate-
to-Distribute Model and the Role of Banks in Financial Intermedia-
tion." *FRBNY Economic Policy Review* 18:21–34.
Bubb, Ryan, and Prasad Krishnamurthy. 2015. "Regulating against
Bubbles: How Mortgage Regulation Can Keep Main Street and Wall
Street Safe—From Themselves." *University of Pennsylvania Law
Review* 163:1539–630.
Buehler, Kevin, Hamid Samandari, and Christopher Mazingo. 2009.
"Capital Ratios and Financial Distress: Lessons from the Crisis
2." Working Paper no. 15. McKinsey & Co., Washington, DC.
Burnham, Peter. 2010. "Class, Capital and Crisis: A Return to Funda-
mentals." *Policy Study Review* 8:27–39.
Calem, Paul, and Michael LaCour-Little. 2004. "Risk-Based Capital Re-
quirements for Mortgage Loans." *Journal of Banking and Finance* 28:
647–72.
Calomiris, Charles W., and Peter J. Wallison. 2008. "Blame Fannie
Mae and Congress for the Credit Mess." *Wall Street Journal*, September 23, 2008. https://www.wsj.com/articles/SB122212948811
465427.
Carlson, Mark, and David Wheelock. 2012. "The Lender of Last Resort:
Lessons from the Fed's First 100 Years." Working Paper no. 2012-
056-B. Federal Reserve Bank of St. Louis.
Carter, J. Preston. 2015. "$50B SIFI Threshold Questioned at Hear-
ing." *Banking and Finance Law Daily*, July 9, 2015. http://www.daily
reportingsuite.com/banking-finance/news/_50b_sifi_threshold
_questioned_at_hearing.
Davis, Marc. 2008. "Top 6 US Government Financial Bailouts."
Investopedia. http://www.investopedia.com/articles/economics
/08/government-financial-bailout.asp.
DeAngelo, Harry, and Renee Stulz. 2013. "Liquid Claim Production,
Risk Management, and Bank Capital Structure: Why High Leverage
Is Optimal for Banks." Working Paper no. 2013-03-08. Fisher College
of Business, Columbus, OH.
Dennis, Brady. 2009. "AIG Executives' Promises to Return Bonuses
Have Gone Largely Unfulfilled." *Washington Post*, December 23,
2009. http://www.washingtonpost.com/wp-dyn/content/article
/2009/12/22/AR2009122203788.html.

Dennis, Brady. 2010. "AIG Plans to Pay $100 Million in Another Round of Bonuses." *Washington Post*, February 3, 2010. http://www .washingtonpost.com/wp-dyn/content/article/2010/02/02 /AR2010020203036.html?noredirect=on.

Diamond, Douglas W., and Philip H. Dybvig. 1983. "Bank Runs, Deposit Insurance, and Liquidity." *Journal of Political Economy* 91: 401–19.

Elliott, Douglas J. 2010. *The Importance of Capital*. Washington, DC: Brookings. https://www.brookings.edu/research/the-importance -of-capital/.

Elliott, Douglas J. 2014. "Bank Liquidity Requirements: An Introduction and Overview." Working paper. Brookings, Washington, DC. https://www.brookings.edu/wp-content/uploads/2016/06/23_bank _liquidity_requirements_intro_overview_elliott.pdf.

FDIC (Federal Deposit Insurance Corporation). 2018. "Section 2.1: Capital." In *Risk Management Manual of Examination Policies*, 2.1-1–2.1-16. Washington, DC: Federal Deposit Insurance Corporation. https://www.fdic.gov/regulations/safety/manual/section2 -1.pdf.

Federal Reserve Board. 1934. *Federal Reserve Bulletin*. Washington, DC: US Government Printing Office.

Federal Reserve System. 1997. *Framework for Risk-Focused Supervision of Large Complex Institutions*. https://www.federalreserve .gov/boarddocs/srletters/1997/sr9724a1.pdf.

Feinman, Joshua N. 1993. "Reserve Requirements: History, Current Practice, and Potential Reform." *Federal Reserve Bulletin*, June 1993. https://www.federalreserve.gov/monetarypolicy/0693lead.pdf.

Finkle, Victoria. 2014. "How the Fight over the $50B 'Systemic' Cutoff Will Play Out." *Bank Investment Consultant*, October 23, 2014. http://www.bankinvestmentconsultant.com/news/practice/how -the-fight-over-the-50-billion-systemic-cutoff-will-play-out -2690861-1.html.

FNMA (Federal National Mortgage Association). 2014. *Annual Report (Form 10-K)*. http://www.fanniemae.com/resources/file/ir /pdf/quarterly-annual-results/2014/10k_2014.pdf.

Froud, Julie, Adriana Nilsson, Michael Moran, and Karel Williams. 2012. "Stories and Interests in Finance: Agendas of Governance Before and After the Financial Crisis." *Governance* 25:35–59.

FSOC (Financial Stability Oversight Council). 2013. *Basis of the Financial Stability Oversight Council's Final Determination Regarding American International Group, Inc.* Washington, DC: US Department of the Treasury.

FSOC (Financial Stability Oversight Council). 2014a. *Explanation of the Basis of the Financial Stability Oversight Council's Final Deter-*

mination That Material Financial Distress at MetLife Could Pose a Threat to US Financial Stability and That MetLife Should Be Supervised by the Board of Governors of the Federal Reserve System and Be Subject to Prudential Standards. Washington, DC: US Department of the Treasury.

FSOC (Financial Stability Oversight Council). 2014b. *Views of the Council's Independent Member Having Insurance Expertise.* Washington, DC: US Department of the Treasury.

Greenspan, Alan. 2004. "Remarks at the HM Treasury Enterprise Conference." Presented at the HM Treasury Enterprise Conference, London, January 26. http://www.federalreserve.gov/boarddocs /speeches/2004/20040126/default.htm.

Grenadier, Steven R., and Brian J. Hall. 1995. "Risk-Based Capital Standards and the Riskiness of Bank Portfolio Credit and Risk Factors." Working Paper no. 5178. National Bureau of Economic Research, Cambridge, MA.

Hackley, Howard. 1973. *Lending Functions of the Federal Reserve Banks: A History.* St. Louis: Federal Reserve Bank of St. Louis.

Hamm, Adam. 2014. *View of Adam Hamm, the State Insurance Commissioner Representative.* Washington, DC: National Association of Insurance Commissioners.

Havemann, Joel. 2009. "The Financial Crisis of 2008." Encyclopedia Britannica Online. http://www.britannica.com/topic/Financial -Crisis-of-2008-The-1484264.

Hoenig, Thomas M. 2012. "Back to Basics: A Better Alternative to Basel Capital Rules." Speech at the American Banker Regulatory Symposium, Washington, DC, September 14. https://www.fdic.gov/news /news/speeches/chairman/spsep1412_2.html.

Hoenig, Thomas M., and Charles S. Morris. 2012. *Restructuring the Banking System to Improve Safety and Soundness.* Working paper. Federal Deposit Insurance Corporation, Washington, DC. https://www.fdic.gov/about/learn/board/restructuring-the-banking -system-05-24-11.pdf.

Huff, John. 2013. *View of Director John Huff, the State Insurance Commissioner Representative.* Washington, DC: National Association of Insurance Commissioners. https://www.naic.org/documents /index_fsoc_130920_huff_dissent_prudential.pdf.

Kauko, Karlo. 2011. *Why Is Equity Capital Expensive for Banks?* Presentation at VI Seminar on Risk, Financial Stability and Banking of the Banco Central do Brasil, São Paulo, August 11. https://www .bcb.gov.br/pec/depep/Seminarios/2011_VISemRiscosBCB /Arquivos/2011_VISemRiscosBCB_17h00_KarloKauko.pdf.

Kelly, Kate. 2007. "Bear CEO's Handling of Crisis Raises Issues." *Wall Street Journal,* November 1, 2007. https://www.wsj.com/ar ticles/SB119387369474078336.

Klein, Aaron, and Laura Hall. 2014. "Five Financial Reform Priorities for Congress in 2015." Bipartisan Policy Center blog, December 23, 2014. http://bipartisanpolicy.org/blog/five-financial-reform -priorities-for-congress-in-2015/.

Labonte, Mark. 2015. *Designating Systemically Important Financial Institutions (SIFIs)*. CRS Insights report. Washington, DC: Congressional Research Service. https://fas.org/sgp/crs/misc/IN10141.pdf.

Levisohn, Ben. 2008. "Bear Stearns Big Shots Reaped Big Paydays." *Bloomberg Businessweek*, March 19, 2008. http://www.nbcnews .com/id/23711023/ns/business-us_business/t/bear-stearns-big -shots-reaped-big-paydays/#.VnB1Bk1Ig4A.

Linter, John. 1965. "The Valuation of Risk Assets and the Selection of Risky Investments in Stock Portfolios and Capital Budgets." *Review of Economics and Statistics* 47:13–37.

Lockhart, Robert. 1998. *Introduction to Statistics and Data Analysis for the Behavioral Sciences*. New York: Freeman.

Macey, Jonathan. 2000a. "The 'Demand' for International Regulatory Cooperation: A Public Choice Perspective." In *Transatlantic Regulatory Co-Operation: Legal Problems and Political Perspectives*, edited by George A. Bermann, Matthias Herdegen, and Peter L. Lindseth, 147–66. Oxford: Oxford University Press.

Macey, Jonathan. 2000b. "US and EU Structures of Governance as Barriers to Transatlantic Regulatory Cooperation." In *Transatlantic Regulatory Co-operation: Legal Problems and Political Perspectives*, edited by George A. Bermann, Matthias Herdegen, and Peter L. Lindseth, 357–72. Oxford: Oxford University Press.

Macey, Jonathan. 2006. "Government as Investor: Tax Policy and the State." *Journal of Social Philosophy and Policy* 23:255–86.

Macey, Jonathan, and James Holdcroft. 2011. "Failure Is an Option: An Ersatz-Antitrust Approach to Financial Regulation." *Yale Law Journal* 120:1368–418.

Macey, Jonathan, and Maureen O'Hara. Forthcoming. "Bank Corporate Governance: A Paradigm for the Post-Crisis World." *Economic Policy Review*.

Markowitz, Harry. 1970. *Portfolio Selection: Efficient Diversification of Investments*. New Haven: Yale University Press.

Martin, Kristen, and Michael Scotto. 2010. *Bailouts and Bonuses on Wall Street*. Case Study BRI-1007. Business Roundtable Institute for Corporate Ethics, Charlottesville, VA. http://www.corporate -ethics.org/pdf/BRI-1007_Bailout_Bonus_Wall_Street.pdf.

Miller, Henry. 2010. "Federal Agencies: Waning Integrity, Dwindling Trust." *Forbes*, July 21, 2010. http://www.forbes.com/2010/07/18 /fda-epa-regulation-trust-opinions-columnists-henry-i-miller.html.

Mitchell, Mark, and Janina Jolley. 2013. *Research Design Explained*, 8th ed. Belmont, CA: Wadsworth Cengage Learning.

Modigliani, Franco, and Merton H. Miller. 1958. "The Cost of Capital, Corporation Finance and the Theory of Investment." *American Economic Review* 48:261–97.

NAIC (National Association of Insurance Commissioners). 2011. "Capital Markets Special Report: Securities Lending in the Insurance Industry." http://www.naic.org/capital_markets_archive /110708.htm.

NAIC (National Association of Insurance Commissioners). 2013. "Capital Markets Special Report: US Insurance Industry's Investment Exposure to the Financial Sector." http://www.naic.org /capital_markets_archive/130405.htm.

NAIC (National Association of Insurance Commissioners). 2014. "Capital Markets Special Report: Investment Strategies and Return on Invested Assets." http://www.naic.org/capital_markets _archive/140911.htm.

National Information Center. 2018. "Holding Companies with Assets Greater Than $10 Billion." https://www.ffiec.gov/nicpubweb /nicweb/HCSGreaterThan10B.aspx.

Neiman, Richard H., and Mark Olson. 2014. *Dodd-Frank's Missed Opportunity: A Road Map for a More Effective Regulatory Architecture*. Washington, DC: Bipartisan Policy Center. https:// bipartisanpolicy.org/library/dodd-franks-missed-opportunity-road -map-more-effective-regulatory-architecture-2/.

New York Times. 2011. "Adding Up the Government's Total Bailout Tab." July 24, 2011. https://archive.nytimes.com/www.nytimes .com/interactive/2009/02/04/business/20090205-bailout-totals -graphic.html?_r=0.

Neyman, Jerzy, and Egon Pearson. 1933a. "On the Problem of the Most Efficient Tests of Statistical Hypotheses." *Philosophical Transactions of the Royal Society of London: Series A* 231:289–337.

Neyman, Jerzy, and Egon Pearson. 1933b. "The Testing of Statistical Hypotheses in Relation to Probabilities A Priori." *Mathematical Proceedings of the Cambridge Philosophical Society* 29:492–510.

Office of the Comptroller of the Currency. 2017. *Activities Permissible for a National Bank, Cumulative*. Washington, DC: Office of the Comptroller of the Currency. https://www.occ.gov/publica tions/publications-by-type/other-publications-reports/pub-other -activities-permissible-october-2017.pdf.

Office of the Comptroller of the Currency. 2018. "Licensing." US Department of the Treasury. http://www.occ.treas.gov/topics /licensing/index-licensing.html.

Paulson, Henry M., Jr. 2010. *On the Brink: Inside the Race to Stop the Collapse of the Global Financial System*. New York: Hachette.

Plantin, Guillaume, and Jean-Charles Rochet. 2007. *When Insurers Go Bust: An Economic Analysis of the Role and Design of Prudential Regulation*. Princeton, NJ: Princeton University Press.

Rivlin, Alice. 2009. *Systemic Risk and the Role of the Federal Reserve*. Philadelphia: Pew Task Force on Financial Reform. https://www.brookings.edu/research/systemic-risk-and-the-role-of-the-federal-reserve/.

Robb, Greg. 2008. "Treasury Details Key Role in Bear Stearns Bailout." *Marketwatch*, April 2, 2008. http://www.marketwatch.com/story/correct-treasury-details-extensive-role-in-bear-stearns-bailout.

Rosen, Richard J. 2010. "The Impact of the Originate-to-Distribute Model on Banks Before and During the Financial Crisis." Working Paper no. 2010-20. Federal Reserve Bank of Chicago.

Ryan, Peter. 2014. "Raising the Bank 'SIFI Threshold' Would Make the Financial System Safer." Bipartisan Policy Center blog, April 16, 2014. https://bipartisanpolicy.org/blog/raising-sifi-threshold-would-make-financial-system-safer/.

Scott, Hal S., and Philip A. Wellons. 1999. *International Finance: Transactions, Policy and Regulation*, 6th ed. New York: Foundation.

Sharpe, William. 1964. "Capital Asset Prices: A Theory of Market Equilibrium under Conditions of Risk." *Journal of Finance* 19:425–42.

Shinkle, Kirk. 2008. "AIG: The Biggest Bailout." *US News and World Report*, September 17, 2008. http://money.usnews.com/money/blogs/the-ticker/2008/09/17/aig-the-biggest-bailout.

Shojai, Shahin, and George Feiger. 2013. *Risk Management in Financial Institutions*. London: Euromoney Institutional Investor.

Simmons, Beth A. 2001. "The International Politics of Harmonization: The Case of Capital Market Regulation." *International Organization* 55:589–620.

Skeel, David. 2011. *The New Financial Deal: Understanding the Dodd-Frank Act and Its (Unintended) Consequences*. Hoboken, NJ: Wiley.

Sun, Yangfan, and Hui Tong. 2015. "How Does Post-Crisis Bank Capital Adequacy Affect Firm Investment?" Working Paper no. 15/145. International Monetary Fund, Washington, DC.

Swagel, Phillip. 2009. "The Financial Crisis: An Inside View." *Brookings Papers on Economic Activity*, Spring 2009. https://www.brookings.edu/wp-content/uploads/2009/03/2009a_bpea_swagel.pdf.

Tarbert, Heath Price. 2000. "Are International Capital Adequacy Rules Adequate? The Basle Accord and Beyond." *University of Pennsylvania Law Review* 148:1771–849.

Tarullo, Daniel K. 2008. *Banking on Basel: The Future of International Financial Regulation*. Washington, DC: Peterson Institute for International Economics.

Taylor, John B., and John C. Williams. 2009. "A Black Swan in the Money Market." *American Economic Journal: Macroeconomics* 1:58–83.

Tobin, James. 1958. "Liquidity Preference as Behavior Towards Risk." *Review of Economic Studies* 25:65–86.

Todd, Walker. 1993. "FDICIA's Emergency Liquidity Provisions." *Federal Reserve Bank of Cleveland Economic Review* 29:16–23.

US Department of the Treasury. 2009. *Financial Regulatory Reform: A New Foundation: Rebuilding Financial Supervision and Regulation.* Washington, DC: US Department of the Treasury. https://www.treasury.gov/initiatives/Documents/FinalReport_web.pdf.

Wall Street Journal. 2009. "Obama Wants to Block AIG Bonuses." *Washington Wire* (blog), March 16, 2009. https://blogs.wsj.com/washwire/2009/03/16/obama-wants-to-block-aig-bonuses/.

Wallison, Peter J. 2009. "The True Origins of This Financial Crisis." American Enterprise Institute. http://www.aei.org/publication/the-true-story-of-the-financial-crisis/.

Wallison, Peter J. 2011. *Dissent from the Majority Report of the Financial Crisis Inquiry Commission.* Washington, DC: American Enterprise Institute. http://www.aei.org/publication/dissent-from-the-majority-report-of-the-financial-crisis-inquiry-commission-2/.

Comment on "Error and Regulatory Risk in Financial Institution Regulation"

Keith N. Hylton*

I agree with just about everything Jonathan Macey (2017) says in his symposium contribution. His claim that bureaucratic tendencies toward *regularity*—specifically, treating like cases alike—generate errors in categorization seems appropriate to me. His explanations of the pathologies in financial regulation should fall in the category of essential or required reading for anyone who chooses to write on the topic. Where I differ from Macey is in the choice of framework, or perspective from which to view the pathologies. Whereas Macey adopts an "error cost" framework, which is clearly appropriate for this symposium, I would build explicitly on a "public choice" framework.[1]

Margaret Thatcher famously said that "Europe was created by history. America was created by philosophy." One could unpack Thatcher's statement further by saying that Europe was created by accidents, catastrophes, and wars, whereas America, and particularly the American Constitution, developed at least in outline form from a well-considered design (see, e.g., *The Federalist Papers*).[2]

* William Fairfield Warren Distinguished Professor, Boston University; Professor of Law, Boston University School of Law. I thank Jack Beermann for helpful comments.

[1] Public choice can be described as the application of economics to political science. I refer generally to the theory that government actors engage in self-interested, utility-maximizing behavior. On public choice theory, see Mueller (1989) and Niskanen (1971). Although I distinguish the error-cost model adopted by Macey from the public choice model, the two models are by no means mutually exclusive. Moreover, Macey has contributed substantially to the public choice literature himself (see, e.g., Macey 1988). For a critique of Macey's public choice arguments, see Beermann (1991).

[2] Obviously, one could quibble that the US Constitution itself is the result of history (wars, catastrophes, accidents, trial and error). But even a casual reader of a found-

Electronically published: December 6, 2018

One can offer a similar division in explaining a particular regulatory framework: it is either a creation of history or of philosophy—or some mixture of both. Macey's thesis that bureaucratic tendencies toward order generate regulatory pathologies suggests a vision of bureaucrats who at least try to play the role of philosophers or "intelligent designers" of regulation. I would start with a very different view of regulatory bureaucrats.

I believe history carries much more weight than philosophy in accounting for the shape of most regulatory frameworks in finance. Financial regulation responds to accidents and catastrophes—such as the Great Recession of 2008. In the wake of these accidents, legislatures respond with new regulations, and factions consisting largely of incumbent pressure groups move in with versions of reform suitable to their interests. The result is a legislative "solution" that often fails to resolve the pathologies that caused the catastrophes because so many compromises and carve-outs have had to be included to satisfy the incumbent factions. The most powerful interest groups typically do not lose their advantages over rivals at the end of the reform process and often emerge from the ashes of reform with even greater competitive advantages. The groups that received the largest subsidies from the state before the catastrophe continue to receive their subsidies after the reform.

Increasingly, the statutes that emerge from regulatory reform introduce a new regulatory infrastructure as well. The statutes generate new rules that firms must follow to gain regulatory approval or to avoid punishment. In the wake of the Dodd-Frank Wall Street Reform and Consumer Protection Act (Dodd-Frank), banks have had to hire numerous employees (private bureaucrats) to help them figure out how to comply with the many rules embedded in the statute. Modern reform statutes increasingly generate agencies that must be staffed by government bureaucrats and that are charged with producing more rules. For example, the Consumer Financial Protection Bureau, created by Dodd-Frank, now employs nearly 2,000 people, and the agency worked diligently, until the change in administration in 2017, to develop new rules to regulate lenders. These agencies are overseen ultimately by courts, but they often work initially to create a barrier between the regulated parties and the courts.

Stepping a bit further into generality, in the wake of financial catastrophes, reform legislation sets initial conditions for new law that will regulate the finance industry. This new law often will be a "negotiated product" resulting from deals made among legislators and incumbent

---

ing document such as *The Federalist Papers* would be astounded by the depth of analysis—of economics, of history, of alternative institutions—reflected in the work.

factions (large firms, regulatory pressure groups). From these initial conditions, bureaucratic action can either exacerbate the inefficiencies built into the initial bargain or mitigate the inefficiencies. Whether bureaucratic actions will mitigate or exacerbate the inefficiencies depends, in turn, on other factors: whether the sitting administration is committed to addressing the inefficiencies (although very often the administration will introduce new inefficiencies or biases) and the extent to which the courts oversee the regulatory regime. As a general rule, where courts play a strong and direct role in administering the statute, such as the Sherman Antitrust Act of 1890 (Sherman Act), the inefficiencies in the initial design tend to be mitigated through court review.[3] Conversely, where courts are somewhat removed from administration because of the existence of an administrative agency burdened with enforcing an enormous regulatory statute (e.g., health-care regulation), there is a greater likelihood that bureaucratic action will exacerbate inefficiencies built into the framework from the start.

I just offered the Sherman Act as an example because it is a regulatory statute with such a thin set of rules at its base that courts have been left to administer the statute with virtually no direct administrative or bureaucratic input by executive-branch agents. The executive-branch agents who help to administer the Sherman Act do so only as enforcers—that is, essentially as plaintiffs who come to court and attempt to persuade the court to apply or to change the law in order to advantage the enforcer. Sherman Act enforcers, however, play no direct role in the creation or interpretation of the law. The result has been a consistent move toward relatively simple and discretionary rules that have tended to be efficient. The general trend of antitrust law has been away from per se prohibitions and toward "rule of reason" tests that enable courts to consider the efficiency of a particular practice before deciding whether it should be declared unlawful under the statute.

Macey's contribution addresses regulation within an administrative or bureaucratic framework—in contrast to the courts. This is an appropriate focus, in this case, because it is consistent with the nature of financial regulation. Unlike the Sherman Act example, the statutes Macey examines are mostly elaborated and developed through direct bureaucratic involvement. Agency officials working on financial regulation generally develop and explicate statutory provisions—the most famous example of which is the Volcker rule, which involves hundreds of pages of bureaucratic law development.

---

[3] For an elaboration of this claim about the relationship between statute and common law, though in the context of federal labor law, see Hylton (1993, 1996).

Within the agency framework Macey studies, we observe the errors he describes and correctly attributes to bureaucratic action. The tendency toward regularity—of treating like cases alike—I would attribute to the possibility and risk of court review rather than a general tendency or desire for order among bureaucrats. I think bureaucrats seek orderly explanations for their actions because those actions eventually will be exposed to judicial scrutiny. If those actions were never to be exposed to judicial scrutiny, the bureaucrats would care a lot less about generating the appearance of order. The other tendency Macey attributes to bureaucrats, which is to avoid the costs of erroneous regulatory inaction, reflects the asymmetric political costs of action and inaction. Erroneous action can always be defended ex post, often by referring to the horrible events that might have resulted without action. Erroneous inaction, however, always leaves the bureaucrat exposed to charges that he failed to act appropriately and in time.[4] Such charges are often politically motivated.

Macey offers several examples to support his thesis of bureaucratic error. One is the "systemically important financial institution" (SIFI) status categorization for firms administered by the Financial Stability Oversight Council (FSOC), an agency created by Dodd-Frank. The SIFI categorization has been imposed on firms too aggressively, Macey argues, inappropriately burdening some firms with the status (e.g., MetLife). Although I agree with Macey's description of the process as prone to error, I am equally impressed by the competitive effects of the FSOC's actions. The SIFI designation imposes costly regulatory obligations that clearly favor the largest firms within the industry. Firms directly below achieving SIFI status have no incentive to expand into the status. Firms with the status have incentives to increase in scale, because by increasing they can reduce the unit cost of regulation.

The same pattern holds for Dodd-Frank generally. The regulatory costs of the statute have advantaged larger banks, because they can spread the fixed costs of regulatory compliance over a much larger revenue base. At the same time, the regulatory costs have pushed a substantial share of the smaller, community-oriented banks out of business (or into forced consolidations) and throttled the entry of new community banks.

The Community Reinvestment Act shows the same pattern (see Macey and Miller 1993; Hylton and Rougeau 1996). The statute aims

---

[4] It is important, in this argument, that the bureaucrat's actions are publicly observable and monitored by hostile political factions. If the bureaucrat's actions were not observable, then inaction would be an attractive option because it would allow the bureaucrat to enjoy a more leisurely work environment. When, for example, public enforcement agents are not consistently monitored, the problem of motivating them to enforce the law becomes a central concern (see Becker and Stigler 1974).

to promote investment in economically decaying inner cities. Large banks have found it relatively easy to comply compared with their smaller rivals. The interesting feature here is that the smaller rivals most burdened by the statute often consist of minority-owned banks that entered the industry with the aim to serve businesses in the predominantly minority communities of inner cities.

Sometimes regulatory errors are apparent, but they remain in place because the cost of correction for large incumbents is too high. For this, probably the best illustration is the work of credit rating agencies with respect to mortgage-backed securities. One of the questions generated by the 2008 banking crisis is why the credit rating agencies moved in parallel fashion by awarding high credit ratings to mortgage-backed securities long after evidence emerged suggesting that a downgrade would be appropriate (for an insightful discussion, see Hill [2010]). One obvious possible explanation is that the credit rating agencies did not really compete against each other, suggesting that the high credit ratings given to mortgage-backed securities resulted from tacit collusion. However, as Macey makes clear, large banks had "herded" into these securities because of the erroneously high credit ratings. The result was an equilibrium in which banks and credit rating agencies joined in a rational disbelief of bad news. Too much was at stake for the credit rating agencies to rationally update their assessments and consequently downgrade the securities.

The general pattern is simple: large banks manage the statutory reform process so that it produces a regulatory framework that advantages them relative to their smaller rivals. The result is that the banking industry moves toward greater concentration, increasing the degree of financial risk. Substantial subsidies, such as the one provided by federal deposit insurance (coupled with inefficient pricing of the insurance), remain in place despite numerous rounds of reform.

In sum, I am in full agreement with Macey on the processes and tendencies of bureaucratic error. However, I would identify the source of those tendencies within incentives created, often deliberately, by participants in the statutory reform process.

REFERENCES

Becker, Gary S., and George J. Stigler. 1974. "Law Enforcement, Malfeasance, and Compensation of Enforcers." *Journal of Legal Studies* 3:1–18.

Beermann, Jack M. 1991. "Interest Group Politics and Judicial Behavior: Macey's Public Choice." *Notre Dame Law Review* 67: 183–230.

Hill, Claire A. 2010. "Why Did Rating Agencies Do Such a Bad Job Rating Subprime Securities?" *University of Pittsburgh Law Review* 71:585–608.

Hylton, Keith N. 1993. "Efficiency and Labor Law." *Northwestern University Law Review* 87:471–522.

Hylton, Keith N. 1996. "A Theory of Minimum Contract Terms with Implications for Labor Law." *Texas Law Review* 74:1741–82.

Hylton, Keith N., and Vincent D. Rougeau. 1996. "Lending Discrimination: Economic Theory, Econometric Evidence, and the Community Reinvestment Act." *Georgetown Law Journal* 85:237–94.

Macey, Jonathan. 2017. "Error and Regulatory Risk in Financial Institution Regulation." *Supreme Court Economic Review* 25:155–92.

Macey, Jonathan R. 1988. "Transaction Costs and the Normative Elements of the Public Choice Model: An Application to Constitutional Theory." *Virginia Law Review* 74:471–518.

Macey, Jonathan R., and Geoffrey P. Miller. 1993. "The Community Reinvestment Act: An Economic Analysis." *Virginia Law Review* 79:291–348.

Mueller, Dennis C. 1989. *Public Choice II*, 2nd ed. Cambridge: Cambridge University Press.

Niskanen, William A., Jr. 1971. *Bureaucracy and Representative Government*. Chicago: Aldine-Atherton.

Wrongful Convictions, Deterrence, and Stigma Dilution

Murat C. Mungan[*]

There is no consensus in the economics of law enforcement literature regarding the likely effects of wrongful convictions on deterrence. Although many assert that wrongful convictions and wrongful acquittals are likely to cause similar reductions in deterrence, others have claimed that certain types of wrongful convictions are unlikely to affect deterrence. However, the stigmatizing effects of convictions are not taken into account in the formalization of either view. Frequent wrongful convictions naturally make criminal records less meaningful, because they reduce the proportion of truly guilty individuals among the convicted population. This stigma dilution effect, along with similar effects regarding the probability of stigmatization, are formalized via a model wherein criminal records act as noisy signals of offenders' characteristics. The analysis reveals that when criminal records cause stigmatization, wrongful convictions reduce deterrence, even if they are caused by adjudication mistakes that were previously shown to have no effect on deterrence. This suggests that prodefendant biases in various criminal procedures can potentially be explained through interactions between stigmatization and wrongful convictions.

[*] Professor, Antonin Scalia Law School at George Mason University. I thank two anonymous referees and the participants of the *Supreme Court Economic Review* Roundtable on the Economics of Legal Error for valuable comments and suggestions.

Electronically published: December 19, 2018

1. INTRODUCTION

This article explains how wrongful convictions can reduce the expected stigma attached to committing crime and thereby lead to reductions in deterrence. The effect occurs through two different channels: by diluting the stigma attached to a conviction and by reducing the gap between the likelihood with which one is stigmatized upon committing crime and not committing crime. Moreover, even wrongful convictions due to mistakes of identity, which were previously argued to cause no sizable effects on deterrence, generate these effects. These findings are described in the context of criminal law enforcement, but they easily extend to noncriminal contexts where a finding of liability generates a reputational loss or stigma. A brief description of the standard economic approach to analyzing legal error is useful for explaining the dynamics behind these results as well as for putting them in context.

An intuitive notion held by many, perhaps nearly all, people is that the punishment of the innocent is unjust.[1] The implications of this statement, however, are unclear because it does not answer important questions, such as, what social costs should we be willing to pay to reduce wrongful punishments? The standard welfare economics answer to this question is that the frequency of wrongful punishment (type I error) ought to be reduced as long as doing so results in marginal social benefits that are greater than the marginal social costs that need to be borne.

Marginal costs that come with reducing type I errors depend on how this reduction is achieved. For instance, if we use higher standards of proof in trials to reduce the probability of false positives, we naturally increase the probability of false negatives, and this may generate costs, perhaps in the form of reduced deterrence. Other ways to reduce type I errors are to increase the amount of evidence that is generally available or to increase the quality of law enforcers, and both methods require costly investments. Consequently, it is difficult to ascertain the magnitude of such costs without specifying the mechanism through which type I errors are to be reduced.

A less complicated, and antecedent, question relates to the marginal benefits of reducing type I errors. An obvious and quite important benefit comes from reducing the suffering that the innocent face from being punished.[2] These and other benefits have been identified and an-

---

[1] See, e.g., Givati (2014) arguing not only that people have preferences against the punishment of the innocent, but also that the average intensity of these preferences varies across cultures.

[2] Rizzolli and Saraceno (2013) formalize the point that an increase in type I errors results in social losses when punishment is costly (i.e., nontransferable as in the case of imprisonment). This point was also previously discussed in Posner (2007).

alyzed in the literature without much debate.[3] A particular question that has led to some debate is to what extent (if any) a reduction in the frequency of type I error leads to benefits in the form of enhanced deterrence. This article demonstrates that a reduction in type I errors can lead to significant deterrence benefits by affecting the likelihood and importance of being stigmatized as a result of committing crime. Explaining how the presence of stigmatization costs affects the deterrent effect of type I errors requires a brief review of the results obtained in the prior literature.

A statement that is often made is that type I and type II errors exert the same effect on deterrence. This claim is incorrectly attributed to Png (1986) and is actually more consistent with the setup introduced in Polinsky and Shavell (2007), which is one of the most comprehensive book chapters on the economic theory of public law enforcement.[4] The primary idea is illustrated by assuming that the probabilities of wrongful conviction and wrongful acquittal, conditional on a fixed probability of adjudication (p), are respectively ε_1 and ε_2. It follows that a person will violate the law if $b - p(1 - \varepsilon_2)s > -p\varepsilon_1 s$, where s is the sanction for the offense and b is a person's benefit from violating the law. This implies that a person violates the law if his benefit from violation is greater than a threshold benefit $b^* = p(1 - \varepsilon_1 - \varepsilon_2)s$. Because b^* is equally responsive to ε_1 and ε_2, it follows that the two types of error have the same effect on deterrence.

This equal-deterrence result breaks down under many important and realistic circumstances, for example, when the sanction is harm based or the choice set is nonbinary.[5] However, in one particular setting, results deviate greatly from the equal-deterrence result—namely, when the type I errors in question are generated by mistakes of identity, which occur when a court convicts a person for a crime committed by someone else. This setting was proposed and explained by Lando (2006), who noted that a person who commits crime does not eliminate the possibility of being wrongfully convicted for another person's crime. In other words, the possibility of being wrongfully convicted due to a mistake of identity, holding all else constant, does not affect a person's decision making, because it increases the expected punishment cost associated with committing crime and not committing crime equally. The implication of this observation is that eliminat-

---

[3] Other benefits include potential reductions in chilling behavior (Kaplow 2011), reductions in socially costly precautions to reduce type I errors (Mungan 2011), and fairness-related gains (Lando [2002] and Demougin and Fluet [2005]).

[4] For a more detailed explanation of the point made by Png (1986) and the way it was misinterpreted in the literature, see Lando and Mungan (2018).

[5] For a more detailed discussion of these issues, see Lando and Mungan (2018).

ing mistakes of identity cannot generate any direct deterrence benefits. Thus, there can exist no purely deterrence-based rationale for sacrificing gains elsewhere to reduce the frequency of mistakes of identity.

Lando's point was later contested by Garoupa and Rizzolli (2012), who pointed out that a reduction in wrongful convictions can reduce wrongful acquittals and thereby increase deterrence. Recently, in Lando and Mungan (2018), we pointed out that to assess the effect of wrongful convictions on their own, one can construct policies that only affect wrongful convictions without affecting the rate at which wrongful acquittals occur. In this setting, the original point made by Lando (2006), namely, that mistakes of identity have no effect on deterrence, reemerges, and its implications (e.g., vis-à-vis the optimal standard of proof) continue to be discussed (Obidzinski and Oytana 2017).

One feature of all the models discussed above is that they consider formal sanctions and ignore informal sanctions, that is, the stigmatizing effect of convictions.[6] However, informal sanctions act as an important deterrent, and, therefore, the interactions between type I errors and the likelihood and magnitude of stigmatization can play an important role. In fact, a result that emerges in the current article is that once informal sanctions are incorporated, even mistakes of identity, as conceived of by Lando (2006) and Lando and Mungan (2018), reduce deterrence.

To formalize the impact of informal sanctions on the deterrent effects of type I errors, I consider a law enforcement model in which convictions (imperfectly) signal a person's productivity. In equilibrium, criminals have lower productivity than noncriminals; thus, a criminal record signals to third parties that the person is likely to have lower productivity than another person with a clean criminal record. Type I errors reduce the informativeness of the signals provided through criminal records by increasing the proportion of innocent individuals who are convicted. This dilutes the stigma attached to a conviction.[7]

---

[6] One may naturally wonder whether convictions are likely to lead to significant stigmatization. There exists ample empirical support for this proposition. For instance, a very recent article investigates whether criminal records reduce employment prospects, and finds that convictions lead to a lower likelihood of job applicants being called back by employers (Agan and Starr 2017). The same article contains references to previous studies finding similar results. Demonstrating that these stigmatizing effects in fact lead to deterrence may be a more difficult task, and I am unaware of empirical studies undertaking this task.

[7] This is very similar to the "stigma dilution" concept introduced in Mungan (2016a) in the context of overcriminalization as well as Galbiati and Garoupa (2007). In both articles, the stigma attached to a conviction is lowered when the legal system attaches liability to people who have either not committed wrongdoings, or who have committed minor offenses. This possibility is also mentioned in n. 5 in Lando (2006).

Type I errors similarly reduce the incremental probability with which a person is stigmatized as a result of committing crime, which reduces the expected incremental informal sanction associated with committing crime further. Moreover, this is true for type I errors generated by mistakes of identity, as well as those that occur due to incorrect assessments of a defendant's lawful act.

The results described are formalized in the next two sections, which separately analyze mistakes of identity (sec. 2) and mistakes of act (sec. 3). Concluding remarks are presented in section 4.

2. MISTAKES OF IDENTITY

This section considers a model in which criminal records provide signals about individuals' productivity to third parties. These criminal records are produced through an imperfect enforcement mechanism, which generates type I and type II errors. In this section, it is assumed that all errors result from mistakes of identity. Section 3, which considers mistakes of act, borrows many of the tools and concepts introduced in this section. In particular, it makes references to average productivity derived in section 2.1, and it relies on the equilibrium properties explained in section 2.4.

2.1. Criminal Benefits and Productivity

I consider people who receive varying benefits (b) from committing crime. The density of individuals with any criminal benefit $b \in [0, \infty)$ is described by the density function $f(.)$ and the corresponding cumulative distribution function $F(.)$. Individuals also have varying degrees of productivity (q), which is private information. Moreover, an individual's productivity may be negatively correlated with his or her criminal benefit, and the commission of crime may result in a reduction in a person's productivity.[8] These effects are captured by the productivity function $q(b, a)$, which is continuous in b, and $a = 1$ denotes that the

---

[8] One may question why an offender may have lower productivity. There are at least two potential sources that may lead to this result, which are formalized via expressions (1) and (2). First, a person's characteristics (e.g., weak sense of morality, or low intelligence as noted by Rasmusen [1996]) may be correlated with propensity to commit crime as well as net contribution to an employer. Second, a person who commits crime may simply become a better criminal, and may thus generate greater costs at the workplace. The importance of the latter consideration becomes more apparent when one notes that a person's net contribution is what the person contributes minus the costs the person causes, such that "if he produces 10 widgets, but spoils two, steals three, and interferes with the neighboring worker enough to reduce his output

person has committed crime and $a = 0$ denotes that the person has not. Potential negative correlations between a person's productivity and his or her criminal benefits and/or criminal actions are captured by the following assumptions:

$$q_b(b, a) \leq 0 \text{ for all } b \text{ and } a \in \{0, 1\}; \tag{1}$$

$$q(b, 1) \leq q(b, 0) \text{ for all } b. \tag{2}$$

It is worth noting that when assumption (2) holds with strict inequality and assumption (1) holds with equality, we have a setting similar to that in the moral hazard model in Rasmusen (1996). Conversely, when assumption (2) holds with equality and assumption (1) holds with strict inequality, we have a version of the adverse selection model considered in Mungan (2016b) and Fluet and Mungan (2017).[9] To formalize the effect of type I errors on deterrence, it is not necessary to rely on a specific source of variation in individuals' productivity. In other words, it is sufficient for either assumption (1) or (2) to hold with strict inequality. This is because, as will become apparent in the proceeding analysis, for any given set of policies, in equilibrium, people commit crimes only if their criminal benefits exceed a threshold benefit b^t.[10] Thus, criminals have lower productivities, on average, than noncriminals if either assumption (1) or (2) holds with strict inequality, which is why criminal records can serve as an (imperfect) signal of individuals' productivity. This can be formalized by deriving the average productivity of individuals as follows:

$$\nu \equiv \frac{\int_0^{b^t} q(b, 0)f(b)db}{1 - \theta}; \text{ and } \lambda \equiv \frac{\int_{b^t}^{\infty} q(b, 1)f(b)db}{\theta}, \tag{3}$$

where

$$\theta \equiv 1 - F(b^t) \tag{4}$$

is the crime rate. Here, ν and λ denote the average productivity of noncriminals and criminals, respectively. It immediately follows that

---

by four, our worker's marginal product is not 10, but one" (Rasmusen 1996, 522). As will become apparent, the validity of either of these considerations is sufficient for the analysis conducted here.

[9] A different adverse selection model, where some low-productivity individuals always choose to commit crime, is considered in Rasmusen (1996). The possibility of individuals' benefits being inversely related to their productivity is considered in Iacobucci (2014).

[10] This result is explained in the beginning of sec. 2.3.

$\nu - \lambda > 0$ if either assumption (1) or (2) holds for some $b > 0$. Thus, in the remainder of the article, I assume that this condition holds to formalize the signaling function of criminal records.

2.2. Wages and Stigma

Individuals commit crime if the expected net benefit from this option offsets the expected net benefits they face from not committing crime. These expected net benefits have three primary components: (i) expected formal sanctions, (ii) expected benefits receivable from third parties, and (iii) criminal benefits. If a person is convicted, he or she receives a formal sanction (s) in addition to external benefits from third parties that equal w_C. On the other hand, if a person is not convicted, he or she receives a transfer from third parties that equals w_N. In addition to these, a person who commits crime receives criminal benefits of b.

Here, w_N and w_C can be thought of as wages or any other transfer that one obtains from third parties. The defining characteristic of these transfers is that they are increasing with the person's reputation, where reputation is measured by the person's expected productivity, given all information that is publicly available about the person. To abbreviate expressions, in the remaining parts of this article, I call these transfers "wages."

Wages offered by third parties to individuals depend on the average productivity of individuals in each observable group, namely, "convicted people" and "nonconvicted people." Average productivities, in turn, depend on the crime rate as well as the frequency of wrongful convictions due to mistakes of identity. To capture these mistakes, I assume that individuals are caught and punished for their own crimes with probability p and that they are caught and punished for someone else's crime with probability $\varepsilon \in (0,1)$. Moreover, following Lando (2006), I assume that committing crime, or being convicted for one's own crime, does not eliminate or affect the probability of being erroneously convicted for someone else's crime.

These assumptions imply that a person who commits crime is punished only for his or her own crime with a probability of $p(1 - \varepsilon)$, punished only for someone else's crime with probability $\varepsilon(1 - p)$, punished twice (one of which is for someone else's crime) with probability $p\varepsilon$, and not punished at all with probability $(1 - p)(1 - \varepsilon)$. In contrast, ε proportion of noncriminals are punished due to mistakes of identity, and $(1 - \varepsilon)$ avoid punishment. These observations imply that $\varepsilon + p(1 - \varepsilon)$ proportion of criminals and ε proportion of noncriminals end up obtaining a criminal record. Thus, the average productivity of people with records is given by

$$w_C = (\nu - \lambda) \frac{(1 - \theta)\varepsilon}{\theta(\varepsilon + p(1 - \varepsilon)) + (1 - \theta)\varepsilon} + \lambda = (\nu - \lambda) \frac{(1 - \theta)\varepsilon}{\varepsilon + \theta p(1 - \varepsilon)} + \lambda, \quad (5)$$

because within this population, which has measure $\theta[\varepsilon + p(1 - \varepsilon)] + (1 - \theta)\varepsilon$, only a measure of $(1 - \theta)\varepsilon$ people are not criminals, and, thus, their productivity is $(\nu - \lambda)$ greater than the remaining population.[11] Expression (5) highlights the—so far implicit—assumption that third parties can only observe whether a person has a criminal record or not and that they cannot distinguish between people who have been convicted once versus twice. This assumption is relaxed in section 2.6, which considers the case in which third parties can perfectly distinguish between different types of criminal records and illustrates that results are preserved under a very broad set of conditions.

Conversely, $(1 - p)(1 - \varepsilon)$ proportion of criminals and $(1 - \varepsilon)$ proportion of noncriminals evade punishment. Thus, the average productivity of people without records is

$$w_N = (\nu - \lambda) \frac{(1 - \theta)(1 - \varepsilon)}{\theta(1 - p)(1 - \varepsilon) + (1 - \theta)(1 - \varepsilon)} + \lambda = (\nu - \lambda) \frac{1 - \theta}{1 - p\theta} + \lambda \quad (6)$$

Thus, the wage differential or, alternatively, the stigma attached to having a criminal record is given by

$$\sigma \equiv w_N - w_C = (\nu - \lambda)(1 - \theta) \left(\frac{1}{1 - p\theta} - \frac{\varepsilon}{\varepsilon(1 - \theta p) + \theta p} \right). \quad (7)$$

Expressions (5)–(7) reveal a few important preliminary observations. First, expression (7) illustrates that stigma is always positive for any interior crime rate, meaning that people without criminal records receive higher wages than people with criminal records. The same expression also reveals that, holding all else equal, an increase in ε reduces stigma. Inspecting expressions (5) and (6) reveals that this is because w_N is unresponsive to the error rate, ε, whereas w_C is increasing with it. The reason for the former point is that a change in ε causes the same percentage change in the measure of nonconvicted guilty and nonconvicted innocent individuals, thus w_N is independent of ε. Alternatively, an increase in ε increases the wages of convicted individuals by diluting the presence of truly guilty individuals in this group. This is rather intuitive, because ε is the rate at which people are convicted for other people's crimes, and thus an increase in this rate increases the percentage of innocent individuals convicted. These points are noted as follows.

[11] To simplify the analysis, wages are assumed to equal the average productivities of the people to whom they are offered. Allowing wages to be any increasing function of these productivities has no effect on the analysis.

Observation 1. (i) The wages for nonconvicts are higher than the wages for convicts, which implies that $\sigma > 0$. (ii) An increase in the frequency of mistakes of identity, holding all else equal, causes a reduction in the stigma attached to a criminal conviction.

This observation plays an important role in identifying the effects of mistakes of identity on the crime rate. However, the observation relates to the isolated effect of ε on σ and is silent on potential interactions between ε and other considerations, including the crime rate. These interactions naturally depend on the way people respond to changes in the probability of type I error, which is analyzed next.

2.3. Individuals' Decision-Making Process

Individuals simultaneously decide whether or not to commit crime. Their joint decisions generate a crime rate, which, in turn, determines the wages (w_N and w_C) offered by third parties, as explained in the previous subsection. A preliminary and intuitive result is that any equilibrium profile must involve a threshold criminal benefit, b^t, as noted in section 2.1, such that only individuals with benefits exceeding b^t commit crime. This is because at a given strategy profile, all individuals face the same expected costs and wages from committing crime, but individuals with high bs obtain greater criminal benefits than individuals with low bs. Therefore, at any profile where there is a person with benefit b^l who commits crime and another with benefit $b^h > b^l$ who does not commit crime, at least one of these individuals has a profitable deviation. This is the reason for why the analysis focuses only on strategy profiles where there is a cutoff benefit that determines whether people commit crimes.

Given this observation, individuals' best responses to the behavior of all other individuals can be ascertained by considering the net benefits they expect to obtain from committing and not committing crime, for any given b^t. In particular, a person's expected net benefit from committing crime is

$$b + (p(1 - \varepsilon) + \varepsilon(1 - p))[w_C - s] + p\varepsilon[w_C - 2s] + (1 - p)(1 - \varepsilon)w_N, \quad (8)$$

because he expects to be punished for only his own crime with probability $p(1 - \varepsilon)$, punished only for another person's crime with a probability of $\varepsilon(1 - p)$, punished twice with a probability of $p\varepsilon$, and not punished at all with a probability of $(1 - p)(1 - \varepsilon)$.[12]

---

[12] The derivation of expression (8) assumes that a person punished twice receives the same sanction for each crime. This assumption is employed to abbreviate expressions, and n. 15 explains that results are preserved as long as the sanction for the sec-

In contrast, a person who does not commit crime is nevertheless punished with probability ε for someone else's crime and is not punished with a probability of $(1 - \varepsilon)$. Therefore, not committing crime yields an expected net benefit of

$$\varepsilon[w_C - s] + (1 - \varepsilon)w_N. \tag{9}$$

Therefore, a person's best response to a strategy profile[13] where people with $b > b^t$ are committing crimes is to commit crime if

$$b^r(b^t, \varepsilon) \equiv p(1 - \varepsilon)\sigma(b^t, \varepsilon) + ps < b, \tag{10}$$

where σ is defined in (7) and is a function of b^t, because $\theta = 1 - F(b^t)$.

2.4. Equilibrium Characterization

A strategy profile constitutes an equilibrium if all individuals' strategies are best responses to each other. In particular, a type b person's best response to a threshold b^t is to commit crime if, and only if

$$b - p(1 - \varepsilon)\sigma(b^t, \varepsilon) - ps > 0. \tag{11}$$

Thus, we can define the following function to identify an equilibrium:

$$C(b, \varepsilon) \equiv b - p(1 - \varepsilon)\sigma(b, \varepsilon) - ps. \tag{12}$$

The best responses of individuals identified via expression (11) implies that a threshold benefit, b^*, is an equilibrium if

$$C(b^*, \varepsilon) = 0. \tag{13}$$

To demonstrate that an equilibrium exists, note that $\sigma(b, \varepsilon)$ is finite and nonnegative for all b and all ε. Thus, $C(0, \varepsilon) < 0$ and $\lim_{b \to \infty} C(b, \varepsilon) = \infty$. Thus, there exists a cutoff criminal benefit b^* that satisfies expression (13). The uniqueness of the equilibrium cannot be guaranteed without imposing additional assumptions. However, as I have shown in similar contexts elsewhere, it is possible to guarantee that the equilibrium is unique under plausible assumptions.[14] Moreover, even when multiple equilibria exist, one can focus on stable equilibria to

---

ond crime is not greater than $\sigma + s$ in equilibrium, i.e., the sum of the formal sanctions for the first offense and stigma.

[13] Here, this phrase refers to the profile of strategies played by all individuals except the one being considered.

[14] See Mungan (2018) showing, in a similar context, that the equilibrium is unique as long as there are diminishing marginal deterrence effects from increasing the total sanction.

conduct comparative statics. Therefore, in what follows, to ease the description of results, I assume that the equilibrium is unique for any given ε.

A property of the equilibrium is that

$$C_b(b^*, \varepsilon) > 0, \tag{14}$$

because, as noted earlier, $C(0,\varepsilon) < 0$. This property implies that a change in ε that leads to a reduction in the incremental expected stigmatization costs, namely, $p(1 - \varepsilon)\sigma(b,\varepsilon)$, leads to a reduction in deterrence because $(db^* / d\varepsilon) = -(C_\varepsilon / C_b)$. This observation can more compactly be noted as follows.

Observation 2.

$$sgn\left(\frac{db^*}{d\varepsilon}\right) = -sgn(C_\varepsilon).$$

This observation implies that, while conducting comparative statics, one can focus on the effects of ε on the incremental expected stigmatization costs from committing crime. This is the objective of the next subsection.

2.5. The Effect of Mistakes of Identity on Stigma and Deterrence

The incremental expected stigmatization costs from committing crime faced by any individual is given by

$$p(1 - \varepsilon)\sigma(b^*, \varepsilon). \tag{15}$$

This expression demonstrates that mistakes of identity affect expected stigmatization costs through two channels. The first one, reflected by the term $p(1 - \varepsilon)$, captures the increased likelihood with which a person suffers stigmatization when he or she commits crime. An increase in ε trivially reduces this probability and, thus, causes a reduction in deterrence through this first channel. The second effect is the impact that ε has on the magnitude of stigma. This effect, too, is negative,[15] as noted by observation 1. Hence, an increase in the frequency of mistakes of act reduces both the extent to which committing crime increases the like-

---

[15] If the sanction for a person's second conviction differs from s, the expected increase in the marginal sanction from committing crime also depends on ε. In particular, expression (10) becomes $b'(b^t, \varepsilon) \equiv p(1 - \varepsilon)\sigma + ps + \varepsilon p(s^r - s)$, where s_r is the punishment for the second offense. Thus, it follows that for $C_\varepsilon > 0$ to continue to hold, it is sufficient that $\sigma > s^r - s$.

lihood of stigmatization as well as the magnitude of stigmatization costs. This implies, via observation 2, the following proposition.

Proposition 1. An increase in the frequency of mistakes of identity reduces deterrence.

Proof. The proof follows immediately from the comments in the text. However, it can be summarized as follows:

$$\frac{db^*}{d\varepsilon} = -\frac{C_\varepsilon}{C_b} = -p\frac{\sigma - (1-\varepsilon)\sigma_\varepsilon}{C_b} < 0, \tag{16}$$

because $C_b(b^*, \varepsilon) > 0$, as noted earlier in expression (14), and $\sigma > 0$ and $\sigma_\varepsilon < 0$, as noted in observation 1. QED

Proposition 1 reveals that when one incorporates informal sanctions into the standard law enforcement model, even mistakes of identity cause a reduction in deterrence. The next subsection is devoted to explaining the effects of simplifying assumptions, and section 3 identifies similar effects when mistakes concern defendants' acts.

2.6. When Criminal Records Can Be Perfectly Distinguished

The preceding analysis assumes that third parties can only ascertain whether people have criminal records and that they cannot distinguish between individuals who were convicted once and individuals who were convicted twice. When parties can distinguish between criminal records, there are three (instead of two) groups of individuals: people who were never convicted, people who were convicted once, and people who were convicted twice. The average productivity of the first group is given, as before, by w_N, because there continue to be $\theta(1-p)(1-\varepsilon)$ criminals without records and $(1-\theta)(1-\varepsilon)$ innocent people without records. The average productivity of people who are convicted twice is simply λ, because only criminals are convicted twice. Finally, to calculate the average productivity of individuals who have been convicted only once, note that there are $\theta[p(1-\varepsilon) + \varepsilon(1-p)]$ criminals who are convicted once and $(1-\theta)\varepsilon$ innocent people who are convicted once. Thus, the average productivity of these individuals is given by

$$w_1 \equiv (\nu - \lambda)\frac{(1-\theta)\varepsilon}{\theta(p(1-\varepsilon) + \varepsilon(1-p)) + (1-\theta)\varepsilon} + \lambda. \tag{17}$$

Third parties' abilities to observe criminal records in detail also changes the incentives of potential offenders. In particular, an offender who commits crime has an expected net benefit of

$$b + (p(1 - \varepsilon) + \varepsilon(1 - p))[w_1 - s] + p\varepsilon(\lambda - 2s) + (1 - \varepsilon)(1 - p)w_N. \quad (18)$$

Conversely, a person who does not commit crime has an expected net benefit of

$$(1 - \varepsilon)w_N + \varepsilon(w_1 - s). \quad (19)$$

Thus, a person commits crime if

$$b > p((1 - \varepsilon)\bar{\sigma} + \varepsilon\underline{\sigma} + s), \quad (20)$$

where

$$\bar{\sigma} \equiv (w_N - w_1) \text{ and } \underline{\sigma} \equiv (w_1 - \lambda) \quad (21)$$

are, respectively, the stigma from obtaining a criminal record and the increase in stigma from being convicted of a second crime. Intuitively, one would expect that $\bar{\sigma} > \underline{\sigma}$, because this would correspond to a situation where the stigma attached to a criminal record is diminishing with the number of crimes of which one has been convicted. A comparison between $\bar{\sigma}$ and $\underline{\sigma}$ reveals that this intuitive conjecture holds as long as $p\theta > \varepsilon$.[16] Proposition 2, below, uses this observation to derive a sufficient condition under which more frequent mistakes of identity reduce deterrence.

Proposition 2. When criminal records containing different numbers of convictions are perfectly distinguishable, an increase in the frequency of mistakes of identity reduces deterrence as long as min $\{1/2, p\theta\} > \varepsilon$.

Proof. Let $\tilde{C}(b^*, \varepsilon) = b^* - p((1 - \varepsilon)\bar{\sigma} + \varepsilon\underline{\sigma} + s)$ be the modified equilibrium condition when third parties can distinguish between different types of criminal records. It follows that $(db^* / d\varepsilon) \leq 0$ if and only if $\tilde{C}_\varepsilon \geq 0$ because $(db^*/d\varepsilon) = (\tilde{C}_\varepsilon/\tilde{C}_b)$ and $\tilde{C}_b(b^*, \varepsilon) > 0$. Next, note that

$$\tilde{C}_\varepsilon = -p[(1 - \varepsilon)\bar{\sigma}_\varepsilon + \varepsilon\underline{\sigma}_\varepsilon - (\bar{\sigma} - \underline{\sigma})]$$

$$= -p\left[\frac{\partial w_1}{\partial \varepsilon}(2\varepsilon - 1) - (\bar{\sigma} - \underline{\sigma})\right] \quad (22)$$

and that

$$\frac{\partial w_1}{\partial \varepsilon} = (\nu - \lambda)(1 - \theta)\frac{p\theta}{(\varepsilon(1 - 2p\theta) + p\theta)^2} > 0.$$

[16] To see this, note that plugging eqq. (6) and (17) into eq. (21) yields $\bar{\sigma} - \underline{\sigma} = (\nu - \lambda)[(1 - \theta)/(1 - p\theta)] - 2(\nu - \lambda)\{[(1 - \theta)\varepsilon]/[p\theta + \varepsilon(1 - 2p\theta)]\}$, which simplifies to $\bar{\sigma} - \underline{\sigma} = (\nu - \lambda)(1 - \theta)\{[p\theta - \varepsilon]/[1 - p\theta][p\theta + \varepsilon(1 - 2p\theta)]\}$.

Therefore, $\tilde{C}_\varepsilon > 0$ as long as $(2\varepsilon - 1) < 0$ and $(\bar{\sigma} - \underline{\sigma}) > 0$. The latter condition holds when $p\theta > \varepsilon$, as shown in expression (14). Thus, $\min\{0.5, p\theta\} > \varepsilon$ implies that $\tilde{C}_\varepsilon > 0$, and, therefore, $(db^* / d\varepsilon) < 0$. QED

Proposition 2 illustrates that when third parties can distinguish between people who were twice convicted versus once convicted, the effect of mistakes of identity on deterrence is no longer unambiguous. However, if the frequency of mistakes of identity is low to begin with, an increase in it reduces deterrence.

It is worth making a brief clarification regarding the condition in proposition 2. When $p\theta < 1 / 2$, the condition holds if $(\varepsilon / p) < \theta$. Here, ε / p denotes the ratio between the unconditional probabilities of wrongful and correct convictions. These unconditional probabilities can be formalized as the probabilities of being adjudicated and subsequently being convicted. Thus, ε / p is likely to be a small number even in circumstances where the probability of adjudication is small. Nevertheless, the condition may still be violated if the crime rate is sufficiently small.

3. MISTAKES OF ACT

In this section, I consider the effect of mistakes of act, rather than mistakes of identity, on deterrence. Although the analysis differs slightly from that of mistakes of identity, the two models share a lot in common. In particular, the average productivity of criminals and noncriminals previously explained in section 2.1 can be transplanted into this section without any modification. Similarly, most of the arguments regarding equilibrium characterization remains equally valid. Thus, only two primary sets of expressions need to be modified to conduct the analysis, namely, the equilibrium wages offered by third parties and the best responses of individuals. These are derived next.

3.1. Wages and Stigma

A *mistake of act* occurs when the court incorrectly assesses the nature of an act committed by an individual, as opposed to a *mistake of identity*, where the court incorrectly attributes an act committed by another person to the defendant.[17] I note by α the probability with which a court erroneously concludes that an innocent person has

---

[17] In this section, I consider act-based sanctions imposed on defendants due mistakes of act. As demonstrated in Lando and Mungan (2018), if sanctions are instead harm based, the deterrent effects of type I errors are likely to be smaller, because then the noncommission of the dangerous act reduces the likelihood with which harm results and therefore the probability with which a sanction must be imposed.

committed a criminal act and continue to assume that it correctly convicts a criminal with a probability of $p > \alpha$. Hence, θp individuals are correctly convicted, whereas $(1 - \theta)\alpha$ individuals are wrongfully convicted, resulting in a total of $\theta p + (1 - \theta)\alpha$ convictions. Similarly, $(1 - \theta)(1 - \alpha)$ innocent individuals evade conviction, whereas $\theta(1 - p)$ individuals evade punishment despite committing crime, producing a total of $\theta(1 - p) + (1 - \theta)(1 - \alpha)$ individuals without convictions. Given these numbers, the average productivity of convicts (w_C) and non-convicts (w_N) can be calculated as follows:

$$w_C = (\nu - \lambda)\frac{(1 - \theta)\alpha}{\theta p + (1 - \theta)\alpha} + \lambda \qquad (23)$$

and

$$w_N = (\nu - \lambda)\frac{(1 - \theta)(1 - \alpha)}{\theta(1 - p) + (1 - \theta)(1 - \alpha)} + \lambda. \qquad (24)$$

This implies that the stigma attached to having a criminal record is

$$\sigma = (\nu - \lambda)(1 - \theta)\left(\frac{(1 - \alpha)}{\theta(1 - p) + (1 - \theta)(1 - \alpha)} - \frac{\alpha}{\theta p + (1 - \theta)\alpha}\right). \qquad (25)$$

As in the previous section, the way stigma responds to α plays a crucial role in determining deterrence effects. A quick inspection of w_N and w_C reveals that the former wage is decreasing, while the latter wage is increasing, in α. This implies the following.

Observation 3. An increase in the frequency of mistakes of act, holding all else equal, causes a reduction in the stigma attached to a criminal conviction.

3.2. Individuals' Decision-Making Process

As in the case of mistakes of identity, in a situation where only all individuals with $b > b^t$ are committing crime, a person's best response is to commit crime if doing so generates a higher expected net benefit than not committing crime. The expected net benefit from crime can be calculated as

$$b + p(w_C - s) + (1 - p)w_N, \qquad (26)$$

whereas the expected net benefit associated with not committing crime is

$$\alpha(w_C - s) + (1 - \alpha)w_N. \qquad (27)$$

Therefore, a person's best response is to commit crime if and only if his or her benefit from crime is such that $(p - \alpha)(s + \sigma(b^t, \alpha)) < b$.

3.3. The Effect of Mistakes of Act on Stigma and Deterrence

An equilibrium is obtained when only people with $b > b^*$ commit crime where b^* satisfies the following requirement:

$$C(b^*, \alpha) = b^* - (p - \alpha)(s + \sigma(b^*, \alpha)) = 0. \tag{28}$$

A simple investigation of this equality reveals the following result.

Proposition 3. An increase in the frequency of mistakes of act reduces deterrence.

Proof. Manipulating the expression for σ in expression (25) reveals that it equals

$$\sigma = \frac{(\nu - \lambda)(1 - \theta)\theta}{(1 - (\theta p + (1 - \theta)\alpha))(\theta p + (1 - \theta)\alpha)}(p - \alpha). \tag{29}$$

Thus, $\sigma \geq 0$. This implies that $C(0,a) < 0$ and, therefore, that $C_b(b^*,\alpha) > 0$. Hence, C_α and $(db^* / d\alpha) = -(C_\alpha / C_b)$ have opposite signs. Differentiating the expression for C in expression (28) with respect to α reveals that

$$C_\alpha = s + \sigma - (p - \alpha)\sigma_\alpha > 0, \tag{30}$$

where the inequality follows from observation 3, and the facts that $s > 0$ and $p > \alpha$. QED

Proposition 3 verifies that the incorporation of informal sanctions into the standard law enforcement model does not affect the conclusion that an increase in the frequency of mistakes of act reduces deterrence. Although this result is less novel than that concerning mistakes of identity, it is reported to verify that the inclusion of informal sanctions does not lead to unexpected dynamics wherein type I errors have positive deterrence effects.

4. CONCLUSION

There is an ongoing debate regarding the effects of wrongful convictions on deterrence. This article demonstrates that even in cases where, absent informal sanctions, wrongful convictions have no effect on deterrence, negative relationships between deterrence and type I errors emerge when one considers the stigmatizing effects of convictions. Thus, the severely stigmatizing effects of criminal convictions may supply a rationale for the prodefendant biases that are unique to the criminal context. Therefore, future research focusing on the stigma effects of specific prodefendant biases employed in the criminal justice system (e.g., the use of high standards of proof and exclusionary evidence rules) may be able to provide deterrence-based rationales for these biases.

It is worth noting that the model provided is meant to capture the stigma-diluting effect of erroneous convictions and its effect on deterrence in the simplest way possible. In doing so, it abstracts from many potentially relevant issues, some of which may exacerbate this dilution effect. The analysis assumes, for instance, that employers can costlessly obtain information regarding an employee's criminal record. When information acquisition is costly, employers' willingness to pay for criminal records would be negatively related to the noisiness of criminal records as signals. This, in turn, would cause fewer employers to inform themselves, which would cause a further drop in the expected stigma from having a criminal record. Further exploration of this and other dynamics related to stigma dilution can enhance our understanding of the full range of effects that erroneous convictions may generate.

REFERENCES

Agan, Amanda, and Sonja Starr. 2017. "The Effect of Criminal Records on Access to Employment." *American Economic Review* 107:560–64.
Demougin, Dominique, and Claude Fluet. 2005. "Deterrence versus Judicial Error: A Comparative View of Standards of Proof." *Journal of Institutional and Theoretical Economics* 161:193–206.
Fluet, Claude, and Murat C. Mungan. 2017. "The Signal-Tuning Function of Liability Regimes." Law and Economics Research Paper no. 17–37. George Mason University, Fairfax, VA.
Galbiati, Roberto, and Nuno Garoupa. 2007. "Keeping Stigma out of Administrative Law: An Explanation of Consistent Beliefs." *Supreme Court Economic Review* 15:273–83.
Garoupa, Nuno, and Matteo Rizzolli. 2012. "Wrongful Convictions Do Lower Deterrence." *Journal of Institutional and Theoretical Economics* 168:224–31.
Givati, Yehonatan. 2014. "Legal Institutions and Social Values: Theory and Evidence from Plea Bargaining Regimes." *Journal of Empirical Legal Studies* 11:867–93.
Iacobucci, Edward M. 2014. "On the Interactions between Legal and Reputational Sanctions." *Journal of Legal Studies* 43:189–207.

Kaplow, Louis. 2011. "Optimal Proof Burdens, Deterrence, and the Chilling of Desirable Behavior." *American Economic Review* 101: 277–80.

Lando, Henrik. 2002. "When Is the Preponderance of the Evidence Standard Optimal?" *Geneva Papers on Risk and Insurance* 27:602–8.

Lando, Henrik. 2006. "Does Wrongful Conviction Lower Deterrence?" *Journal of Legal Studies* 35:327–37.

Lando, Henrik, and Murat C. Mungan. 2018. "The Effect of Type I Error on Deterrence." *International Review of Law and Economics* 53:1–8.

Mungan, Murat C. 2011. "A Utilitarian Justification for Heightened Standards of Proof in Criminal Trials." *Journal of Institutional and Theoretical Economics* 167:352–70.

Mungan, Murat C. 2016a. "Stigma Dilution and Over-criminalization." *American Law and Economics Review* 18:88–121.

Mungan, Murat C. 2016b. "A Generalized Model for Reputational Sanctions and the (Ir)relevance of the Interactions between Legal and Reputational Sanctions." *International Review of Law and Economics* 46:86–92.

Mungan, Murat C. 2018. "Statistical (and Racial) Discrimination, 'Ban the Box,' and Crime Rates." *American Law and Economics Review* 20:512–35.

Obidzinski, Marie, and Yves Oytana. 2017. "How Does the Probability of Wrongful Conviction Affect the Standard of Proof?" Working Paper. https://hal.archives-ouvertes.fr/hal-01462844/document.

Png, I. 1986. "Optimal Subsidies and Damages in the Presence of Judicial Error." *International Review of Law and Economics* 6:101–5.

Polinsky, A. Mitchell, and Steven Shavell. 2007. "The Theory of Public Enforcement of Law." In *Handbook of Law and Economics*, vol. 1, edited by A. Mitchell Polinsky and Steven Shavell, 403–54. Amsterdam: North-Holland.

Posner, Richard. 2007. *Economic Analysis of Law*. New York: Aspen.

Rasmusen, Eric. 1996. "Stigma and Self-Fulfilling Expectations of Criminality." *Journal of Law and Economics* 39:519–43.

Rizzolli, Matteo, and Margherita Saraceno. 2013. "Better That Ten Guilty Persons Escape: Punish Costs Explain the Standard of Proof." *Public Choice* 155:395–411.

Comment on "Wrongful Convictions, Deterrence, and Stigma Dilution"

*Albert H. Choi**

1. INTRODUCTION

Whenever a defendant gets convicted in a criminal proceeding, it is well documented that the defendant will not only be responsible for the consequent legal sanctions, such as incarceration, monetary penalty, and so forth, but also be subject to nonlegal penalties. Nonlegal penalties can include restricted employment opportunities, lower wages, difficulty finding housing, and more general "reputational" harm, including being shunned by family, friends, and acquaintances. These types of nonlegal sanctions, imposed by agents outside of the criminal law system, are well known. What is, however, interesting is whether such nonlegal sanctions are based on other agents' "rational" behavior and, if we presume that the other agents are acting rationally, why such nonlegal sanctions occur (in equilibrium) and what the legal system can or should do in response. It is in that vein that I found Murat Mungan's (2017) "Wrongful Convictions, Deterrence, and Stigma Dilution" to be an extremely informative and thought-provoking article.

Ostensibly, the article addresses a somewhat narrower question of whether a particular kind of wrongful conviction, where one agent can be held responsible for some other agent's crime (the case of mistaken identity), can affect deterrence. Lando (2006) argued that mistaken identity-based wrongful convictions do not affect deterrence because they increase the expected punishment cost associated with

* University of Virginia School of Law.

Electronically published: December 19, 2018
© 2018 by the University of Chicago. All rights reserved. 978-0-226-64653-4/2017/0025-0012$10.00

217

committing crime and not committing crime equally. That is, holding everything else the same, when an agent is deciding whether to commit a crime, because the agent knows that there is a chance that he or she may be punished for a crime committed by someone else, regardless of whether the agent commits the contemplated crime, the possibility of such wrongful conviction will not affect the decision. What Mungan convincingly shows in his article is that this irrelevance (or neutrality) result will disappear when we take into consideration the "stigma" attached to criminal convictions. The core insight of the article is that when rational agents impose nonlegal sanctions (e.g., lower wages, fewer employment opportunities) against agents with criminal records, wrongful conviction reduces the informational content of a conviction and, therefore, dilutes the impact of nonlegal sanctions. This stigma dilution, in turn, will affect deterrence.

As a person who principally deploys economic analysis to law, I found the article, written in the tradition of law and economics style, a real pleasure to read. The theoretical model has been reduced down to the core elements so that the reader does not have to deal with (or wonder about) how and why certain variables or analyses are being presented; the mathematical analysis (along with the proofs) is clean, elegant, and thorough; and the main insights from the model are presented in an easy-to-understand format that, I expect, even the non-law-and-economics audience can access relatively easily. The surrounding discussion is also well organized, to the point, and succinct, allowing the reader to get the core insight without having to read through unnecessary digressions. Furthermore, this thoughtful article has given me a chance to think about broader issues associated with legal versus nonlegal sanctions (including stigmatization), and this comment attempts to share some thoughts on such issues.

2. OPTIMAL LEGAL DETERRENCE REGIME

The article's primary objective is to examine, in the presence of "stigmatization," what effect wrongful conviction will have on deterrence. Stigmatization is modeled as agents with criminal conviction receiving lower wages ($W_C \leq W_N$ where the subscripts C and N stand for "conviction" and "nonconviction," respectively). Paying lower wages is rational in the model because criminal conviction leads to lower productivity: for instance, $q(b, 1) \leq q(b, 0)$ for all b where $q(\cdot)$ measures one's (marginal) productivity, b stands for the benefit the agent receives from committing the crime, and the second argument $a \in \{0,1\}$ denotes whether the agent has been convicted or not. Given that there is a possibility of wrongful conviction, the other agents in the economy will infer the average productivity of the agent with criminal conviction and set the wage in accordance (W_C or W_N). Also, when an agent is convicted, he or she will have to pay the monetized penalty of s. The article examines what happens to the level of deterrence as the probability of false conviction (represented as $\varepsilon \geq 0$) rises, when the other agents rationally update their beliefs about the impact of conviction on productivity and set the wage in accordance, while holding everything else the same.

Although the focus of the article is on the effect of wrongful conviction on deterrence, I was intrigued by the possibility of designing the optimal legal sanctions in light of the stigmatization effect. That is, when we know that such a stigmatization effect exists and the impact of stigmatization on deterrence, how should we think about modifying the legal sanctions mechanism? Instead of holding the size of legal sanctions (s) and the litigation mechanism (p and ε) the same, the social planner (or the government) can design the sanctions in response to the effect of stigmatization. One possibility is to think about the absolute size of s. In the presence of stigmatization, should we increase or lower s? Another possibility is to think about whether we should condition s on multiple convictions. At least in the model, only the agents who commit crime can be convicted twice, once for their own crime and second for someone else's crime, whereas innocent agents can be convicted only once (for someone else's crime). From the designing perspective, this implies that we should perhaps impose a harsher penalty on the repeat offenders or those who are convicted multiple times. Although the fact that only the agents who commit crime can be convicted twice comes from the stylized nature of the model, I think this point can be made more generally. Perhaps this can lead to the justification about systems such as the "three strikes" rule.

The other possibility is to think about what the legal system can do in terms of affecting the probabilities of conviction, represented by p and ε in the model. Again, the central focus of the article is to see the effect on deterrence as the probability of wrongful conviction (ε, along with the probability of correct conviction, p) changes. Presumably, however, the changes in probability must be stemming from some underlying changes in the legal system. This renders another possible avenue for further exploration. Should the legal system be designed to generally increase or decrease the probabilities of conviction? Should we make it easier or more difficult for the prosecutors to obtain a guilty judgment or a guilty plea? What about the burden of proof? Should the system impose a higher or lower burden on the prosecutor to show whether the defendant has, in fact, committed a crime? In the presence of stigmatization (and other nonlegal sanctions), how should we think about Blackstone's ratio ("It is better that ten guilty persons escape than one innocent suffer")? In short, the article lends itself some nice research questions about design of the legal sanctions in the presence of stigmatization and other nonlegal sanctions.

3. INTERACTION BETWEEN LEGAL AND NONLEGAL SANCTIONS

Another interesting avenue of research and discussion that the article stimulates is the idea about how legal and nonlegal mechanisms are intertwined and interact with each other. The primary nonlegal sanction that the article explores is the poorer employment outcome (in the sense of lower wages, $W_C \leq W_N$), and this, in turn, in equilibrium, is justified based on lower productivity for those who have been convicted. The article suggests motivation for the lower productivity based on two rationales: (1) a person who commits a crime may simply have a weaker sense of morality and a higher propensity of not abiding by law; and (2) a person who commits a crime becomes a "better criminal" or becomes more efficient in committing crime and imposes a larger cost on the workplace. The first rationale is based on simple correlation, whereas the latter invokes some type of "learning by doing" story. I would guess that there could also be a third rationale: when a person is convicted and is imprisoned for some time, the person loses the (productive) human capital accumulated prior to conviction and may also learn, within the prison system, other ways of committing future crime. Although the learning story would be similar to the second rationale proposed in the article, the human capital atrophy story could provide a different basis for the lower productivity story.

What is interesting is that depending on which story we decide to adopt, how we should think about the criminal justice system differs. If, for instance, we adopt the correlation story (the first justification), unless we can design a system in which we could change the preferences of criminals (or their "characteristics"), the optimal response by the legal system would likely be to increase the accuracy of the conviction, adjust the sanctions appropriately, and let the public be aware of one's past criminal history. Alternatively, if the justification is based on some type of learning or human capital atrophy, new possibilities emerge, particularly through the system of rehabilitation. One possibility is to reduce the chances and the length of prison sentence and focus more on retraining and rebuilding of human capital. By giving the convicted agents a chance to rebuild human capital, the legal system can change their marginal propensity to commit (future) crime. Furthermore, if incarceration and prison sentence were to lead to destruction of human capital (or becoming more efficient at committing crime), perhaps the better system would be to encourage the prosecutors to rely less on prison sentences and more on nonprison rehabilitation, possibly through deferred or nonprosecution sentences. To the extent that a criminal record creates a stigmatization effect, we can also combine the rehabilitation program with the system that makes it more difficult for the public to uncover one's past criminal record. The latter, for instance, can also be done by allowing guilty pleas to be subject to a nondisclosure arrangement.

Lower or restricted employment outcome is certainly an important element of nonlegal sanctions, but the article also encourages us to think more broadly about other types of nonlegal sanctions and, perhaps more importantly, how the nonlegal and legal sanctions interact. An important contribution made by the article is the informational value created by legal sanctions: how a criminal record can allow the public to update their belief about an agent's productivity. This idea suggests that the relationship between nonlegal and legal sanctions can be quite complementary: information produced by a legal sanction can trigger or facilitate nonlegal sanctions. In a couple of articles I wrote with Scott Baker, we examine this issue more broadly in a repeated game theoretic framework (see Baker and Choi 2015, 2018). There, we argue that oftentimes the information generated by the liability regime (e.g., being found liable in a product liability suit) can facilitate more efficient nonlegal, reputational sanctions by allowing the other agents to tailor their sanctions based on the information. We also suggest that the informational benefit can also flow in the opposite direction: how one's past behavior can inform the legal system in determining liability issues. One intriguing possibility here, in the context of criminal conviction, is whether to take into consideration one's past behavior in determining conviction and sentencing. This is, at least briefly, mentioned above in thinking about how to treat repeat offenders. But, more broadly, should an agent's preconviction behavior be taken into consideration when the court is determining liability and subsequent sentence?

Finally, although the article's primary focus is on the employment outcome for agents convicted of crime, the article also encourages us to think about other types of nonlegal sanctions. People with criminal convictions are known to suffer not only worse employment outcomes but also face restricted access to housing, poorer chances of marriage, and other types of adverse "reputational" consequences. Sometimes the nonlegal sanctions can work in the opposite direction. Tax lawyers who have been found guilty of creating ingenious tax shelters can possibly find better postconviction employment opportunity in helping legislature fill the gaps in the tax code or a convicted securities trader, with intricate knowledge of the securities market, can perhaps find better opportunities in operating a hedge fund. Depending on the type of nonlegal sanctions (and their magnitude), one could think about designing a different legal system. For instance, should we design a more lenient system for people who have suffered serious restriction in housing choices? How should the legal system respond when we expect the criminal to have an even better employment outcome after conviction? These are all intriguing avenues for future research.

4. CONCLUSION

Mungan's (2017) article, "Wrongful Convictions, Deterrence, and Stigma Dilution," adds an important and valuable insight into how we should think about the interaction between legal sanctions (e.g., criminal convictions) and nonlegal mechanisms (e.g., employment outcomes or other reputational sanctions). The law and economics analysis in the article is elegantly executed and makes a very convincing case. Although the article focuses on a narrow question about stigma dilution, it presents many avenues for future research from which, I believe, other scholars can benefit.

REFERENCES

Baker, Scott, and Albert Choi. 2015. "Contract's Role in Relational Contract." *Virginia Law Review* 101:559–607.
Baker, Scott, and Albert Choi. 2018. "Reputation and Litigation: Why Costly Legal Sanctions Can Work Better Than Reputational Sanctions." *Journal of Legal Studies* 47:45–82.
Lando, Henrik. 2006. "Does Wrongful Conviction Lower Deterrence?" *Journal of Legal Studies* 35:327–37.
Mungan, Murat. 2017. "Wrongful Convictions, Deterrence, and Stigma Dilution." *Supreme Court Economic Review* 25:199–216.